HONG KONG FROM BRITAIN TO CHINA

To my parents

who struggled to bring up their children
during the harsh and difficult years of
postwar Hong Kong

Hong Kong from Britain to China
Political cleavages, electoral dynamics and institutional changes

LI PANG-KWONG
Lingnan University
Hong Kong

LONDON AND NEW YORK

First published 2000 by Ashgate Publishing

Reissued 2018 by Routledge
2 Park Square, Milton Park, Abingdon, Oxon OX14 4RN
711 Third Avenue, New York, NY 10017, USA

Routledge is an imprint of the Taylor & Francis Group, an informa business

Copyright © Li Pang-kwong 2000

All rights reserved. No part of this book may be reprinted or reproduced or utilised in any form or by any electronic, mechanical, or other means, now known or hereafter invented, including photocopying and recording, or in any information storage or retrieval system, without permission in writing from the publishers.

Notice:
Product or corporate names may be trademarks or registered trademarks, and are used only for identification and explanation without intent to infringe.

Publisher's Note
The publisher has gone to great lengths to ensure the quality of this reprint but points out that some imperfections in the original copies may be apparent.

Disclaimer
The publisher has made every effort to trace copyright holders and welcomes correspondence from those they have been unable to contact.

A Library of Congress record exists under LC control number: 99075552

ISBN 13: 978-1-138-70037-6 (hbk)
ISBN 13: 978-1-138-70034-5 (pbk)
ISBN 13: 978-1-315-20478-9 (ebk)

Contents

List of Figures	*vi*
List of Tables	*vii*
Acknowledgements	*ix*
List of Abbreviations	*xi*
1 Introduction	1
2 Historical Setting: The State and the Society	20
3 The Rise of the Centre-Periphery Cleavage	37
4 State Expansion and Consumption Cleavage	86
5 Development and Alignment of Political Forces	135
6 The Embryonic Electoral Market in the 1990s	175
7 Institutional Design and Conflict Management	208
8 Conclusion	229
Bibliography	*242*
Index	*276*

List of Figures

Figure 1.1	Cleavage Transformation	12
Figure 1.2	The Typology of Political Conflicts	16
Figure 5.1	The Budding Party Market in 1991: A Sketch	172
Figure 5.2	The Budding Party Market in 1998: A Sketch	173
Figure 7.1	A Sketch of the Electoral Market of Hong Kong in 1998	222
Figure 7.2	The Dynamics within the LegCo	224
Figure 7.3	The Twin Cleavages and the LegCo	225
Figure 8.1	Possible Dimensions of Electoral Support	238

List of Tables

Table 3.1	Comparison of 1984 Green and White Papers -- LegCo's Composition	58
Table 3.2	Comparison of 1984 Green and White Papers -- ExCo's Composition	59
Table 4.1	The Authorized Population of Cottage Resettlement Areas and Multi-storey Resettlement Estates, 1954-73	88
Table 4.2	The Number of Senior Posts in the Government Secretariat and Department Level 1970-98	99
Table 4.3	Changes in Composition of the Executive Council and the Legislative Council, 1947-98	101
Table 4.4	The Composition of the Urban Council and the Regional Council, 1947-91	104
Table 4.5	The Composition of the District Boards, 1982-97	105
Table 4.6	The Number of Government Advisory Bodies, Selected Years	107
Table 4.7	The Growth of the Civil Servants (Actual Strength) by Selected Function Areas, Selected Years	110
Table 4.8	The Actual Revenue and Expenditure of Hong Kong, 1947-97 (At Current Market Prices)	112
Table 4.9	The Actual Revenue and the GDP, 1974-97 (At Current Market Prices)	114
Table 4.10	The Main Components of Actual Revenue, 1947-97 (%)	116
Table 4.11	Capital Works Reserve Fund and the Actual Revenue, 1986-97 (HK$ million)	118
Table 4.12	Selected Components of the Inland Revenue, 1955-98 (%)	120

Table 4.13	Statistics of Salaries Tax, Selected Years	122
Table 4.14	Salaries Tax Allowances and Inflation, 1973/74-1997/98	122
Table 4.15	Actual Expenditure and the GDP, 1974-97 (At Current Market Prices)	125
Table 4.16	Public Expenditure by Policy Area Group, 1971-99 (%)	126
Table 4.17	Subventions of Selected Social Services Programmes (Recurrent and Capital Expenditure) (%)	128
Table 4.18	Government Contribution to Public Housing and Total Actual Expenditure, 1978-94 (HK$ million)	130
Table 5.1	The Electorate of the UrbCo and Population of Hong Kong, 1952-81	142
Table 5.2	Performance of Political Groups in 1985 District Boards Elections	154
Table 6.1	The Electorate and Population of Hong Kong, Selected Years	177
Table 6.2	The Number of Candidates in the Three-tier Legislature Elections by Years	178
Table 6.3	Contest of Political Groups by Constituencies in the 1991 LegCo Popular Elections	181
Table 6.4	Membership of Selected Political Groups before 1991	183
Table 6.5	Comparison of the 1991, 1995 and 1998 Popular Elections Results	189
Table 6.6	Vote Share of the 1991 LegCo Popular Elections	191
Table 7.1	The Composition of the Post-1997 Legislature	215
Table 7.2	Access to the Constitution-making and Decision-making Processes by the General Public	219

Acknowledgements

This book is developed from my Ph.D. thesis on elections and political mobilization in Hong Kong submitted to the London School of Economics and Political Science. Thanks are therefore due to my supervisors, Professors Tom Nossiter and Michael Yahuda. I would also like to express my gratitude to the following individuals for granting me an interview: Philip C.K. Kwok, Allen Lee, Patrick Shiu Kin-ying and Tsang Yok-sing; and to the following political groups for supplying the relevant information: the Democratic Alliance for Betterment of Hong Kong, the Democratic Party, the Hong Kong Democratic Foundation, the Liberal Democratic Federation of Hong Kong, the Liberal Party, the New Hong Kong Alliance, and the Reform Club of Hong Kong; and for election data: the Registration and Electoral Office, Constitutional Affairs Branch (Bureau), Hong Kong Government Secretariat.

In the process of revising the manuscript, the institutional change of Hong Kong has been included as one of the main components of this book. As a result, I carried on board my relevant works on institutional design and electoral change of Hong Kong. The author therefore thanks The Chinese University Press for permission to reuse the following articles in Chapters 6 and 7: "Executive and Legislature: Institutional Design, Electoral Dynamics and the Management of Conflicts in the Hong Kong Transition," in Li Pang-kwong, ed., *Political Order and Power Transition in Hong Kong*, pp. 53-78 (Hong Kong: The Chinese University Press, 1997) and "Elections, Politicians, and Electoral Politics," in Stephen Y.L. Cheung and Stephen M.H. Sze, eds., *The Other Hong Kong Report 1995*, pp. 51-65 (Hong Kong: The Chinese University Press, 1995). I also thank David Newman for allowing me to reproduce part of our joint article, and the Institute for Far Eastern Studies, Kyungnam University for permission to reuse it in Chapter 6: Pang-kwong Li and David Newman, "Give and Take: Electoral Politics in Transitional Hong Kong," *Asian Perspective* 21 (1997):213-32.

Tribute must also be paid to Brian Bridges, Pun Wing-chung and Raymond Yeung Wai-man for their advice, comments and criticisms; to Ada Yeung Shui-yin for editorial assistance; to Carmen Chung Sui-lin,

Jennifer Lee Fung-yee, Anthony Ng Kwai-wah and Stella Yu Lai-ngo for their unfailing support and assistance. The usual disclaimer applies.

My deepest thanks should go to my parents and family members for their continuous support, concern and encouragement; to my wife, Oi-ling, and my daughter, Wan-yi, who have suffered from my busy academic life and endless public engagements. Without their support and understanding, this book project could not have come into reality.

Li Pang-kwong
June 1999

List of Abbreviations

123DA	123 Democratic Alliance
BL	Basic Law
BLCC	Basic Law Consultation Committee
BLDC	Basic Law Drafting Committee
CCP	Chinese Communist Party
CDO	City District Officer Scheme
CE	Chief Executive
CPPCC	Chinese People's Political Consultative Conference
CRC	Cooperative Resources Centre
DAAs	District Affairs Advisors
DAB	Democratic Alliance for Betterment of Hong Kong
DBs	District Boards
DP	Democratic Party
EC	Election Committee
ExCo	Executive Council
FC	Functional Constituency
FTU	Federation of Trade Unions
HKAAs	Hong Kong Affairs Advisors
HKADPL	Hong Kong Association for Democracy and People's Livelihood
HKAS	Hong Kong Affairs Society
HKASPDMC	Hong Kong Alliance in Support of the Patriotic Democratic Movement in China
HKCA	Hong Kong Civic Association
HKCF	Hong Kong Citizen Forum
HKDF	Hong Kong Democratic Foundation
HKMAO	Hong Kong and Macau Affairs Office
HKO	Hong Kong Observers
HKPA	Hong Kong Progressive Alliance
HKPTU	Hong Kong Professional Teachers' Unions
HKSAR	Hong Kong Special Administrative Region
HOS	Home Ownership Scheme
JD	Sino-British Joint Declaration
JLG	Joint Liaison Group
KMT	Kuomintang

KTMCA	Kwun Tong Man Chung Association
LDF	Liberal Democratic Federation
LegCo	Legislative Council
MP	Meeting Point
NCNA	New China News Agency
NHKA	New Hong Kong Alliance
NPC	National People's Congress
NTA	New Territories Alliance
NTAS	New Territories Association of Societies
NWSC	Neighbourhood and Workers Service Centre
OR	October Review
PE	Popular Election
PHKS	Progressive Hong Kong Society
PRC	People's Republic of China
PSPS	Private Sector Participation Scheme
PWC	Preliminary Working Committee
RCHK	Reform Club of Hong Kong
RegCo	Regional Council
SCOPG	Standing Committee on Pressure Groups
SoCO	Society for Community Organisation
TUC	Trades Union Council
UA	United Ants
UDHK	United Democrats of Hong Kong
UrbCo	Urban Council

1 Introduction

After more than 150 years of British rule, Hong Kong has become a part of China since July 1997. The transition from a British colony to a Chinese special administrative region was not only a transfer of sovereignty, but also touched upon a very important issue of political transition generated by the Sino-British Joint Declaration signed in December 1984. The Sino-British Joint Declaration had provided an impetus to reform the colonial political structure by the injection of election into the political system. Later in 1990, the Basic Law (the mini-constitution for post-1997 Hong Kong) had furthered a step by stipulating that the Chief Executive (CE) and all the LegCo members of the Hong Kong Special Administrative Region (HKSAR) be ultimately returned by popular election. The transformation of the mode of political recruitment through appointment to one through election has redefined the rule of the political game and the associated value system and norms of behaviour.

From an institutional perspective, the introduction of popular election into the District Boards (DBs) and the Legislative Council (LegCo) in 1982 and 1991, respectively, had kicked off a long process of political transformation. However, political change in Hong Kong in the 1980s and 1990s has its uniqueness. First of all, it is clear that Hong Kong would never have become an independent state after the "decolonization" process. Chinese government, whether under the rule of the Kuomintang (KMT) or the Chinese Communist Party (CCP), has never failed to assert its sovereignty over Hong Kong and has claimed to be able to restore it when they think fit. Unlike other British colonies, therefore, the transfer of power has not been from the colonial government to the native people but to another sovereign state--China. Thus, the normal Westminster decolonization process leading to the establishment of a parliamentary sovereign state would not happen in Hong Kong. The destiny of Hong Kong was finally fixed in 1984 when Britain agreed to return Hong Kong to China in 1997.

Second, there has been a lack of widespread nationalist movements in Hong Kong since the 1940s. Without the intense mobilization in society witnessed in the independence movements of other decolonizing colonies, Hong Kong has failed to create an integrated political force and a popular leadership to represent the people's views and interests, and to provide a vision of change. On the one hand, the traditional and economic elites have been isolated from the masses for decades and it has been very difficult to enlist support from the masses because of differences in values and interests between them. On the other hand, the newly emerging middle-class political activists have had some social support, but they have been rather loosely organized and not equipped well with the "will and might" to challenge the political status quo.

Third, the "pre-emptive" political reforms in the 1980s initiated by Britain have unleashed the "frozen" political force.[1] At the organizational level, group-building efforts attempted by the political activists were induced in the early 1980s by the expected devolution of power as stipulated in the Sino-British Joint Declaration in 1984 and the Chinese promise of "Hong Kong people governing Hong Kong" after 1997. This gave an institutional push to defrost the "frozen" political forces and eventually created a political market through which various political groups compete among themselves for the devolved political goods. At the individual level, the mass public was suddenly exposed to the still-in-the-making political market and subject to frequent political mobilization drives by the political activists. Their political horizons were, in one way or another, extended, because "politics" was no more a taboo in society. The demystification of politics had removed psychological hurdles and eventually made society prone to political mobilization. Moreover, the enfranchised public was reminded to think politically by the periodic advent of elections. More important is that the reform from above created a situation where the political power devolved in an orderly way to the local society. This development contradicted the wishes of the Chinese government. Any reforms, without the blessing of the Chinese government, would not be accepted because Beijing questions the motive behind the reform and wants as little change in political structure as possible in the transitional period. But the ball was not in the Chinese court. The British government still had the legitimate right to initiate as well as carry out its own policy in the transitional period, although consultation with China was required as stipulated in the Sino-British Joint Declaration of 1984. Moreover, the situation was further complicated by the fact that the democrats,[2] whose political value and orientation differed from that of the Beijing government, especially after the Tiananmen Incident in 1989, were supported by the majority of Hong Kong voters from the 1991 LegCo first-ever popular elections.[3] In the 1991 LegCo popular elections, out of the 18 popularly-elected seats, the democrats won 16. More important was the fact that none of the leftist candidates were elected (*Oriental Daily News*, 17 September 1991, p. 3; *Sing Tao Jih Pao*, 17 September 1991, p. 23). It is very strange to have such a complicated and subtle relationship between the colonial government, the colonized, and future sovereign state of the colonized.

Under such peculiar circumstances, how to comprehend the collective behaviour of the Hong Kong voters and the results of the LegCo popular elections are, thus, important topics to explore. Individuals do not live in isolation. They are social beings and, thus, cannot avoid interaction with society. So, individual behaviour has its social and contextual dimensions. In other words, the electoral choice of voters, though made individually, has something to do with the specific social configurations and conditions which prevailed at the election time. With this understanding in mind, what this book plans to study is the identification of the social cleavage lines that help shape the voters' choice and serve as the basis of mobilization during the LegCo popular elections. It also attempts to explore the following related questions: what specific social conditions in the 1980s contributed to the salience of particular cleavage lines among the political elites? How did these cleavage lines structure the development of political groups (parties) in the 1980s? Under what political conditions do these political groups establish linkage and network with the electorate? How effective are the mobilization efforts of these political groups? What implications do these cleavages have for the future political change of Hong Kong in general, and the development of the party system and electoral competition in particular?

Amid the introduction of popular election and the emergence of a particular cleavage system, the institutional arrangements and design of a political system are also important in managing the political conflicts created by the emerging political market, in which partisan alignment, de-alignment and realignment have taken place. This book therefore also explores the dynamic relationships between as well as the institutional designs of the executive and legislature in the post-1997 Hong Kong and to examine the institutional arrangements, as stipulated in the Basic Law, in terms of their capacity for conflict resolution and management.

Literature Review

Given that universal suffrage in Hong Kong was only introduced at the district level in 1982 and at the central level in 1991, it is not surprising to find that there were not many academic electoral studies in the 1980s. As one study has suggested, there were altogether 67 voting behaviour surveys in the period 1970-91, and nearly half of them (N=32) were conducted in 1991 (Louie and Wan, 1992:27, appendix 2). Furthermore, most of them were conducted by civic or community groups, or commissioned by the mass media. The objective of the former in conducting voting behaviour surveys was to mobilize the mass public's electoral awareness, while that of the latter was to attract readers' or audiences' attention by predicting the winners in the electoral "horse races". Thus, nearly all of these surveys are descriptive in nature rather than explanatory. As shown in the same study, only nine voting surveys (with reports) were conducted by academics (Louie and Wan, 1992:22-4). Nevertheless, over twenty papers on the 1991 elections and eleven papers on the 1995 elections were added to the stock of voting studies in Hong Kong in late 1992 and 1993 as well as in 1996 (Kwok, Leung and Scott, 1992; Lam and Lee, 1992a, 1992b; Lau and Louie, 1993; Kuan, Lau, Louie and Wong, 1996).

Humans do not live in isolation. They interact with each other to form a closely-knit social network and community. It is therefore believed that if one is going to understand the collective action of individuals, a possible way out is to put their actions into context and then have them analysed. Election behaviour, or more specific voters' choice, has therefore had its social foundation. This social cleavage approach has directed the researchers' attention to the electoral expression of social contradiction and its relations with electoral support.

As political conflicts are of different natures and forms in different societies, political cleavages will then be organized along the different bases of social divisions. Although there are various types of cleavage, only a few of them may find electoral expression and serve as the basis for partisan alignment. The salience of particular cleavages may depend on the availability and nature of political cleavages presented at the time of the introduction of universal franchise.

As a result, social or economic divisions that have found political (electoral) expression may serve as the basis of cleavage, cutting or cross-cutting the electorate into several slices. Party competition and electoral battles would, then, be fought along these lines of cleavage.

There have been four articles adopting the cleavage approach in analysing Hong Kong's voters' choice. Two of them were written by Leung Sai-wing (1993, 1996). Leung argues that "it was the socialization of alienation through political events, with the June 4th Incident as the climax, during the transitional period of Hong Kong that resulted in the besieging of pro-China candidates by an anti-Communist China sentiment and in the landslide victory of the democratic camp in the 1991 [LegCo] direct election" (Leung, 1992:192). Furthermore, Leung also indicates that some Hong Kong people, especially the younger generation, have evolved an "anti-Communist China syndrome". The syndrome that he refers to is "an integrated set of political attitudes, with the distrust of the Chinese government as the centrifugal force, from which other related political attitudes, or even political actions, are derived" (Leung, 1992: 219-20). Leung also predicts that "the space for development of the democratic camp is limited by this [anti-Communist China] sentiment" because "the democrats have to bear risks of many kinds by continuing to say 'no' to the Chinese government after 1997" (1996: 233 & 234).

The other two were written by this author (Li, 1993, 1996). One of them studied the urban-rural cleavage in the 1991 District Boards elections and the other advanced a dual cleavage model to account for the voters' behaviour in the 1995 LegCo popular elections. The basic argument of the latter paper is that: the effect of the Tiananmen Incident complex or the "anti-Communist China syndrome" on Hong Kong voters' choice is the function of the domestic conflicts here in Hong Kong and its linkage (interaction) with this complex. The emotional feelings attached to this complex would be sustained for a long period of time only if it finds a manifestation in the local conflict or cleavage system which is believed to have a more permanent effect on voters' choice.

The popular reason advanced to account for the landslide victory of the democrats, especially those of the United Democrats of Hong Kong (UDHK) and the Meeting Point (MP), in the 1991 first-ever LegCo popular elections was the Tiananmen Incident complex or the "anti-Communist China syndrome" among the Hong Kong voters. It is true that the events in the Tiananmen Square in 1989 had reinforced the Hong Kong people's long-term distrust of the communist Chinese government, and thus contributed to their support for the democrats' candidates. But it might not be the sole factor in shaping the voters' electoral choices. What is left untouched are the domestic political contradictions and their linkages with China. In the mid-1980s, two conflicts seem to occupy the domestic political scene. First, the political conflict between the Hong Kong government, the conservatives[4] and the leftists[5] on the one hand, and the democrats on the other, over the political reforms in the transitional period, as well as between the conservatives and the democrats over the future political model of the HKSAR. Second, the conflict between the Hong Kong government and Hong Kong society over the privatization scheme and related measures. The picture becomes more complicated because of China's growing involvement in Hong Kong's domestic politics. It is a logical development as Hong Kong becomes part of China after 1997. The problems are: under what conditions do the two sides meet with each other, and what attitude does the Chinese government adopt to frame the new political relationship and order between itself and Hong Kong.

Theoretical Framework

It is useful to clarify a number of terms and concepts, such as democratization, political cleavage, political mobilization, partisan alignment, institutional design and conflict management, which have been the subject of academic debate, so as to provide a theoretical framework for this study.

Democratization and Elections

As advanced by Samuel P. Huntington (1991:45-106), there are several conditions contributing to the democratization of the non-democratic regimes. They are:

- declining legitimacy and the performance dilemma;
- economic development and economic crises;
- religious changes;
- new policies of external actors; and
- demonstration effects or snowballing.

Although the relative significance of the above-mentioned objective conditions may vary, Huntington has included in his analysis a subjective dimension of democratic transition, that is, the "will and skill" of political leaders throughout the democratization process. To borrow his words,

> General factors create conditions favorable to democratization. They do not make democratization necessary, and they are at one remove [sic] from the

factors immediately responsible for democratization. A democratic regime is installed not by trends but by people. Democracies are created not by causes but by causers. Political leaders and publics have to act. . . . (Huntington, 1991:107)

What is democratization, then? Put simply, democratization denotes the process of transition from authoritarian to democratic rule. In the process of democratization, Stein Rokkan (1970:79-96) has identified four sequential thresholds:

- legitimation: the recognition of the right of petition, criticism against the regime, and the protection of the rights of assembly, expression, etc;
- incorporation: the granting of equal right to choose representatives to the opposition and their potential supporters;
- representation: the lowering of institutional barriers for the representation of the opposition; and
- executive power: the opening of the executive organ to legislative pressure, or the direct influence of the legislature on executive decision-making.

The emergence of competitive mass politics depends on the crossing of the first two thresholds, while the institutional development of mass politics relies on the crossing of the last two thresholds. The lowering of one threshold would sooner or later generate pressure on the change of the other, but the transition to other higher thresholds would not be automatic.

Furthermore, Rokkan (1970:227) has also suggested "four steps of change" in the process of electoral mobilization:

- incorporation: the inclusion of the former disfranchised publics;
- mobilization: the mobilization of the enfranchised in electoral contests;
- activation: the encouragement of direct participation in public life; and
- politicization: the intrusion of national parties into local elections.

Although scholars and the public have different interpretations of the word "democracy" and the exact constitution of democratic rule, one thing that can be certain is the minimum institutional requirement that the top decision-makers should be elected periodically by means of an open, fair, popular and competitive election.

If we use this ideal criterion to measure Hong Kong's political reforms implemented to date, we can only describe the moves so far as "liberalization" rather than "democratization" of the political structure; for liberalization means "the partial opening of an authoritarian system short of choosing governmental leaders through freely competitive elections" (Huntington, 1991:9). In the context of Hong Kong (as of 1999), although only 20 seats, out of 60 seats, are opened for popular election and the post of chief executive is still not determined by means of popular election, the various LegCo popular elections held in 1991, 1995 and 1998 can be regarded as a competitive one because the participants, whether candidates or voters, are free to enter or exit the election. The distribution of the remaining 40 members are as follow: 30 elected members through functional constituency and 10 members returned by electoral college.

Whatever it may be, liberalization or democratization, once the competitive elections and universal franchise have been put in place in a state, the institutional threshold of political participation will be lowered. The absorption of the newly mobilized persons into the "network of electoral institutions" may have a "deinstitutionalizing effect" on the existing political order. As a result, the "decay of institutionalized patterns of behavior" has given the original, excluded politicians an opportunity of jockeying for power through the newly instituted competitive electoral system (Przeworski, 1975:49-67). Subsequently, modern mass political parties would be formed to fight the electoral battle. Through the help of political parties, the public have been, in one way or another, incorporated into the national political process. Joseph LaPalombara and Myron Weiner (1966:9) have aptly described the situation:

> Where the suffrage is greatly restricted, local electoral committees are simply not needed; where it is expanded, the need to woo the masses is strongly felt. What was once a struggle limited to an aristocratic elite or small groups of notables now becomes a major drama in which large segments of the citizenry play an active role.

The most controversial and critical issue during the transition seems to be "the production of contingent consent" on a set of election rules that the ensuing national elections will be based upon (O'Donnell and Schmitter, 1986:59). All the concerned parties will try to shape the election rules to their favour, "for the party that wins the transition election plays a key role in the consolidation of democracy, often writing a new constitution, deciding the fate of the old guard, and rewriting the 'rules of the game'".[6] Guillermo O'Donnell and Philippe C. Schmitter (1986:59-60) highlight three critical dimensions in finding such consent of procedural democracy:

- eligibility of participants and threshold for representation;
- electoral formula ("workable majorities" vs. "accurate representation"); and
- "the structure of offices for which national elections are held" ("parliamentarism" vs. "presidentialism").

At a "founding election", it is said that the election outcome would be highly uncertain because of the inexperience of voters in choosing candidates, weak identity of voters with parties, unclear candidates' image, and the unreliability of survey results.[7]

Nancy Bermeo (1987:213), however, has proposed three structural factors that may have "the strongest effect" on the outcome of the "transition election":

- the patterns of regime transformation: revolution or reform;
- the class configurations; and
- the critical role of semiopposition.

The term "semiopposition" is used by Juan Linz (1973:191-2) to describe groups "that are not dominant or represented in the governing group but that are willing to participate in power without fundamentally challenging the regime" and thus, can be considered as "[b]eing partly 'out' [of] and partly 'in' power".

Concept of Political Cleavages

If the statement "politics arises from the existence of cleavages" is assumed to be true (Rae and Taylor, 1970:21), then, social cleavages exist in every political community, no matter what the form of government or political system may be. The problem is by what means can we identify these cleavages. Probably, elections may provide the appropriate occasion to detect them, as elections are said to serve as "a measure of social divisions" and "provide information on the extent to which society is organized and divided by such factors as religion, class and ethnicity" (Harrop and Miller, 1987:173). This is particularly the case in "competitive" elections.

Douglas W. Rae and Michael Taylor (1970:1) have defined cleavages as:

> the criteria which divide the members of a community or subcommunity into groups, and the relevant cleavages are those which divide members into groups with important political differences at specific times and places.

Ronald Inglehart (1984:25) indicates that if a political community is divided into groups that particularly favour certain policies and parties for a period of time, political cleavages are said to be present. He described political cleavages as "relatively stable patterns of polarization" in a political system.

As political conflicts are of different natures and forms in different societies, political cleavages will then be organized along different bases of social divisions. The following scholars have put forward various types of cleavages.

Seymour M. Lipset and Stein Rokkan (1967:14) suggest four critical cleavages:

- subject-dominant culture (centre-periphery);
- church-government (church-state);
- primary-secondary economy (land-industry); and
- workers-employers (worker-owner).

The first two and the last two cleavages are the direct products of national and industrial revolutions, respectively.

Rae and Taylor (1970:1) have differentiated three types of cleavage:

- ascriptive (race or caste);
- attitudinal ("opinion" cleavages as ideology or preference); and
- behavioural ("act" cleavage elicited through voting and organizational membership).

Huntington (1974:163-91) suggests that three major cleavages will develop when society moves from being industrial to post-industrial:

- group cleavage: that is divisions between declining and rising social forces; between declining forces; and between rising social forces in terms of social status, economic position, and numerical strength.

- institutional cleavage: that is party conflict, legislative-executive conflict, state-national conflict, executive bureaucracy-mass media conflict.
- ideological (political goals and values) cleavage: that is between modern and traditional groups; among modernizing groups of bourgeoisie, the military, and intellectuals over values of development, efficiency, and egalitarianism.

In the past decade, the literature on electoral cleavage is mainly divided over the discussion of production-based (class) and consumption-based (sectoral) cleavages. Before the late 1970s, class voting research had received wide acceptance in Western academic circles, especially in Britain. In the late 1970s, this trend was challenged by Patrick Dunleavy (1979, 1980a, 1980b), who incorporated the concept of consumption cleavages in explaining electoral behaviour. Dunleavy argues that with the expansion of state activities and state intervention into the consumption process, sectoral cleavages (collective vs. individualized consumption) would emerge and crosscut the existing class cleavages. Hence, class voting may decline and give way to accommodate sectoral voting. The sectoral cleavage model is basically developed out of the thesis of collective consumption in urban politics advanced by Manuel Castells (1978: chapter 2) in 1972.

Inglehart (1977, 1984) argues that the value-based polarization of materialist-postmaterialist issues has entered into the political arena. He suggests that when the postmaterialist issues, such as environmentalism, the women's movement, the peace movement, the consumer advocacy movement, come to the centre of political debates, the materialist reaction of much of the working class would be stimulated to reassert the traditional materialist value of economic growth, security, and law and order. This may help to neutralize the class-based cleavage and eventually pave the way for electoral and partisan change. Parties of the Left will be divided over the postmaterialist issues and, thus, suffer a net flow of support to the Right. This perspective is also known as the "new politics thesis" (Knutsen, 1986:235-63).

In a review article discussing cleavage models, Arend Lijphart (1990:143-50) has included foreign policy, regime support, participatory democracy, and ecological dimensions on the top of those types proposed by Lipset and Rokkan.

12 Hong Kong from Britain to China

Political Mobilization, Political Party and Partisan Alignment

Although there are various types of cleavage, as mentioned above, only a few of them may find electoral expression and serve as the basis for partisan alignment (see Figure 1.1). The salience of particular cleavages may depend on the availability and nature of political cleavages presented at the time of introduction of universal franchise. Given that the election results would decide who or which party has the mandate to rule within a pre-defined period of time, and the legitimacy to allocate or distribute political goods and social resources, different political forces would align with those of similar values to form political groups or parties and mobilize people for electoral support. Thus, political parties would act as an agent to politicize the cleavages and to mobilize them for electoral support.

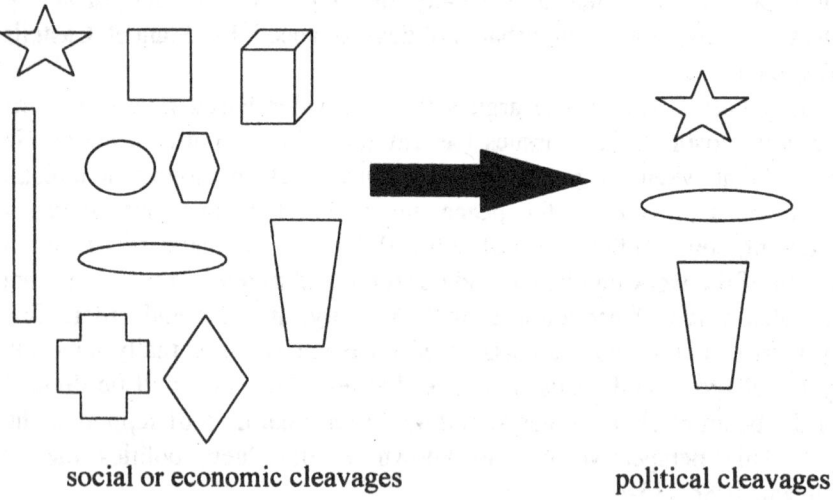

social or economic cleavages   political cleavages

Figure 1.1   Cleavage Transformation

Mobilization, here, is conceptualized as a composite process involving several stages:

(a) the existence of values and goals requiring mobilization.
(b) action on the part of leaders, elites or institutions seeking to mobilize individuals and groups.
(c) the institutional and collective means of achieving this mobilization.
(d) the symbols and references by which values, goals and norms are communicated to, and understood as well as internalized by, the individuals involved in mobilization.
(e) the process by which mobilization takes place in terms of individual interaction, the creation and change of collectivities and structure, the crystallization of roles, the effect on subsystems and their boundaries.
(f) estimates of the numbers of people (or proportion of a population) mobilized and the degree of such mobilization for different sectors or strata of the population (Nettl, 1967:33).

In other words, political mobilization "is to be considered as differential commitment and support for collectivities based on cleavages" (Nettl, 1967:126).

The seminal work of Lipset and Rokkan (1967:1-64) in *Party Systems and Voter Alignments* provided the theoretical linkage between cleavage structure, party systems, and voter alignment. They argued that the incorporation of rank-and-file voters into the electoral process as a result of the introduction of universal franchise in most European countries and the presence of social cleavages in the political community would help to shape the development of party systems. Political parties are said to be an "agent of conflict and instrument of integration". On the one hand, a political party is only a "part" of the political system; it needs to compete with others for power. Conflict, thus, is hard to prevent. On the other hand, when a party is engaged in the established political game, it certainly works to mobilize voters to support its own cause. As a result of such mobilization, the former, loosely knitted local community would be integrated with the national political process.

Alan S. Zuckerman (1982:137-40) argues that the nature and extent of political cleavage depends on the interplay between party leadership and the "variable strength of the social bonds". The term "social bonds" is described as "tightly knit networks of interaction" in which "most individuals interact with others on many dimensions and exist within variably bound groups". Therefore, its meaning is different from Karl Marx's concept of class. He also argues that only politicized networks of interaction would give rise to the persistent political divisions, and political divisions would be either widespread or persistent, and vice versa.

Political parties make use of the media and the "tightly knit networks of interaction" to convey their respective value systems and policy positions to the public. In order to differentiate from other political parties, the traditional view of conducting election campaigns has been said to adopt a "direct confrontation" method and focuses on the party difference over a set of issues or policies. But Ian Budge and Dennis Farlie (1983:269-72) point out that parties actually tend to emphasize selectively their "own" issue or policy areas. That is what they call the "saliency theory" of party competition.

As a result, social or economic divisions that have found political (electoral) expression may serve as the basis of cleavage, cutting or cross-cutting the electorate into several slices. Party competition and electoral battles would, then, be fought along these lines of cleavage. Although Lipset and Rokkan (1967) have claimed that the Western party system has been frozen for nearly half-a-century, the shift of the cleavage line may actually cause the realignment of political forces. Parties that have responded adequately to the new shift and absorbed the new cleavages into their own programmes will survive. Parties that have failed to adapt will witness a significant decline of electoral support and fade away eventually. Electoral volatility may then happen and pave the way for dealignment or realignment of political forces. The study of electoral volatility (change, dealignment, realignment) therefore has received much attention from scholars in the field (Bartolini and Mair, 1990; Budge, 1982; Butler and Strokes, 1974; Clubb, Flanigan, and Zingale, 1990; Crewe and Denver, 1985; Dalton, Flanagan, and Beck, 1984; Salisbury and MacKuen, 1981; Sundquist, 1983).

The ebb and flow of a particular social cleavage will cause a long-term change in the party system. As suggested above, the rise of postmaterialist values in Western Europe has crosscut the parties of the left. The line of reasoning is that when a party fails to respond to the emerging critical cleavages, the decline of electoral support may be expected, and those parties that can represent the new cleavage may witness a significant gain of vote.

But the same logic would not apply to the type of election that has taken place in a "non-competitive" system. Since the whole exercise of election is devised to legitimatize the pre-determined outcome, the electoral result would not really reflect the societal cleavages. There is no such thing as partisan alignment and party system change in that kind of election. So, some scholars describe this as "state-controlled" elections (Hermet, 1978; Furtak, 1990a).

Institutional Design and Conflict Management

Elections have been regarded as an instrument to detect the presence of social conflicts and their intensity. The conflicts, or what we call cleavages for those conflicts which are durable and have political significance, that find political or electoral expression may serve as a dividing line that cuts across the electorate and a mobilising basis that helps the political groups or parties to fight the election battle.

Conflicts may take different forms and be of different natures. The minimum requirement that a political community needs to survive is the spread of "we-group" feeling among members, based upon which the sense of nationhood is built.[8] Therefore, if there is conflict over national identity, political instability would then follow. A typical example is Northern Ireland. The nationhood (statehood) crisis can be regarded as the basic challenge to the very survival of a political community.

Less critical, but it does not mean that it is not important and significant, in threatening the survival of a political community is the conflict over the kind of regime that would be constituted. Regime is defined as:

> ... that part of the political system which determines how and under what conditions and limitations the power of the state is exercised. ... [R]egime embody the norms and principles of the political organization of the state, which are set out in the rules and procedures within which governments operate. (Lawson, 1993:187)

The conflict over regime type is a reflection of the way members of that community diverged on the basic principles of organising the polity and of dispersing political power and social resources.

Under the broad political framework, members may further have conflicts over how to transform the accepted principles into corresponding institutional rules and decision-making procedures (institutional arrangements). That means there may be more than one way to operate the same principles. As Krasner (1983:3) rightly points out:

Principles and norms provide the basic defining characteristics of a regime. There may be many rules and decision-making procedures that are consistent with the same principles and norms. Changes in rules and decision-making procedures are changes within regimes, provided that principles and norms are unaltered.

Therefore, the conflicts over the rules and decision-making procedures can be regarded as "changes within regime" and do not necessarily relate to the conflicts over the regime type itself. The latter conflict can be regarded as "regime change" which will touch upon the fundamental principles of the regime.

Conflicts over public policy may be located at the lowest level of political conflicts. Compared with the conflicts over institutional arrangements, the policy conflicts are more narrow in scope and specific in content. As long as the conflict resolution mechanisms (decision-making procedures) are effective, the policy conflict may not transform into a higher level of political conflict.

In considering whether a cross-level, either upward or downward, transformation of conflicts would be developed, the nature of the conflicts may have a role to play. If the conflict is categorized as an "encapsulating" one, the possibility of a downward cross-level transformation of conflicts may be higher, and vice versa. Figure 1.2 illustrates those relationships graphically.

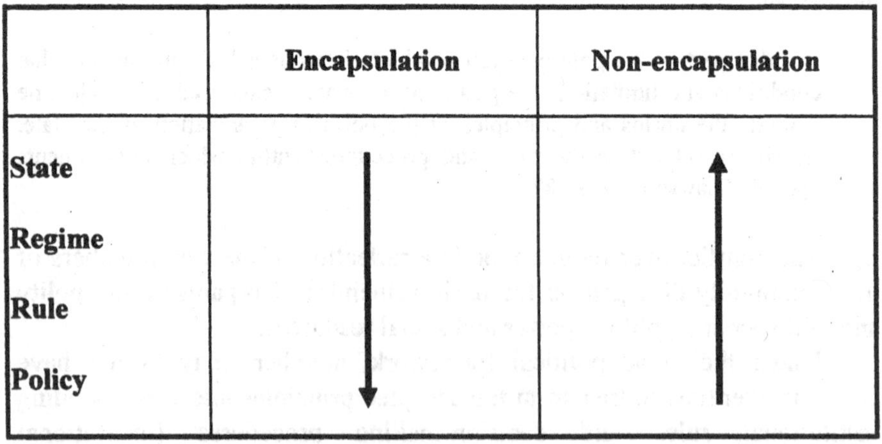

	Encapsulation	Non-encapsulation
State	↓	↑
Regime		
Rule		
Policy		

Figure 1.2   The Typology of Political Conflicts

The concept of "encapsulated conflicts" is borrowed from Amitai Etzioni. He describes "encapsulation" as "the process by which conflicts are modified in such a way that they become limited by rules". Etzioni indicates that encapsulation "does not require that the conflict be resolved or extinguished but only that the range of expression be curbed" and "hostile parties are more readily 'encapsulated' than pacified" (Etzioni, 1964:242-3).

One of the functions of a constitution is to provide a legitimate channel for conflict management or resolution. Although the nature and scope of conflicts varies across societies, the way these conflicts are being resolved does have a tremendous impact on the political order and stability of a society. The effectiveness of the channel to settle conflicts depends on whether the conflicting parties regard the existing institutional arrangements as just and legitimated. That kind of feeling or judgement, in turn, depends on (1) how high is the institutional threshold of allowing the political elites, groups or parties to represent their perceived social conflicts in the resolution process if they see fit (the lower the better, but not that low as this will overload the process) and (2) how effectively the conflicts are being resolved within the exiting institutional arrangements.

Organization of the Book

Following on from this introductory chapter (Chapter 1), the remainder of the book is organized as follows:

The political context under which the political reforms in the 1980s took place is examined in Chapter 2. Topics included are: the nature of the Colonial state, the social compositions and their political orientations, the reasons for no serious challenge to colonialism, and the unusual decolonization process in the early 1980s. By putting in this context, subsequent developments can be properly comprehended. Chapter 3 charts the development of centre-periphery cleavage in the 1980s, in which the contradiction between the British-Hong Kong government and the Hong Kong society was gradually transformed to that of the Chinese government and Hong Kong society. The focal point is the pace and direction of political liberalization or democratization in the transition period as well as the degree of autonomy enjoyed after 1997. Attempts are also made to examine the efforts of all the concerned parties to mobilize support for their favoured political models before and after 1997. The fourth chapter demonstrates the expanding activities of the Hong Kong state and the formation of the consumption cleavage. The reason for privatization since the mid-1980s is also examined and the example of public housing programmes is used to illustrate the trend of privatization. The more the government intervenes in the society, the greater the impact of the government policies upon society; the more the government policies grow in scope and depth, the higher the proportion of people being drawn into the political process. As a result, any change in policy direction will meet with protest from the affected sector(s) and any move to privatize the collective consumption goods, such as public housing, hospital service, education, and so on, will cause shifts in electoral support.

Chapter 5 examines the various stages of development of political forces within Hong Kong and their alignments since the 1970s. The structural factors leading to the transformation of pressure groups into election-oriented political groups are also studied. Social origin of the political forces and their ideology as well as policy location are examined so as to ascertain the nature of the forces and the political (electoral) universe in which the electorates weigh each political force and cast their votes accordingly. By tracing the origins and the alignment of various political forces in the 1980s and 1990s, a budding party system emerges. The sixth chapter focuses on the mobilization efforts the relevant electoral participants had made in the 1991, 1995 and 1998 LegCo popular elections, including both the Chinese and the British governments. It also explores the election results of these LegCo popular elections and tries to comprehend the results in the context of the emerging electoral market and party development. Faced with the tremendous political transformation mentioned in previous chapters, the designing of a new institution that has the capability to cope with the turbulence of realignment of political forces is significant and critical to the political stability of Hong Kong and the legitimacy of the emerging political order. Chapter 7, therefore, aims to explore the dynamic relationships between as well as the institutional designs of the executive and the legislature in the post-1997 Hong Kong and to examine the related institutional arrangements in terms of their capacity for conflict resolution and management. Finally, in conclusion, there is a discussion and evaluation of various possible scenarios that may occur in the post-1997 political and electoral markets.

Notes

1   The word "frozen" is used to describe the rather static nature of the politics of Hong Kong before the 1980s. See Harris (1978:132).
2   The democrats are those who support faster pace of democratization and high degree of autonomy as well as those who advocate more welfare to the low-income groups and the poor. The democrats mostly come from the new middle-class of professionals, intellectuals, social workers, lawyers, and so on.
3   Throughout this book, the word "popular election(s)" is used to denote the elections returned by universal franchise, instead of the word "direct elections", except within quotation.
4   The conservatives are those who support the political status quo and want as little political reform as possible, and who also value the efficiency of the market and oppose greater spending on welfare. The conservatives mostly come from the business sector, rural and local communities.
5   The term "leftists" is used, throughout this book, to denote those people or organizations that are affiliated with the Chinese Communist Party (CCP) or its related organizations, and also those who are the supporters of the CCP.
6   "Transition election" is "the first national electoral contests which follow the restoration of political freedom". See Bermeo (1987:213).
7   "Founding elections" means "for the first time after an authoritarian regime, elected positions of national significance are disputed under reasonably competitive conditions". See O'Donnell and Schmitter (1986:57 & 61).
8   Conceptually, there are differences between "state" and "nation". However, for convenience, I make no attempt to differentiate them in this book. For a simple definition of the two words, see Vernon Bogdanor, ed., *The Blackwell Encyclopaedia of Political Institutions* (Oxford: Basil Blackwell, 1987), pp. 380-381. Although the word "nation" is defined as "a named human community with a myth of common ancestry, historical memories and standardized mass culture, possessing a single territory, division of labour and legal rights for all members", the word "state" is defined as "a set of public institutions, autonomous of other institutions, differentiated, centralized and possessing the monopoly of coercion and extraction in a demarcated and recognized territory".

2 Historical Setting: The State and the Society

Hong Kong as a British Colony

The British Crown Colony of Hong Kong comprised three parts: the Island of Hong Kong, the Kowloon Peninsula, and the New Territories. Hong Kong Island and Kowloon were ceded in perpetuity to Britain in 1842 and 1860, respectively. The New Territories were leased to Britain for a period of 99 years from 1898.

Like other British colonies, Hong Kong was headed by a powerful governor, who was formally appointed by the Queen (King) of the United Kingdom (Miners, 1991). The Governor was supported administratively by the Government Secretariat.[1] Before the 1980s, the highest level of the government bureaucracy was dominated by non-Chinese expatriates. As in other colonies, an appointed Executive Council (ExCo) and LegCo were set up to advise and assist him to rule the colony.[2] Although the power was highly concentrated in the Governor's hands, he was kept under the supervision and co-ordination of the Foreign and Commonwealth Office.[3] In fact, Britain seldom intervened into local affairs, except for those matters related to security and foreign relations, after the Second World War. This was especially the case after the granting of financial autonomy to Hong Kong in 1958. John Walden (1987:89), the former Director of Home Affairs who retired in 1980, outlined the relations between the British and the Hong Kong governments as follows:

> ... the British Government gave the Governor of Hong Kong and his small team of civil servants an almost unfettered hand in the way they governed Hong Kong. The Government, though colonial in origins, was in no sense a creature of the British Government.... Britain rarely tried to exert pressure upon the Hong Kong Government.

In addition, the Governor himself was generally a British civil servant without any vested interest in Hong Kong and was subject to a fixed term of service. Because of such a peculiar relationship, the Hong Kong government was operated actually by bureaucrats who were insulated from public pressure. Nevertheless, "the well-meaning traditional paternalism of British Colonial Governors" would be to care about the welfare of the colonial people (Walden, 1983:9). Otherwise, the colonial authority would have been in deep trouble in maintaining the law and order of Hong Kong.

Under the pressure to have more overseas markets as a result of the tremendous enhancement of productive capacity brought about by industrialisation since the sixteenth century, the British traders, like their counterparts in other European countries, had travelled to Asia for the sake of trade expansion. The colonization of Hong Kong was, therefore, initiated by British traders and arose solely out of economic considerations. It seemed quite normal that the ensuing colonial government often came under the influence of those who have a vested interest in trading with China. Their influence can be well reflected in their nearly exclusive appointment to the LegCo and the ExCo.[1] Furthermore, these traders maintained strong ties with Britain (Endacott, 1962:157-62). The presence of these metropolitan capitalists dominated the input from society in the early period of colonial rule, probably up to the 1920s (Chan, 1991: chapters 2-4).

Accompanying the establishment of the Crown Colony was the flourishing of the entrepot trade and relevant economic development. By taking advantage of the economic boom, some indigenous businessmen promptly adapted to the newly emerged economic order and gradually built up their sphere of influence. In order to accommodate the emerging indigenous economic forces, the Hong Kong government resorted to co-opting the Chinese elite by appointing them to prestigious positions at various levels of government. This corporatist approach of politics is reflected in the appointment of them to the LegCo and the ExCo in 1880 and 1926, respectively (Endacott, 1964:89-96 & 135-49; Cheng, 1969).

The predominant position of the traders and big business representatives in the state structure has been maintained up to the present, though the pool of appointment was extended to the "new rich" and middle-class professionals in the mid-1970s. Some scholars have argued that the state power seems to be used to protect and enhance the privileges of the capitalist class (Davies, 1977). An often-quoted sentence reads: "Power in Hong Kong . . . resides in the Jockey Club, Jardine and Matheson, The Hong Kong and Shanghai Bank, and the Governor--in that order" (Hughes, 1976:23). H.J. Lethbridge (1969:127) also argues that: "It is a Colony run today-- though this is not a result of deliberate Government policy but faute de mieux--for a small group of Chinese and European businessmen, experts in the technique of making money". This line of reasoning is in line with the Marxist argument that the capitalist state is only "a committee for managing the common affairs of the whole bourgeoisie" (Marx and Engels, 1967:82). That means the state does not have its own autonomy at all.

But we would argue that in order to maintain the capitalist mode of production, the state would have to act in contradiction to the will of some capitalists. In analysing post-colonial societies in South Asia, Hamza Alavi (1972, 1990) has put forward his thesis of the "plurality of economically dominant classes" of metropolitan bourgeoisie, indigenous bourgeoisie and landed bourgeoisie that have regulated and controlled the military-bureaucratic oligarchies through "the needs and demands, the logic, of peripheral capitalism". That means that the bureaucratic state may have a leverage to balance the interests of the above-mentioned economic classes and has thus enjoyed "relative" autonomy as far as it proceeds according to the "structural imperative of capital". That means the state is able to enjoy autonomy, though it may be a "relative" one (Nordlinger, 1981: chapters 1-2).

Although the colonial Hong Kong government was rather free from mass (electoral) pressure, there were occasional conflicts with the businessmen over the question of taxation. On the one hand, Britain seemed to be reluctant to take up all the financial cost of running the colony, but, on the other, the capitalists wanted to pay as little tax as possible and to maintain a "minimal" government. This kind of conflict often surfaced in the early colonial period (Endacott, 1964: chapters 3-4). Although Hong Kong is a capitalist state, it seemed to enjoy a certain degree of autonomy in the face of capitalists' challenge. Several examples can be cited to illustrate this point.

First of all, despite the resistance from both the shipping companies and its own officials, the state insisted on building the state-owned railway which connected Hong Kong with Canton in the mid-1900s. The then Hong Kong Harbour Master was quoted (Davis, 1949:131) as saying the following in 1906:

> It is a work which those who favour it appear to think will bring new prosperity to Hong Kong. But as the Colony depends entirely upon shipping for its existence I do not feel so hopeful, neither do I see its value or necessity.

Even up to 1934, the shipping companies, which were dominated by European capitalists, still complained about the unfair competition of the state-owned railway.

Second, despite competition from a British firm, the Hong Kong state granted a contract of HK$5,000 million to a Japanese consortium for the construction of the Mass Transit Railway in 1973 (Kuan, 1979:151).

Third, contrary to its economic philosophy of laissez-faire, the government initiated a massive public housing scheme in the early 1970s. The state intervention into the collective consumption process had the effect of stabilizing workers' wages and maintaining its cheap labour edge in the world market (Rabushka, 1973; Schiffer, 1991).

Fourth, following a decade of social protest and movement as well as the flourishing of pressure groups, the state started to co-opt and accommodate the emerging new middle-class critics in the early 1980s by appointing them to various advisory committees and carrying out partial reform of its political structure. In the eyes of the metropolitan and indigenous capitalists, these emerging forces would do harm to the free economy, as they stand for the provision of "free lunch" and the establishment of some form of welfare state.

State Development in the Pre-1945 Period

In the century beginning from the establishment of the colonial state in 1841 to the eve of the Japanese occupation in 1941, there was no substantial social demand on the Hong Kong government, with the exception of the conflict between the earlier Governors and the business community over the problem of taxation and the great labour strikes in 1925. As a whole, the population living there by 1941 did not regard Hong Kong as their permanent domicile but rather as a temporary residence for the sake of economic betterment and emigration. Therefore, the society was of a transient nature in this period of time. Moreover, Hong Kong has served as a doorstep or supporting base for the British and later Chinese businessmen to advance their economic activities in mainland China. Acting as an entrepot, the function of the Hong Kong government was largely confined to maintaining law and order, and the basic port and communication facilities.

Given the least degree of integration, the state relied on a narrow strata of socio-economic elites to communicate with the society which is largely composed of ethnic Chinese (Lethbridge, 1978: chapters 3-5). The co-option of the prominent social and economic figures into the ExCo, the

LegCo, the Sanitary Board (SB)[2] and other advisory bodies served to enhance the legitimacy and efficiency of the Hong Kong government. The Hong Kong government started to appoint non-official members of LegCo and ExCo in 1850 and 1896 respectively.[3] Non-popular election of LegCo non-official members was also instituted in 1884, though it was not a formal process (Miners, 1991:129, n1). The Hong Kong General Chamber of Commerce and the non-official Justices of the Peace each elected one nominee whose name would be put through by the Governor to the Secretary of State in Britain for appointment (Endacott, 1964:102-3). The SB also had its non-official and elected members in 1886 and 1888 respectively. But the franchise of the SB was very restrictive and its function was largely confined to the maintenance of public health. In the New Territories, the Hong Kong government first adopted the principle of indirect rule through village elders, but this was gradually replaced by a district administration system with District Officer as the administrative head there. The state has co-opted the local landed figures through the Heung Yee Kuk (Rural Consultation Committee) since 1926. It has served as an informal senior advisory council and acted as the sole representative body for the indigenous residents there.

After the Japanese occupation in the period 1941-45, the British returned to Hong Kong and reinstalled the pre-war administrative structures there. But what was different from the pre-war period was the readiness of the British-Hong Kong government to carry out political reform in the mid-1940s. Mark Young, the then Hong Kong Governor, announced his intention to reform the colonial political structure in 1946, but the ensuing developments within and without Hong Kong contributed to the dropping of the plan. Chapter 4 will deal with this point in more detail.

A Chinese Society Under British Rule

The Hong Kong people, especially the Chinese, have long been described as politically apathetic. Living in a "borrowed time" and a "borrowed place" (Hughes, 1976), most of the Hong Kong Chinese are said to have emphasized material values, social stability, and short-term time horizons (Lau, 1982:68-72). In addition, they are submissive to authority and lack civic consciousness and a sense of belonging. The submissive attitude of the Chinese people was well described by Lin Yu-tang (1938:44; Miners, 1975:32), a famous scholar, in 1938:

There is so much of this virtue [of Confucian patience] that it has almost become a vice. The Chinese people have put up with more tyranny, anarchy and misrule than any Western people have put up with, and seem to have regarded them as part of the laws of nature. In certain parts of Szechuan [Sichuan] the people have been taxed thirty years in advance without showing more energetic protest than a half-audible curse in the privacy of the household. Christian patience would seem like petulance compared to Chinese patience . . . We submit to tyranny and extortion as small fish swim into the mouth of a big fish.

These orientations owe much to the cultural roots of Confucism and the tumultuous situation in China, particularly in Guangdong Province, from where most of the old Hong Kong Chinese originated. They came to the colony to avoid turmoil in China and seek a better living as well as economic opportunity. Most new-comers from China were labourers, less educated and not wealthy, except those who fled from Shanghai in 1949. The estimated population just before the Japanese occupation in 1941 was 1,600,000, but there was only 500,000 to 600,000 population when the British returned to the colony in 1945. In the late 1940s, there was an influx of refugees because of the civil war in China and the estimated population rose to 1,800,000 (*Hong Kong Annual Report 1954*, p. 16). The population figure doubled by the mid-1960s and amounted to 3,708,920 in 1966 (Census and Statistics Department, 1993:11, Table 2.1). They found Hong Kong to be a promised land, compared with the situation and their life in China. Although the colonial structure was far from perfect and just, it provided a stable environment that was badly needed. With this in mind, they did not bother to challenge the colonial system.

From the mid-1960s, the socio-economic condition has begun to change. The post-war economic boom had failed to narrow the gap between the wealthy and the poor. As Ronald Hsia and Laurence Chau (1978:185) indicated:

Despite the progress made in the 1960's, the distribution of household income in Hong Kong remained highly unequal in 1971. The top quintile of households received 51 per cent of the total income, the lowest quintile got less than 6 per cent, and the next lowest had only 10 per cent. At a low level of overall income, these figures imply a fairly widespread poverty. On a per capita basis, our calculations show that 138,000 persons had a monthly income of less than $50, and another 766,000 had to make do with less than $100. By any standard, these are very poor people indeed.

Furthermore, the working hours were long, usually ten to twelve hours a day and seven days a week in the 1950s and 1960s. As Edward Szczepanik (1958:73) wrote in 1958:

> ... Sunday[s] are very seldom observed, and as a result, work in the Colony goes on almost without interruption the whole year round, often without machines stopping even at night.

Although the workers' average wages increased 73% in the period 1958-65 (Hong Kong Government, 1967a:5-6), it was unlikely to ease their distress caused by the wide gap between their aspirations and the hard reality (Jarvie, 1969:365; England and Rear, 1975: chapter 4). The people's upward mobility through education was also very limited. Only 3,900 university places were available in 1966 and only about 1.7% of the population aged over 5 in the 1960s received university education (Census and Statistics Department, 1975:58 & 61, 1987:16). In addition, it was reported that:

> In 1967, 980,000 pupils were enrolled in schools, but more than 150,000 children of primary school age were unable to attend school and only 39% of 10-14 year olds [sic] and 13% of 15-19 year olds [sic] were enjoying secondary education. (Heaton, 1970:844)

Though the term "sweated labour" is rather an emotional expression, it seems to reflect the feeling of the Hong Kong workers, especially the young workers. In addition, most of them lived in a very congested environment. As described by an official report in 1963:

> The people in these [post-war] buildings may well present a more serious health hazard, and bring up their children mentally, socially, and physically more handicapped or stunted than if they had been in controlled or even uncontrolled squatter shacks on the hillsides. (quoted in Goodstadt, 1969:281)

Although the Hong Kong government had tried its best to provide more resettlement squatter huts, the pace was far behind the demand as there was an enormous influx of refugees from China. According to the estimation of Edvard Hambro in 1954, there were about 385,000 refugees (17.1% of the whole population) in Hong Kong (Hambro, 1955:162). But only 54,559 persons were resettled in cottage resettlement areas and multi-storey resettlement estates by the government in the same year

(Commissioner for Resettlement, 1973:30). Furthermore, according to the 1961 Census report, one-fifth of the urban population lived in housing built of temporary material or in accommodation not designed for domestic use (quoted in Goodstadt, 1969:280).

Under such "a grey industrial world", anomic violence was born. The "social disequilibrium" of Hong Kong, thus, appeared to provide "a logical choice" to start a revolution (Heaton, 1970:840-7). As David Trench, the then Governor of Hong Kong, commented in 1967: ". . . trouble can flare up over any minor matter--a football match or anything else--and it would be foolish to pretend otherwise" (Heaton, 1970:840). The fare increase of the Star Ferry Company in 1966 and the labour strikes of 1967, thus, triggered off a series of protests and riots (Hong Kong Government, 1967a; for the communist view, see Committee of Hongkong-Kowloon Chinese Compatriots of All Circles for the Struggle Against Persecution by the British Authorities in Hong Kong, 1967). Nevertheless, the "China factor" also contributed to the intensification of the conflict. Being inspired by the Cultural Revolution in China at that time and the resulting left-lean policy towards Hong Kong, the local leftists (communists) played a leadership role in the 1967 riots.

After the two riots, the colonial government began to take steps to cool down the tension, namely by the passing of new labour legislation, the reorganization of the Labour Department, the setting up of the Labour Advisory Board and so on (England and Rear, 1975:5-9). Besides, the colonial government came to recognize the fact that there was a large communication gap between the government and the governed. Thus, a series of administrative reforms were carried out, namely the implementation of the City District Officer (CDO) Scheme, the proposal of setting up an ombudsman, and the reorganization and reform of the Civil Service (Scott, 1989:106-70; Hook, 1983: 491-511; King, 1975:422-39).

In the 1970s, the Hong Kong government expanded its activities in social services. The "Ten-Year Housing Programme" and the nine years of compulsory education have signified this tendency (Cheng, 1986). Accompanying these changes were the emergence of social conflicts and the changing perception towards politics. After surveying the nature of social conflicts for the period 1975-1986, one study revealed that:

> The observable pattern of social conflicts in Hong Kong during the period 1975 to 1986 has definitely pointed to an increasing trend of social conflicts which have extended to issues relating to quality of life and civil and political rights. More social conflicts are resorted to for the articulation of sectoral and local interests, with the demands increasingly aiming at long-term

institutional changes and non-material rights.... Besides, participants are getting more and better organized. The presence of more permanent groups of one form or another is becoming a significant feature of social conflicts. (Cheung and Louie, 1991:53)

Another study also recorded a change in attitude towards politics:

While still maintaining a largely anti-political or apolitical predisposition, the Hong Kong Chinese are somehow able, in their values, to lessen subscription to the ideas of political omnipotence, political omniscience and political omnipresence....
The sense of political powerlessness is still the most potent factor in perpetuating political lethargy among the Hong Kong Chinese, but they have become more aware of the multitude of means available to get access to the government, particularly those influence tactics that contain some amount of unconventionality and confrontation.... (Lau and Kuan 1988:115-6)

These slight attitudinal and behavioural changes may probably reflect the emergence of a new generation composed of mostly the local-born Hong Kong people. According to the 1986 by-census figure, the percentage of local-born Hong Kong people for the age groups of "aged under 15" and "aged 15-24" were 90.8% and 84.3%, respectively. These percentages were very high both in absolute and relative terms. The respective percentages for "aged 25-64" and "aged 65 and over" were 42.8% and 11.8%. As a whole, about 59.4% (approximately 3,203,165) of the population had been born in Hong Kong by 1986 (Census and Statistics Department, 1997a:19 and 1997b:7). Their life style as well as value systems had developed to a point that is not hard to detect, and is easily differentiated from their mainland compatriots (Baker, 1983).

Colonialism Without Serious Challenge

During the one and a half centuries of colonial rule, Hong Kong passed through the high tide of nationalism elsewhere without any significant challenge from within. It is also surprising to learn that there were nearly no significant massive national or anti-colonial movements, except the great labour strikes in the 1920s as well as the 1966 and 1967 riots. It seems to many people that this is impossible. But the fact is that it has not only survived but also provided an extended period of stability and prosperity at times when China repeatedly falls into political chaos and social turmoil, especially after the establishment of the People's Republic of China (PRC) in 1949. Why is this so? The answers are probably found in the peculiar domestic condition of Hong Kong and its delicate relations with China.

First of all, the colonial power set up its state structure over a "barren rock" (referring to Hong Kong Island only), where only about 2,000 people were said to live before 1841 and nearly all of them were engaged in some form of farming and fishing (Chan, 1991; Tsai, 1993; Welsh, 1993; Chan, 1993). Their life might well be described as "a primitive, arcadian existence devoid of any ambition beyond their daily wants" (Hurley, 1925:21). Furthermore, Hong Kong was located at the periphery of the Qing imperial state. To borrow Michael Mann's (1984:185-213) concept of state power, Qing China by and large maintained despotic power rather than infrastructural power there.

Second, accompanying the coming of the colonial government was the institutionalization of the capitalist order and development. The idea of acquiring a small piece of land at the mouth of the Pearl River was out of consideration of facilitating trade with China. Naturally, Hong Kong society was shaped to provide the necessary infrastructure in fulfilling this function, such as the development of the transportation facilities, a corresponding legal system, and the spreading of the value of the rule of law. On the other hand, material incentives and the betterment generated in the process of capitalist development have compensated for the loss of statehood which has not been well developed and perceived among the indigenous Chinese population at that moment. There is a widespread old Chinese saying that has well reflected the Chinese attitude towards the government: "Whoever becomes the emperor (ruler), we all have to pay rates (in kind)". Furthermore, Hong Kong has enjoyed a rapid economic growth rate since the late 1950s. For the period 1961-1981, the Gross Domestic Product grew at the average rate of about 9.9% annually in real terms, and at 7.4% per capita (Miners, 1991:34).

Third, most of Hong Kong's population came to reside there well after the setting up of the colonial government (Burns, 1987). That means they were voluntarily subjected to alien rule. Why do they do so? To a large extent, it is the tumultuous situation in China that helps to explain it. When there was social unrest or political instability in China, there would be an influx of people from Canton or nearby provinces into the British colony. Once social order in China was been restored, they moved back to their homeland. This was often the case before the establishment of the PRC in 1949. The influx of people (refugees) therefore was served as a barometer of the stableness of domestic order in China. Furthermore, the capitalist society of Hong Kong has provided the economic opportunity for people originating from the dislocated rural region of China. Given this transient nature, it is difficult for them to develop their identity with Hong Kong. Nor did they seek any social or political reform to the colonial structure. They only regarded Hong Kong as their temporary abode just for the sake of security and economy.

Fourth, the establishment of the PRC in 1949 and the subsequent restless political campaigns as well as social dislocation and economic stagnation have driven those who lived in the colony with a higher standard of living to have little chance to find any romance of nationalism. Furthermore, Hong Kong has been used as an economic and political shelter for those who escaped from the political turmoil in China. This was especially the case after 1949. Although subjected to an alien rule, the Hong Kong Chinese were quite instrumental and pragmatic towards the colonial government. Any national movement aimed at driving out the colonial state would eventually be integrated with its communist mother state. In the face of this dilemma, an old Chinese saying seems aptly applicable: "Among the evils, choose the least one". Under such circumstances, it was easier for the local-born Hong Kong Chinese to develop a separate Hong Kong identity (Baker, 1983).

Fifth, the co-option of the local Chinese elite contributed to the stability of Hong Kong. Through the synarchical rule, prominent Chinese residents were, in one way or another, absorbed into the administrative system and became a part of the colonial establishment. Through such a device, a certain level of elite integration was achieved (King, 1975). Furthermore, the Hong Kong government quite promptly adjusted to the changing environment of Hong Kong once it found the system inadequate or government policy unacceptable to the governed. The timely introduction of the CDO Scheme in 1968 just after the riots of the pro-Beijing leftists in 1967 is an example at hand.

Sixth, the China factor. Although the Kuomintang and the Communists renounced the three "unequal" treaties signed by the Qing government and vowed to restore the sovereignty of Hong Kong at any time, they adopted a cautious and pragmatic approach to solving the issue. As long as the colonial status quo continued to make a contribution to China, Hong Kong would remain as it was. Zhou Enlai, the former Premier of the PRC, was quoted as describing the special role of Hong Kong as "a weather station, an observation point, a meeting place, and a suitable place for things which must be launched and radiated".[4] Moreover, the basic policy of the Beijing government towards Hong Kong since 1949 has been: "Make long-term plans, utilize to the full". This is also known as the "eight-word guiding policy" within the CCP. According to Wong Man-fong, former deputy general secretary of the Hong Kong Branch of the New China News Agency (NCNA) before his retirement in August 1992, the meaning of the "eight-word guiding policy" is:

> "Make long-term plans" refers to the fact that Hong Kong will not be taken back in the near future. Of course, since the central government decided in 1981 to take back Hong Kong after 1997 this part now requires a different kind of explanation.
> "Utilize to the full" refers to making use of all Hong Kong's beneficial conditions to serve China, in particular its economic construction. (*Eastern Express*, 6 July 1994:6)

Unusual Decolonization in the Early 1980s

Regarding the constitutional future of its remaining colonies (dependent territories), Britain made clear its guiding principles in 1968:

> ... Britain will always adhere closely to the cardinal principle to which we have adhered in the past--that the wishes of the people concerned must be the main guide to action--it is not and never has been our desire or intention either to delay independence for those dependencies who want it or to force it upon those who do not. (quoted in Drower, 1992:xiv)

As will be detailed in Chapter 3, the continuous British rule of Hong Kong was hinged on the will of the Chinese government. Any political reforms leading to the drastic change of Hong Kong political structure seemed to invite Chinese intervention. This has long been regarded as one of the reasons not to carry out constitutional reforms since the late 1940s. As David Trench, the former Hong Kong governor, wrote in 1971: "China has made it pretty clear that she would not be happy with a Hong Kong moving towards a representative system" and Hong Kong "has to be either firmly under an old-style colonial government or lose her identity" (Trench, 1971:5; quoted in Lo, 1990:102). But, in the midst of the surge of the 1997 issue, the establishment of elected District Boards by the Hong Kong government at the district level in 1982 signified a revision of the former cautious policy. Some political observers regarded the move as a preparatory stage for the ensuing decolonization process, but others saw it as a logical step to take as the original local administration system had proved to be ineffective (Wong, 1982; Leung, 1982). Whatever the reason(s) behind the local reform in 1982, it was not followed by the usual path of decolonization through transferring power to an independent state, where parliamentary government is operated through periodic elections and universal franchise (Jeffries, 1960; Lee, 1967: chapter 5; Austin, 1980; Darwin, 1988; Miners, 1988). It is because neither the Chinese government would allow Hong Kong to gain independence, nor did the majority of people in Hong Kong want it.

As mentioned before, one of the components of Hong Kong--the New Territories--was bound by a lease treaty which stipulated that the New Territories would be restored to China's sovereignty in 1997. Although Britain had asserted the validity of the various treaties when the question of Hong Kong's future was first raised in early 1980s, it definitely knew that without the New Territories it would be very hard for Hong Kong to survive, because the New Territories cover nearly 90% of the land mass of Hong Kong, have nearly 60 percent of the population living there (Census and Statistics Department, 1981:24, Table 2.3), and have most of the industrial sites located there.

The chance to go independent diminishes when the view and policy of the Chinese government is added to the above objective constraints. As mentioned before, the position of the Chinese government, whether it is the Nationalist or the Communist, has been very clear that Hong Kong is a part of China ceded/leased to Britain under various "unequal treaties" signed by the Qing Dynasty in the nineteenth century. Indeed, the PRC wasted no time in declaring its policy towards Hong Kong once it was admitted to the United Nations in 1972:

> The questions of Hong Kong and Macau belong to the category of questions resulting from the series of unequal treaties which the imperialists imposed on China. Hong Kong and Macau are part of Chinese territory occupied by the British and Portuguese authorities. The settlement of the questions of Hong Kong and Macau is entirely within China's sovereign right and do [sic] not at all fall under the ordinary category of colonial territories. Consequently they should not be included in the list of colonial territories covered by the declaration on the granting of independence to colonial countries and people. With regard to the questions of Hong Kong and Macau, the Chinese government has consistently held that they should be settled in an appropriate way when conditions are ripe . . . . (quoted in Cheng, 1984:54)

Historical Setting: The State and the Society 33

As mentioned above, anticipation of the Chinese objection to political reforms had prevented the British-Hong Kong government from carrying out political reforms since the late 1940s. But the situation was changed in the mid-1980s after the signing of the Sino-British Joint Declaration in 1984 and the Chinese promise of "Hong Kong people governing Hong Kong" after 1997. Given the incompatibility between a "high degree of autonomy" after 1997 and the colonial political structure, it became necessary to reform the colonial structure so as to prepare Hong Kong to exercise autonomy after 1997. It is believed that the reforms proposed in the 1984 White Paper on the development of representative government appeared to have the blessing of the Chinese government at first. But later China withdrew its support, as will be demonstrated in Chapter 3. Nevertheless, the political reforms did provide a push to politicize part of the population. In the three-tier legislature[5] elections in 1994 and 1995 (last election cycle under British rule), the respective number of popularly-elected seats of the DBs, Urban Council (UrbCo), Regional Council (RegCo), and LegCo are 346 (out of 373), 32 (out of 41), 27 (out of 39), and 20 (out of 60); the total number of popularly-elected seats is 425 and the total number of candidates is 942 (DB: 757; UrbCo: 75; RegCo: 60; LegCo: 50).[6] Supposing that each candidate, on average, had been assisted by fifty campaign workers, there would have been an involvement of forty-seven thousands people. Furthermore, the number of registered voters grew tremendously from about 40,000 in 1979 to about 2,795,000 in 1998. The turnout of the 1998 LegCo popular election was about 1,489,000 (nearly 53.3% of the registered voters). As a result, through the partial opening-up of the three-tier legislature and the electioneering process, more and more people became involved in politics.

Meanwhile, the social fabric or composition of Hong Kong is quite different from other British colonies when they were embarking on the road of decolonization. As reported in the Hong Kong 1991 population census, there were all together 2.8 million working population. Among them, twenty-three per cent are managers, administrators, and professionals. Nearly two-thirds of the working population served in the tertiary sector (Census and Statistics Department, 1992a:34). Over 11% of the population aged 15 or above (N=4,370,365) had received some sort of tertiary education (degree and non-degree courses), and another 31% had finished their upper secondary or matriculation education (Census and Statistics Department, 1992b:199, Table 15.1). Given the above figures, it seems that no other decolonizing colony has had a matching quality and quantity.

Decolonization is not merely the transfer of political sovereignty to a new state; it involves also a social and economic restructuring process (Darwin, 1988:5-17). As a result, each of the social forces will try hard to shape it to their own advantage. But the hard fact is that not all the participants carried equal weight in deciding the final product. In addition, the reform has different meanings to different social classes. Their respective attitudes towards the reform in or before 1984 were as follows.

First of all, the businessmen did not want any change in the way of governing. In general, they viewed the reform with scepticism. Some of them argued that the then British administration[7] and non-intervention policy had contributed to the stability and prosperity of Hong Kong. So, why bother to change it. Nonetheless, the business circle is not a homogenous entity. We can roughly differentiate it into the following sub-groups: the European "hongs" and metropolitan capitalists, the indigenous Chinese capitalists (including both the traditional and the New Rich), as well as the small and medium size firm-owners. The first sub-group may probably be more willing to tolerate reform; the second sub-group seems to be reluctant to accommodate reform; and the last sub-group may be hard to assess because of its number, diversity and being rather inactive in politics. Given that these sub-groups have a close economic relationship and interest with China and the fact that their privileges are well assured in the then and future political structure (Chan, 1991: chapters 2-4), their attitude towards political reform may tend to be conservative. That means no reform if possible; if not, favour "gradual" and "orderly" change (for the views of the business circle, see Dunn, 1985).

The middle class has grown out of the rapid social and economic development since the 1970s and comprised mainly managers, technocrats, accountants, social workers, doctors, lawyers, professors, and administrators. The size of this class doubled more than twice from 141,860 (7.7% of the working population) in 1976 to 315,945 (11.9% of the working population) in 1986 (So and Kwitko, 1990:384; Census and Statistics Department, 1987:32 & 38). Accompanying the growth in size is the rise of their political awareness. Some of them want some kind of political reform because the pre-reformed political structure has limited their chance of participation, and the policies that the colonial government adopted favour the business class at the expense of their own interest (taxation is an example at hand). Some of them also think that their contribution to society has barely matched their political influence. As a result, several interest groups were established in the late 1970s and early 1980s, such as the Hong Kong Observers (HKO), the Hong Kong Affairs

Society (HKAS), and the Meeting Point (MP). On the whole, they seem to favour reform but in a gradual and non-violent way. This newly emerging middle class has played a significant role in the campaign for democracy since the mid-1980s.

The general public and the working class still remain politically apathetic. For them, the notion of democracy is so remote that it will make no immediate difference to their life. They work as hard as their predecessors so as to earn a living. Although some of them are quite attentive to public affairs, they are not keen to articulate their interests or participate politically. So, they get used to being the passive actor in the political arena. In addition, the trade unions are loosely organized and have limited bargaining power (England and Rear 1975: chapters 5 & 13). Nevertheless, they will easily be mobilized if their interest and living is at stake. The vigorous protest against government's policy of importing foreign labour is a recent example. Through the active role of the social workers, the "grass roots" are likely to become more organized than before (Wong, 1990; Leung, 1986). Moreover, 34 social workers and social work administrators were elected members of the DBs, UrbCo and RegCo in 1988 (Mok, 1988:251). In general, social workers have tended to support the under-privileged class and the poor as the former regard the poverty and misfortune of the latter as a structural issue, not an individual one. Thus, social workers often resort to direct action to pressure the government to adopt a more interventionist policy or a policy with redistributive effect so as to redress the social injustice and inequality resulting from the market failure (Wong 1993:17-27).

How far the decolonization process can go would depend on the outcome of the negotiation between China and Britain, with the Hong Kong people playing a secondary role in the process. The Sino-British negotiation and the subsequent Basic Law drafting processes could be regarded as competition among China, Britain, and the Hong Kong people to shape the political order of Hong Kong both before and after 1997. We now turn to the efforts of all concerned parties and the rise of the centre-periphery cleavage in that context.

Notes

1. The Government Secretariat was known as the Colonial Secretariat before 1976.
2. For the development of the British colony's legislature before the Second World War, see Wight (1946). The LegCo started to have elective elements from 1985.
3. The Hong Kong government was supervised by the Colonial Office until the reorganization in 1968. Since then, the Foreign Office and the Colonial Office have merged to form the Foreign and Commonwealth Office.
1. A full list of the appointed ExCo and LegCo members before 1941 can be found in Endacott (1964:250-3).
2. The Sanitary Board was set up in 1883 and was, later, replaced by the Urban Council (UrbCo) in 1936.
3. Throughout this book, the term "non-official" member is employed, instead of the more tradition usage of "unofficial" member, except within quotation.
4. Quoted in Wong Man-fong's memoirs (extracts), Eastern Express (Hong Kong) 6 July 1994:6. Wong Man-fong was the Deputy General Secretary and Head of the Taiwan Affairs Department of the Hong Kong Branch of the NCNA before his retirement in August 1992. He is very familiar with Beijing's Hong Kong policy as he was one of the two CCP members assigned to work on Hong Kong affairs in the late 1940s.
5. The three-tier legislature denotes the District Boards at the district level, the Urban and Regional Councils at the regional level, and the Legislative Council at the centre level. Although the word "three-tier legislature" has a connotation of superior-subordinate relations, it in fact does not have such a meaning because those boards and council have their own jurisdiction or scope of powers.
6. The District Boards' figures are supplied by the Home Affairs Department on 18 July 1995; the Urban and Regional Councils', and the LegCo's figures are compiled from the electoral data supplied by the Registration and Electoral Office, Constitutional Affairs Branch, Hong Kong Government Secretariat.
7. Nearly half (49.3%, N=463) of the directorate posts were occupied by expatriates in 1986. And nearly three-quarters of all expatriates were employed in the following six departments: Police (1,098), Engineering (344), Government Secretariat (191), Building (163), Legal (155), and Judiciary (111). See Burns (1988:96).

3 The Rise of the Centre-Periphery Cleavage

The destiny of Hong Kong in the early 1980s was at the cross-roads. The emergence of the 1997 issue had raised the question of whether this tiny Hong Kong would remain a British Colony or not after 1997. After more than two years of negotiation, Britain agreed to hand all of Hong Kong back to China in 1997. The Sino-British Joint Declaration signified the resolution of conflicting claims to sovereignty over Hong Kong, but not the assurance of close cooperation in the transitional period. The question of who had the final say in the lengthy transitional period of 12 years, from the effective date of the Sino-British Joint Declaration in May 1985 to the actual transfer of power in July 1997, proved to be an explosive one. The first controversial issue that emerged after the signing of the Joint Declaration was the pace and the extent of the democratic reforms in the transitional period.

The British "pre-emptive" political reforms in the mid-1980s had first created a political "seller" market, and then a "buyer" market in which the demand for democratic reforms kept growing, especially after the Tiananmen Incident in 1989. From the outset, the Chinese government doubted the motives behind the reform and seemingly regarded it as a British "conspiracy" to obstruct the smooth restoration of sovereignty. Understandably, Beijing wanted as little political reform as possible in the transitional period. Adding to this was the growing support for democratic reforms within Hong Kong society after the Tiananmen Incident in 1989.

The different attitudes of China, Britain, and segments of the Hong Kong people towards democratization have been reflected in their respective attitudes and supports of the pace of democratic reform before 1997 and the different political models after 1997. Hence, three contradictions have been present: between the Chinese and British governments, between the Chinese government and Hong Kong people, and between the British government and Hong Kong people. The interplay of these contradictions would have a significant impact on the subsequent formation of electoral cleavage. Through the political mobilization in the past decade, the various political forces have established a linkage with their potential supporters. As a result, their differences would spill over to the electorate and would then contribute to the emergence of cleavage lines.

Given the decisive role played by China in shaping both the pre- and post-1997 political order, the contradiction between Beijing and Hong Kong would become paramount and thus contribute to the development of centre-periphery electoral cleavage over the proper relationship between the "centre" Beijing government and the "periphery" Hong Kong Special Administrative Region after 1997, i.e. dependency or autonomy and the pace of democratization. For those who support the Beijing government's stance towards and ideas about the HKSAR's pace of democratization and degree of autonomy, we can describe them as "pro-centre grouping". For those who support the faster pace of democratization and a higher degree of autonomy regardless of the Beijing government's view, we can describe them as "pro-periphery grouping". Needless to say, the usage of the term "centre" and "periphery" only denotes the superior-subordinate political relationship between China and Hong Kong, and does not apply to their economic relationship. Neither of these two terms carry the same meaning as those used in the dependency theory. We now turn to the detailed examination of the evolution and emergence of the centre-periphery cleavage.

This chapter examines the rise of the centre-periphery cleavage resulting from the dynamic shift of the contradictions between the British government, the Chinese government, and the Hong Kong people in the context of the reversion of sovereignty and the political reforms of the 1980s. First of all, we examine the conflicts and compromises of China and Britain in settling the question of Hong Kong, and the responses from the Hong Kong people towards the Sino-British Joint Declaration. Second, the rivalry of various political forces over the pace of democratic reforms in the political reforms debates since the mid-1980s. Their respective stances and considerations will also be explored. Third, the clash of the democrats with the Chinese government and the conservatives in the Basic Law drafting process will be used to demonstrate the rise of the centre-periphery cleavage. The successive mobilization efforts of the concerned parties will also be studied.

The Settlement of the 1997 Issue

The uncertainty that loomed over the future of Hong Kong from the late 1970s had not been new to Hong Kong. Whether the Nationalist or the Communist government was in power, the three treaties that helped create the Crown Colony of Hong Kong had been regarded as "unequal" and thus, had to be nullified "when the time is ripe" (Chan, 1973; Wesley-Smith, 1980; Lane, 1990). Furthermore, as mentioned in Chapter 2, over 90% of the Hong Kong territory was subject to a 99-year lease due to expire in June 1997. It was not so surprising that Hong Kong had been described by one observer as a "borrowed place" where people lived on a "borrowed time" (Hughes, 1976).

The time had come to conclude a clear and formal settlement of the peculiar status of Hong Kong when the expiry date of the lease of the New Territories was approaching. Because of the fact that the Hong Kong government did not have legal power to grant land leases in the New Territories beyond July 1997, most of the economic activities would be disrupted if no new arrangement with the PRC was acquired well before 1997. The anxiety of the business community in Hong Kong had prompted the Hong Kong government to act. Under such circumstances, Murray MacLehose, the then Hong Kong Governor, travelled to Beijing in 1979 to discuss the matter with China's then Vice-Premier Deng Xiaoping. When he returned to Hong Kong, the Governor told the public that Deng had asked the Hong Kong investors "to put their hearts at ease". But MacLehose had failed to convey the message at that time that China would reclaim the sovereignty of Hong Kong in 1997.

Later in May of the same year, the Chinese Vice-Foreign Minister Song Zhiguang reiterated the official position that "Hong Kong is part of China" and "when the lease expires, an appropriate attitude would be adopted in settling the question" (quoted in Cheng, 1984:246). In contrast to the vague attitude of the Chinese government, the British and Hong Kong governments wanted to have an early settlement of the status of Hong Kong by pressing for formal talks between Beijing and London.

Regarding the talks, a Chinese official was quoted as saying: "It has been the Socialist policy to allow Hong Kong to stay as it is. We did not ask for the talks. Britain did" (Wilkinson, 1983:447-8). Regardless of the question of which side wanted the talks, the visit of Margaret Thatcher, the then British Prime Minister, to Beijing in 1982 had paved the way for subsequent formal negotiation between Beijing and London over the future of Hong Kong (Cottrell, 1993; Scott, 1989: chapter 5; Tsim, 1984; Cheng,

1984: chapters 1-2; Duncanson, 1988). Although China and Britain had different views on the validity and legality of the three treaties concerned, a joint statement was released on 24 September 1982 when Thatcher concluded her Beijing trip:

> Today, the two leaders of the two countries held far-reaching talks in a friendly atmosphere on the future of Hong Kong. Both leaders made clear their respective positions on the subject.
> They agreed to enter into talks through diplomatic channels following the visit with the common aim of maintaining the stability and prosperity of Hong Kong.

The Setting of the Sino-British Negotiation

The setting of the negotiations was to have an overwhelming effect on the strength and bargaining strategy of the negotiators. For the British government, the whole setting was not favourable. First of all, the uncertain situation had made the governing of Hong Kong more difficult, as any unfavourable developments would promptly have an adverse effect on the incumbent British-Hong Kong government. The immediate concern of the British-Hong Kong government was the continuing effective governing and sound economic development of Hong Kong. Any development that may jeopardize the above concerns would be avoided by the British-Hong Kong government. The British government was being tied down by "the realization that Deng Xiaoping was absolutely serious in his declared determination to allow Hong Kong to be ruined if necessary in order to regain full Chinese sovereignty" (Yahuda, 1993:252).

Second, the institutional setting also did not favour Britain. China denied any representative from Hong Kong the right to join the Sino-British negotiation, as Beijing stressed that the negotiation was between two sovereign states and the whole process should be kept confidential. In addition, Beijing regarded the Hong Kong Chinese as its nationals and thus, the Chinese government claims that it represented its compatriots in Hong Kong. Under these circumstances, the question is: who did the British government represent?

Third, from geographical considerations, Britain had no way to defend Hong Kong in both military and economic terms. Hong Kong is totally different from the Falklands, where no such question of expiration of lease existed and, more importantly, military defence was viable. In addition, the international climate was against the continuance of colonialism. Moreover, the decision-makers in London were very clear that the British interest and importance, both economic and strategic, vested in Hong Kong was declining relatively when compared to the 1960s or before. The break-up of the British Empire, the detente of East-West relations as well as the open door policy of China contributed to the lessening of the importance of Hong Kong.

Fourth, Britain's claim of the validity and legality of the three nineteenth century treaties that formed the basis of Britain's rule over Hong Kong put London in a weak and hard position to defend. If the claim were accepted by China, would the whole of the New Territories be logically handed back to China on the expiry of a 99-year lease? Given that the New Territories cover over 90% of the land territory of Hong Kong, the survival of the remaining tiny area seems not viable.

As a result, the British negotiators were fighting not only an uphill battle but also a no-win one because Beijing would not agree to Britain ruling Hong Kong after 1997. The second best option for London to take was to try to fight for a better terms for the reversion of sovereignty. Because of the reliance on Beijing to produce an acceptable mutual agreement, London adopted a co-operative approach towards the negotiation. Percy Cradock (1994b:92), the architect of Britain's China policy from late 1970s to early 1990s, defended the policy in 1994 that:

> Cooperation does not mean automatic acquiescence in China's views. Tough negotiation has always been necessary and has always been practised. But it does mean recognising that unilateral action and confrontation with China are more damaging to Hong Kong in its special circumstances than a negotiated settlement and are therefore inconsistent with our responsibility to do our best for the territory. The long-term welfare of Hong Kong must be the sole criterion.

Conversely, Beijing seems to have a free hand in dealing with London over the sovereignty of Hong Kong. Taking advantage of not being responsible for direct ruling and the low cost of any immediate economic crisis at the time of negotiation, China exploited the situation skilfully. On the one hand, Beijing knew that timing was in its favour. The time pressure on the British government would be tremendous as the negotiation hinged on an extended period of time. Besides, China had threatened to announce unilaterally the plan to recover the sovereignty of Hong Kong if agreement could not be reached by September 1984.

On the other hand, Beijing tried to remove the fear of the Hong Kong people by appealing to nationalism, and by promising "Hong Kong people governing Hong Kong" and "no change for fifty years after 1997". The idea of "one country, two systems" was put forward by China as a guideline for the subsequent reunification of Taiwan, Hong Kong and Macau (Weng, 1987-88). Under the "one country, two systems" concept, Hong Kong would retain its own capitalist system for 50 years after 1997. Hong Kong was also promised a high degree of autonomy, except in defence and foreign relations.[1] Moreover, only Hong Kong people would qualify to rule Hong Kong.[2] Such an arrangement seemed to be aimed at wooing the Hong Kong people to accept the hard fact of the transfer of sovereignty, and at maintaining the stability and prosperity of Hong Kong during the transitional period and beyond.

The Sino-British Negotiations, 1982-84

Diplomatic talks had started after the visit of Thatcher in September 1982. But no significant advance was made as Britain had insisted that the negotiation should be based on the legality of the treaties concerned. That means London was only ready to discuss the lease issue of the New Territories but not the Hong Kong issue as a whole. For Britain, Hong Kong island and Kowloon Peninsula (south of Boundary Street) was ceded to it in perpetuity and was a part of Britain. Furthermore, Britain argued that only the continuous "presence" of the British could contribute to a more stable and prosperous Hong Kong. The view of the British government more or less reflected the ideas of the Hong Kong business community.

Understandably, China had persistently asserted its claim of sovereignty over Hong Kong by stating that the "unequal treaties" had no binding force and advocating the return of Hong Kong as a whole in 1997. In reacting to Thatcher's claim of "Britain's moral responsibility and duty to the people of Hong Kong" in September 1982, the NCNA made clear the Chinese position in an article entitled "Our Solemn Stand on the Question of Hong Kong" maintaining that:

> Hong Kong is part of China. The treaties concerning Hong Kong signed in the past between the British government and the Qing dynasty were unequal treaties which the Chinese have never accepted. It is the sacred duty of the Chinese government and the Chinese people to recover sovereignty over Hong Kong. This has all along been the just stand of our people on this issue. The British Prime Minister, Mrs Margaret Thatcher, however, once again emphasized on 27 September 1982 in Hong Kong that the Sino-British treaties concerning Hong Kong signed in the previous century were still

'valid' and so were still 'binding'. This is something which the Chinese will never accept.
It must be pointed out that the aforementioned treaties are unequal treaties imposed on China in the wake of the nineteenth-century British imperialistic policy which manifested itself in the invasion of China by the use of 'gunboat diplomacy'. Those treaties are ironclad proof of the plundering of Chinese soil by British imperialism, and have, since their existence, been considered by the Chinese as illegal and invalid. . . .
. . . .
Mrs Thatcher also brought up the point of Britain's 'moral obligation' to the Hong Kong people. It is our belief that the Hong Kong issue is part and parcel of the People's Republic of China with its one billion people (including the Chinese living in Hong Kong), and, as such, falls within the confines of China's national sovereignty and interests. Only the People's Republic of China, being the country with sovereignty over Hong Kong, is entitled to say that it has obligations to Hong Kong. (quoted in Cheng, 1984:55-6)

This loud and clear stance had brought home the message that China would not make any concession on Hong Kong's sovereignty. It was regarded by Beijing's leaders as a subject of principle allowing no compromise.

As mentioned in the previous section, the setting and timing of the negotiation had prevented Thatcher from acting boldly. Although Thatcher's initial claim of the validity of the treaties was quite forceful during her meeting with Deng Xiaoping in September 1982, no high-profile position had been taken, nor was a strong-worded statement delivered, by the British government after that. The first few months of the negotiation could be described as standstill and fruitless as both sides showed no sign of compromise.

The breakthrough came in March 1983 when Britain softened its position over the sovereignty of Hong Kong. Any longer delay in the arrival of a mutually acceptable agreement would be detrimental to the social stability and economic prosperity of Hong Kong. Britain was also tied down by the fact that the British-Hong Kong government was responsible for the continuation of effective governing of Hong Kong. Thatcher (1993:489) confessed in her memoirs that she wrote a letter to Zhao Ziyang, the then Chinese Prime Minister, stating that:

Provided that agreement could be reached between the British and Chinese Government on administrative arrangements for Hong Kong which would guarantee the future prosperity and stability of Hong Kong, and would be acceptable to the British Parliament and to the people of Hong Kong as well as to the Chinese Government, I *would be prepared to recommend* to Parliament that sovereignty over the whole of Hong Kong should revert to China. (italics in original)

As a result, Britain and China entered a new phase of negotiation of substantial matters in July 1983. In the early rounds of negotiation in this phase, Britain tried to convince Beijing by playing up the "economic" cards and stressed that some form of British administrative presence in the post-1997 Hong Kong would be vital to the stability and prosperity in both the transitional period up to 1997 and beyond (Scott, 1989:179-80). In response to a question whether Britain "hope to keep a British presence" in Hong Kong, Thatcher said:

Well, these kind of things are exactly what we're now negotiating about. And obviously we think that the British link is very, very important indeed, because it is partly responsible for the kind of success we've had in Hongkong. (quoted in Cheng, 1984:44)

Britain changed its tone and tried to separate "jurisdiction" from "sovereignty". That means Britain gave up its sovereign claim to China but maintained the right to administer Hong Kong. This idea was also not accepted by China. These new efforts made by the British government had not only failed to convert Beijing, but also sparked off the so-called "megaphone diplomacy" characterized by a series of criticism from the local leftist newspapers and unions. From Beijing's point of view, sovereignty and administration were indivisible. These rising differences had given a blow to the economy of Hong Kong. The Hong Kong dollar had been driven to the record low of $9.55 against the US dollar in late September 1983. In order to rescue the fall of the Hong Kong dollar, the currency board system has been restored by pegging the Hong Kong dollar with that of the United States at an exchange rate of HK$7.8 for a US dollar.

Facing the tremendous pressure from the financial crisis and subsequent social instability, London had made a further concession before the fifth round of negotiations held on 19 October 1983 (Tsim, 1984:37). Thatcher conveyed to Beijing that "we envisaged no link of authority or accountability between Britain and Hong Kong after 1997" (Thatcher, 1993:490). Subsequently, the destiny of Hong Kong was almost fixed when Geoffrey Howe, the then British Foreign Secretary, made it plain and public after his Beijing trip on 19 April 1984 that:

The terms of an agreement between the British and Chinese Governments still have to be worked out, but it is right for me to tell you now that it would not be realistic to think of an agreement that provides for continued British administration in Hong Kong after 1997. (cited by UMELCO *Annual Report 1984*, 1985:6)

After twenty rounds of negotiation, the Sino-British Joint Declaration on the Question of Hong Kong was finally signed in 1984. In the Sino-British Joint Declaration, Britain formally returned Hong Kong's sovereignty to China with effect from 1 July 1997. In return, China had promised to set up a special administrative region in Hong Kong with "high degree of autonomy" (except for foreign and defence affairs) and no change of life style for 50 years after 1997. In the transitional period, "the Government of the United Kingdom will be responsible for the administration of Hong Kong with the object of maintaining and preserving its economic prosperity and social stability; and that the Government of the People's Republic of China will give its cooperation in this connection" and a Sino-British Joint Liaison Group will be set up to "ensure a smooth transfer of government in 1997". In section I of Annex I, the future HKSAR political system will be:

The Hong Kong Special Administrative Region shall be directly under the authority of the Central People's Government of the People's Republic of China and shall enjoy a high degree of autonomy. Except for foreign and defence affairs which are the responsibilities of the Central People's Government, the Hong Kong Special Administrative Region shall be vested with executive, legislative and independent judicial power, including that of final adjudication. . . .
The government and legislature of the Hong Kong Special Administrative Region shall be composed of local inhabitants. The chief executive of the Hong Kong Special Administrative Region shall be selected by election or through consultations held locally and be appointed by the Central People's Government. Principal officials (equivalent to Secretaries) shall be nominated by the chief executive of the Hong Kong Special Administrative Region and appointed by the Central People's Government. The legislature of the Hong Kong Special Administrative Region shall be constituted by elections. The executive authorities shall abide by the law and shall be accountable to the legislature.

In evaluating the Sino-British Joint Declaration, Thatcher (1993:492) highlighted "three main advantages":

First, they [the Joint Declaration] constituted what would be unequivocally binding international agreement. Second, they were sufficiently clear and detailed about what would happen in Hong Kong after 1997 to command the confidence of the people of Hong Kong. Third, there was a provision that the terms of the proposed Anglo-Chinese Agreement would be stipulated in the Basic Law to be passed by Chinese People's Congress: this would in effect be the constitution of Hong Kong after 1997.

Although the terms of the Joint Declaration would be adopted in the Basic Law, the successful conversion would largely rely on the goodwill as well as the same comprehension of the letter and spirit of the Declaration. Subsequent developments proved neither.

Institutional Barriers of Representation

The negotiations were structured as if it was only a matter of two concerned sovereign states. On the insistence of the Chinese government, the British government agreed to keep the negotiations in strict confidence and on a bilateral basis (Bonavia, 1985:102-4; Yahuda, 1993:257; 1996: chapter 3). Direct participation from the Hong Kong people was, thus, prevented. The lack of direct participation could be remedied if there was a sound representation system in place before the negotiation started. Unfortunately, no such kind of mechanism was available. Because of such structural constraints, Hong Kong could only rely on the negotiators from both governments to represent and take care of its opinions.

On the British side, the Governor of Hong Kong acted as a member of the British delegation. Voices from within Hong Kong had to rely on the ExCo, which had been granted an advisory status from the second phase of the negotiation in July 1983. In a statement issued by the British Prime Minister's Office following the visit of all the ExCo members to London on 1 July 1983, Britain "reaffirmed their commitment to Hong Kong and their aim of seeking arrangement which would be acceptable to Parliament, to China and to the people of Hong Kong" and also "emphasised the importance which they attach to the advice of the Executive Council which would continue to be sought throughout the course of the talks" (UMELCO, *Annual Report 1984:*3). But the Hong Kong mass public could hardly regard the ExCo members as representative of their interests because the latter were nominees of the Governor and so insulated from the society (Yahuda, 1993:256, n15). The closed colonial political structure, more or less, contributed to the wide spread of such kind of feelings.

On the Chinese side, Hong Kong deputies to the National People's Congress (NPC), representatives to the Chinese People's Political Consultative Conference, the Hong Kong branch of the NCNA and local leftist organizations had constituted the major channels of reflecting public opinion in Hong Kong. It seemed to many Hong Kong people that the above-mentioned channels were far from adequate and had been regarded as not as neutral as they claimed to be. Without the necessary and widespread legitimacy in the eyes of the Hong Kong people in general, the representation and effectiveness of these channels were seriously called into question.

Furthermore, Beijing had rejected the "three-legged stool" concept totally. The concept was first used in 1971 to describe a tripod of consent among China, Britain and Hong Kong people in maintaining the stability of Hong Kong, and later borrowed to denote the three legs of China, Britain and Hong Kong in supporting the stool of Hong Kong's future after 1997.[3] The conflict was stirred up when Edward Youde[4], the then Hong Kong Governor, was asked who represents the people of Hong Kong in the Sino-British negotiations when he returned to Hong Kong from London on 7 July 1983. He said: "I represent. I am the Governor of Hong Kong . . . Indeed I represent the people of Hong Kong; who else would I represent?" (Quoted in H.K. Lamb, 1985:29; Lane, 1990:97)

Beijing reacted the next day by stressing that the Hong Kong Governor was a member of the British delegation. Moreover, Peter Tsao, the then Director of the Government Information Service, was denied a visa for accompanying the Governor to the Beijing talks. The Chinese stance had been understood to be that only the Chinese government has the right to act on behalf of the Hong Kong people.

Later on, Beijing had also challenged the status of the non-official members of both the ExCo and the LegCo as representatives of Hong Kong people. When receiving Chung Sze-yuen, Lydia Dunn and Q.W. Lee, who visited Beijing at China's invitation, on 23 June 1984, Deng Xiaoping discredited them deliberately by stating that they were there in their private capacities. Deng was quoted as saying: "The Sino-British negotiations will not be subject to external interference" and "[a]s for the so-called 'three-legged stool' situation, we only recognise two legs. There is no third leg". After the meeting, Dunn was said to be surprised "at Deng's initial reference to our individual capacity" (*Far Eastern Economic Review* (hereafter *FEER)*, 5 July 1984).

Given the prevention from participation in the negotiations and the lack of an effective representation mechanism, the Hong Kong mass public seemed to have little faith in the resulting Sino-British Agreement.

The Shifting of Aspirations

In the late 1970s and early 1980s, the Hong Kong people had held a quite optimistic view towards the future of Hong Kong. They believed that China would let Hong Kong remain as it was because of the fact that the Chinese government had tolerated the colony for the past several decades, especially in the years of the Cultural Revolution, as well as because of the importance of Hong Kong in accomplishing its goals of "Four Modernizations". Therefore, they were of an opinion, though somewhat subjective, that the status quo would be maintained after 1997. According to a survey released in March 1982, over three-fourths of the respondents indicated that the probable outcome of the future of Hong Kong after 1997 would be either to maintain the status quo or to become trust territories (Cheng, 1984:85).

As mentioned before, Beijing would not accept any form of British presence after 1997 and this stance was straightforward and not negotiable. The hope to maintain the status quo was dashed as Beijing put across the above message vigorously and firmly during the initial phase of negotiations. In order not to disappoint and frustrate its compatriots in Hong Kong, Beijing put forward the plan of "Hong Kong people governing Hong Kong" (*gangren zhigang*[5]).

This strategic move by the Beijing leaders had succeeded to a certain extent in shaping the preferences of Hong Kong people, as well as offering a hope, at least at the moment, of Hong Kong people governing themselves. In response to the question of what the meaning of "Hong Kong people governing Hong Kong" was in an interview with *Newsweek* on 23 January 1984, Li Chu-wen, the then Deputy Director of the Hong Kong branch of the NCNA, said:

> The demand for democracy on the part of Hong Kong's people is fully justified and should win the sympathy of all those with democratic aspirations -- including the Chinese. If Hong Kong prefers direct elections to determine its officials, then it should strive for that, and it will have the support of the Chinese people.

In early 1984, members of the LegCo had adjusted their attitudes towards the Sino-British negotiations from the one of waiting passively for the outcome to the one of being more active in asserting their right to discuss the matter before London and Beijing have arrived at any agreement. This was largely in response to London's decision to withdraw from Hong Kong in 1997 (Sze Ma, 1984:37-9). Under such a condition, R.H. Lobo, Senior Member of the LegCo, introduced a motion to debate the issue in public on 14 March 1984. The motion reads as follow:

> This council deems it essential that any proposals for the future of Hong Kong should be debated in this council before any final agreement is reached.

During the debate, LegCo members seemed dissatisfied with the way the Hong Kong people were being treated by both Britain and China. For example, Alex Wu used the term "arranged marriage" to denote the treatment Hong Kong people had received; Ho Kam-fai refuted those who regarded the "Lobo motion" as the re-emergence of the "three-legged stool" concept; Stephen Cheong shared the view of Ho and added that the LegCo members were not fighting to have a final say in the negotiations; and Maria Tam argued that the LegCo has the legal status to debate the future of Hong Kong (*UMELCO Annual Report*, 1984:4-5).

When Foreign Secretary Howe had made it clear on 20 April 1984 that Britain would retreat from Hong Kong in 1997, the non-official members of the ExCo and the LegCo issued a position paper arguing that the acceptability of the would-be Sino-British Agreement depended on its:

(i) containing full details of the proposed administrative, legal, social and economic systems applicable after 1997;
(ii) providing adequate and workable assurances that the terms of the Agreement will be honoured;
(iii) stating that the provisions of the Basic Law will incorporate the provisions of the Agreement;
(iv) guaranteeing that the rights of British nationals will be safeguarded. (*UMELCO Annual Report*, 1984:56)

Furthermore, Chung Sze-yuen, Lydia Dunn and Q.W. Lee visited Beijing at China's invitation and met with Deng Xiaoping and Ji Pengfei on 23 June 1984. In the meeting, they made three recommendations to maintain stability and prosperity of Hong Kong both before and after 1997:

(i) ... the Agreement:
-- must be very detailed; it must provide clear and precise definitions of all aspects of Hong Kong's existing systems;

-- must be mutually binding as between the two signing countries of China and Britain;
-- must contain a provision stipulating that the Basic Law of the Special Administrative Region of Hong Kong will be based on the terms in the Agreement. . . .

(ii) In order to enhance confidence, we believe that the Basic Law should be drafted in Hong Kong. It should be included in the Constitution of China after the approval by the Standing Committee of the Chinese National People's Congress (NPC). . . .

(iii) . . . If the Chinese leaders understand the anxiety of the people of Hong Kong and would agree to the establishment of an insulating mechanism, like a dam, between Hong Kong and China, confidence in Hong Kong would be greatly increased. We, therefore, propose the establishment of a Committee consisting of Chinese people of international standing and reputation. This Committee will be appointed by the Government of China. Their responsibility would be to monitor or advise the drafting, and implementation of, and subsequent amendments, if any, to the Basic Law. (*UMELCO Annual Report*, 1984:57-8)

The strong wording in the above quotation did not bring much fruit. As mentioned before, Deng Xiaoping opted to play down their capacities and denied that there was any crisis of confidence in Hong Kong. Nevertheless, a strong distrust of the Chinese government could be detected from the lines. And this probably reflected the state of mind of many Hong Kong people, at least at that moment.

In addition, after the initialling of the Joint Declaration on 26 September 1984, Hong Kong people were invited to submit to the Assessment Office their views on it. One submission from an individual seemed to reflect the powerlessness and actual feeling of the Hong Kong people:

I belong to the middle income group who do not have the means to emigrate to other countries and because I was born and educated in Hong Kong I would wish to stay in Hong Kong. For the purpose of your statistics you can classify me as one of those who would accept the draft agreement but I hope you will also take into account that I only accept it with much reluctance and with many reservations about the feasibility of its implementation. My heart is not truly at ease and I have no full confidence in our future. The whole thing has not been a very fair play to us because we have not had any say and there is no other alternative than not to have an agreement at all. (Assessment Office, 1984:19)

From the above we could see that some of the Hong Kong people had adjusted to accepting whatever arrangements reached by Britain and China on their behalf. Retreating from their high hopes of maintaining the status quo under British rule, they now came down to the earth by accepting, though somewhat reluctantly, the reality that Hong Kong had to return to China in July 1997. The remaining thing they could do was to press for an agreement that promised to keep the existing systems unchanged and then have it codified in the Basic Law, which is the mini-constitution of Hong Kong after 1997.

Their hope and faith for the future of Hong Kong relied on whether the promise of "high degree of autonomy" and "Hong Kong people governing Hong Kong" under the roof of "one country, two systems" would be actually put into practice. Gone was the possibility of having any form of British presence after 1997; thus, the question of how to perfect and realize the concept of "Hong Kong people governing Hong Kong" became paramount.

Rivalry Over the Democratization of Hong Kong

The idea of developing "representative government" in Hong Kong was a recent one. Only after the issue of 1997 had been raised in the early 1980s did the British government make public its intention to have some sort of political reform in Hong Kong. To a certain extent, the late arrival of decolonization was due to the complicated political situation of Hong Kong (Miners, 1988:44-54). Unlike other British colonies, Hong Kong was unlikely to become an independent state. The Chinese government, whether the Communists or the Kuomintang, had never given up its sovereign claim over Hong Kong. Any constitutional reform must take into account the reaction of the Chinese government.

The long-overdue reform of the "Victorian" colonial structure seemed to get China's blessings as stated in the Joint Declaration. Up to the conclusion of the Joint Declaration, there was no elected element, be it popular or non-popular, in the LegCo. But the Joint Declaration stipulates that the chief executive "shall be selected by election or through consultations held locally" and the legislature "shall be constituted by elections". Although there would be reform of the political structure, two outstanding questions remained: when to introduce such reforms, and who has the final say on the pace and direction of the reform. These two questions seem to be separated from each other at first glance, but they are indeed highly related. If Britain and China had arrived at a consensus on the extent of the reform, the question of timing would become less problematic. If not, the timing becomes critical as China would prefer no or limited change during the transitional period. Furthermore, the consensus between Beijing and London on the extent of the political reforms would be vital for building up a basis for Hong Kong's autonomy that would endure after 1997.

Britain seemed to think that it would be responsible for preparing the reform during the transitional period given that the proposed reform was in line with the Joint Declaration. Britain also thought that its sovereignty over Hong Kong would last until 1997, though China would be consulted in the implementation of the Joint Declaration. Furthermore, "the British and Hong Kong Governments appear to have interpreted the Chinese acceptance of central elective institutions for the S.A.R. [Special Administrative Region] *from* 1997 as also acquiescence in their progressive introduction in the interim period to lay the groundwork for full internal autonomy after the reversion of sovereignty" (Slinn, 1987:11; italics in original).

China appeared not to share the same view as Britain. As the following sections will reveal, Beijing wanted to take hold of the pace of reform by stressing that the reform would better converge with the Basic Law which is still under drafting. China could not accept the pre-determination of the Basic Law by the political reforms initiated by the British government. Furthermore, China seemed to regard the right of being consulted by Britain in the implementation of the Joint Declaration during the transitional period as having the right of approval or the veto power.

The divergent views had not only spelt out the difficulty of smooth transition, but also mobilized the local political forces to join in the rivalry. The attempts and bargains made by all these actors (political forces) in shaping the emerging political structure and order have provided the Hong Kong public with an understanding of their political value and stance. This process of development would shape the attitude and behaviour of the public and was bound to have impact on the voters' choice in the ensuing elections.

Different Attitudes Towards Political Reforms

As mentioned before, the item of political reforms had been put on the political agenda by the Sino-British Joint Declaration of 1984. There was no problem about carrying out reform but the pace and the extent of democratization did stir up debate and mobilization among the concerned parties. There were several forces working to shape the political reforms before 1997 and the post-1997 political structure. At the state level, there were only two actors: Britain and China. At the societal level, the following could be identified: the metropolitan capitalists, the indigenous capitalists, the rural gentry, and the new middle class (Kuan, 1991:774-93). The alignment and realignment of the above-mentioned forces will probably help shape and explain the emergent social formation and political order in the transitional and post-1997 period. All of them would like to see Hong Kong remain stable and prosper but they had their own ideas and ways to achieve it. Their interests and calculation are so divergent that conflict and contradiction seemed inevitable.

First of all, China made it clear that Hong Kong would be governed by Hong Kong people and enjoy a high degree of autonomy under the "imaginative" idea of "one country, two systems" after the restoration of Hong Kong sovereignty in 1997. Although the terms "Hong Kong people governing Hong Kong" and "high degree of autonomy" had often been talked about within Hong Kong society in and before 1985, no operational meaning and relevant procedures of implementation were offered by China at the time. This state of affairs could be attributed to the premature nature of the relevant concepts which were originally aimed at wooing the Taipei government for reunification. As the situation came to requiring clarification in mid-1980s onwards, Beijing had added qualifications to its promise. Furthermore, Beijing showed that it would like to see as little change as possible before 1997. The adoption of such conservative approach by the Chinese government seemingly came from Beijing's "suspicion" over the British sincerity at carrying out the pre-emptive political reforms in 1985 and the resulting so-called danger of restoring power to the Hong Kong people by such reforms before 1997. Furthermore, a long list of reasons were also advanced to explain China's resistance to democratization:

(1) the fear that Britain will use it as an excuse to shirk its responsibility of administering Hong Kong until 1997, (2) democratization will release political forces of such magnitudes that continued rule of the Hong Kong [G]overnment will be difficult or impossible, (3) the injection of elements of uncertainty which would wreck the stability and prosperity of Hong Kong before China is in a position to take over, (4) the possibility that power will be transferred to political groups which are pro-Britain, hostile to China or predisposed to place the interests of Hong Kong before those of China, (5)

China being compelled to openly organize politically in order to participate in the competition for the transferred power, thus bringing about detrimental consequences for Hong Kong, (6) democratization will disrupt the capitalist system of Hong Kong by scaring away local and foreign capital and by forcing the government to adopt excessive welfare measures and restrictive economic regulations, (7) the possibility of turning mass elections into occasions for the people of Hong Kong to periodically pass judgments on the popularity of China, and (8) the fear that the 'democratic forces' in Hong Kong will eventually become subversive of political tranquility in China by sheer demonstration effects and by their purposive promotion of Western-style 'democracy' in China. (Lau, 1987:6).

Because of being "[n]ot sure of Britain's intentions and unable to completely prevent some forms of power transfer from taking place, China for strategic reasons and out of an instinctual predisposition not to leave power to chance, feels compelled to compete in any power-grasping game" (Lau, 1987:10). Under such a perception, China would try to resist any constitutional change that will let Hong Kong out of its control and would like to maintain the executive-led government and related structures after 1997. This intention was well reflected in the content of the Basic Law. By concentrating nearly all the power in the hands of the executive head, China would easily control the use of state power in post-1997 Hong Kong.

For Britain, the best outcome of the negotiation with China was the continuation of the British rule after 1997. As shown in previous sections, Britain had failed to achieve that goal and subsequently agreed to hand back Hong Kong to China in 1997. The remaining questions for the British government to resolve just before the conclusion of the Sino-British Joint Declaration in late 1984 were how to ensure institutionally the continuation of the existing freedom and life style after 1997, and how to convince the British Parliament to approve the said Joint Declaration (Walden, 1987:73).

As a result, the British government had swiftly issued Green and White papers in 1984 aiming at the establishment of representative government before 1997. After that, the British concern was whether it could maintain an effective rule over Hong Kong in the transitional period. The unusual 12-year long transitional period brought out the question as to which government had the ultimate say in that period. The intervention of China in the transitional period aroused British suspicion about the extent of the autonomy the future HKSAR government would have. The intensive and prolonged controversy over the constitutional reforms and the building of Chek Lap Kok airport in early 1990s have been typical examples. Democratization therefore became one of the necessary steps to take so as to maintain Britain's effective and legitimate rule as well as to counter the expanding Chinese intervention in Hong Kong affairs.

The metropolitan capitalists, the indigenous capitalists and the rural gentry seemed to try to avoid any involvement in the Sino-British dispute. Although their common interests in maintaining the capitalist system in Hong Kong were the same, they had conflicts over their respective roles and influence in the colonial state as well as in the future HKSAR state. Accompanying the restoration of Hong Kong to China was the rise of economic nationalism. The influence of the metropolitan capitalists seemed to be contained and might give way to the indigenous capitalists and the rural gentry as 1997 approached. Furthermore, due to their extensive investment in China as well as the diminishing power of the British-Hong Kong government, the indigenous capitalists, the rural gentry and some British businessmen would tend to support China if conflict existed between China and Britain. Nevertheless, the metropolitan capitalists are not without counteracting power. The very success and further development of Hong Kong as well as the economic reform in China hinged on the present and on the supply of adequate financial capital by the metropolitan capitalists, and the latter's strategic position in the world capitalist system.

The new middle class had long been deprived of representation in the colonial state, at least up to the early 1980s. Through the writing of critics in the newspapers and the organization of protest, the activists in this class had started to challenge the colonial state from the 1970s.[6] (So and Kwitko, 1992 : 32-43; Campbell, 1980 : 8-9 & 12). They were not satisfied with the colonial political order and wanted to see some sort of democratic reform (Cheng, 1989). They were therefore given the label of "democratic faction". The reunion with China and the maintenance of a high degree of autonomy for Hong Kong after reunion were their political principles in the 1980s, but the latter one seems to have gained more emphasis after the Tiananmen Incident in 1989. Although rising to the status of semi-opposition through electoral competition, their vulnerability lay in their limited (though growing) mobilization capacity and the lack of cohesive leadership (Lau, 1990). More important than that is whether they would have the will to remove the institutional barriers set by the present and future sovereign states (Doron and Maor, 1991; Holcombe, 1991). Meanwhile, a pro-Beijing faction does exist in this class. This had a close relationship with the Chinese authorities and their organs in Hong Kong. For them, nationalism is more important than the principle of autonomy.

Unlike in other British colonies, the public in Hong Kong seemed to have played a minor and passive role in the politics of decolonization. Insulated from politics under the colonial rule, discouraged from participation by its future sovereign state, and lacking leadership and organization, their influence would be peripheral. Their voice could only be heard spontaneously in protest movements and hopefully in elections. This segment of population comprised largely the refugees from China after 1949 and their offspring. Their political orientation towards Communist China is quite negative and their trust in it is very limited (Wong, 13 July 1994:160-4). Regarding the political reform, they tended to be crosscut by the national sentiment and the principle of a high degree of autonomy.

Given the closed and concentrated nature of the Hong Kong government which had developed since 1841 and was likely to remain in place after 1997, the successful jockeying for influence or power of particular social forces lies in their coincidence of interest with the sovereign state. In the meantime, the state may probably be constrained by its paramount aim of capitalist development and therefore may occasionally accommodate demands that seem to have effect on the stability and prosperity of the Hong Kong capitalist society.

The Political Reforms from Above

While the Sino-British negotiations were still in progress in July 1984, the Hong Kong government put forward a Green Paper entitled "The Further Development of Representative Government in Hong Kong". One of the aims stated in the Paper is:

> ... to develop progressively a system of government the authority for which is firmly rooted in Hong Kong, which is able to represent authoritatively the views of the people of Hong Kong, and which is more directly accountable to the people of Hong Kong; ... (Hong Kong Government, 1984a:4)

Following the District Administration Reforms launched in 1980-81 which led to the establishment of the consultative DBs system, the Paper proposed to reform the "central organs of the Government" of the LegCo, the ExCo, the Governor and their relationships with each other.

The move seemed to indicate Britain's decision to further reform the political structure in Hong Kong, though in a very cautious and manageable way. This can be detected from the Green Paper's praise of the existing "consensus politics" and the somewhat less favourable comments on the introduction of popular election. In highlighting the unique feature of Hong Kong's political system, the Green Paper put it in this way:

> The most distinct feature of the present system of government in Hong Kong is that it operates on the basis of consultation and consensus. It is not a system based on parties, factions and adversarial politics but one of broad agreements which seeks to take a pragmatic approach to the problems of the day.... The very real advantages of this system, which have enabled Hong Kong to enjoy sustained periods of economic growth and internal stability, must not be forgotten, or lightly thrown aside, in developing plans for the introduction of more representative institutions in Hong Kong. (Hong Kong Government, 1984a:8)

Regarding popular election, the Green Paper described it as not a "universally successful as a means of ensuring stable representative government" and it "would run the risk of a swift introduction of adversarial politics, and would introduce an element of instability at a crucial time". On the contrary, the adoption of non-popular election, especially in the form of functional constituencies, seemed to have the consideration that "full weight should be given to representation of the economic and professional sectors of Hong Kong society which are essential to future confidence and prosperity" (Hong Kong Government, 1984a:9).

The then Hong Kong Governor, Edward Youde, had also hinted that the views from Beijing had also been taken into consideration when framing the proposal. In introducing the Green Paper to the LegCo in July 1984, he stated:

> In drawing up our proposals we have had regard to the special circumstance of Hongkong and the need to maintain our good relationship with our mainland neighbour. We have also done our utmost in framing these proposals to ensure that there need be no conflict with the principle of continuity between the systems in force both before and after 1997. [7]

As shown in Table 3.1, the LegCo proposed to have 12 (25%, N=48) and 24 (48%, N=50) non-popularly-elected members (half from the electoral college and half from functional constituencies) in 1985 and 1988, respectively. In 1991, the number would be raised to 28 (56%) under option 1 and 40 (80%) under option 2. Though there was no proposed change in the ExCo in 1985, the Green Paper had proposed that 4 (25%)

and 8 (57%) members would be elected from among the LegCo's non-official members in 1988 and 1991, respectively (see Table 3.2). Because of the above changes in the LegCo and the ExCo, the Governor would cease to be the President of the LegCo and his power in the ExCo would be reviewed in due course. Furthermore, the Green Paper also indicated that:

> The future method of selecting candidates for appointment as Governor will also need to be considered. One possible development would be for the Governor himself, in his capacity as Chief Executive, to be selected, once the process described in this Paper is complete, through an elective process, for example, through election by a college composed of all Unofficial Members of the Executive and Legislative Councils after a period of consultation among them. (Hong Kong Government, 1984a:20)

Table 3.1 Comparison of 1984 Green and White Papers -- LegCo's Composition

	Green Paper: 1984	1985	1988	1991 (1)	1991 (2)	White Paper: Change in 1985
Electoral College*	0	6	12	14	20	12
Functional Constituencies	0	6	12	14	20	12
Appointed Members	29	23	16	12	0	22
Official Members	18	13	10	10	10	10
Total	47	48	50	50	50	56

* It is composed of UrbCo, (new) RegCo and District Board members.

Table 3.2   Comparison of 1984 Green and White Papers -- ExCo's Composition

	Green Paper: 1984	1988	1991	White Paper
Elected by LegCo	0	4	8	No Change in 1985 and no timetable for implementation
Appointed Members	12	8	2	
Ex-officio Members	4	4	4	
Total	16	16	14	

The question here is whether the release of the 1984 Green Paper preceded the Chinese agreement in the Joint Declaration that the future HKSAR legislature should be constituted by elections. The answer was not, as revealed later by Geoffrey Howe.[8] Although showing its disapproval in private briefings, China at last did agree to include the clause in the Joint Declaration (Miners, 1991:25; *FEER*, 29 November 1984). This pre-emptive move to reform had aroused the suspicion of China which was later found to be detrimental to the close cooperation of both countries during the transitional period (for details, see the following section).

One possible explanation for the pre-emptive move by Britain was the British calculation of pressurising China to adopt the relevant clauses in the Joint Declaration. If adopted, it seemed to smooth the way for the subsequent approval of the Joint Declaration by the British Parliament and the Hong Kong people. In addition, the move also served as the constitutional basis for the succeeding democratic reform as well as "Hong Kong people governing Hong Kong".

In fact, the release of the Green Paper has been viewed as a logical move to prepare for the subsequent "Hong Kong people governing Hong Kong". Chung Sze-yuen, the then Senior Member of the ExCo, had stated that:

If there is no problem in the [on-going Sino-British] negotiation, British rule will end on 30 June 1997. China has said to let Hong Kong people govern Hong Kong after regaining sovereignty. At present, Hong Kong is a colony and the Governor--the highest administrator--is appointed [by Britain]. The ordinary people in Hong Kong do wish that the [future] administrator would not be appointed by Beijing, but be elected by the Hong Kong people. Thus, there is no reason for Hong Kong to follow the colonial system in the future. Instead, Hong Kong should follow [to develop] a democratic system. We do not want the Hong Kong Government to continue the existing colonial government until 1996 and then suddenly carry out an election. As a result, [we] should use the remaining 13 years to transform [Hong Kong] into a representative government. . . . (*The Nineties Monthly* 175, August 1984:58; original in Chinese, my own translation)

In the LegCo's motion debate on the Green Paper, Alex Wu also said: "It is especially sensible for the Green Paper to adopt a gradual approach to achieve the objective of 'Hong Kong people to rule Hong Kong'". Yeung Po-kwan said on the same occasion that: "as there are only 13 years to go before Hong Kong is faced with the reality of 'Hong Kong being ruled by Hong Kong people' in 1997, the introduction of reforms into the government system has become an urgent task which admits of no delay" (*Hong Kong Hansard*, 2 August 1984:1354 & 1405).

Although there was a common understanding of the need to reform the central level of government by introducing elected members to the LegCo first and then to the ExCo, the political community was divided over the way the elected members would be recruited. Those who supported the Green Paper's option of non-popular election were mainly ExCo and LegCo members. They argued for a cautious start of political reform so as to maintain stability and prosperity of Hong Kong. Chan Kam-chuen (*Hong Kong Hansard*, 2 August 1984:1373-4), a LegCo member, even hinted that the introduction of popular election would probably favour the well-organized leftist trade unions. He further reminded those who supported popular election that:

> They should be aware of the Chinese saying (螳螂捕蟬，不知黃雀在後) i.e. the mantis preying a cicada is unaware of the oriole behind it. If they count the number of votes they estimate they would get and compare the figure with what the unions would get, they would discover that it will take a lot of hardwork to canvass for the votes of the disorganised silent majority, bearing in mind that the unions are well organised and may use the votes they can canvass as their powerful political weapons.

The advocates of popular election were UrbCo members, activists of pressure groups, trade unions and grass-roots organizations. They united together to form the Joint Conference on the Green Paper on Further Development of Representative Government. The Joint Conference argued that popular election to the LegCo was the key issue of the present political reform and a step to "return governmental authority to the people" as there would be "a democratic and highly autonomous system of self-administration" in 1997. They therefore demanded that there should be no less than one-fifth of popularly-elected LegCo members by 1988 (*South China Morning Post* (hereafter *SCMP*), 17 September 1984).

The subsequent White Paper, released in late November 1984, opted for a speedy pace of introducing non-popularly-elected members to the LegCo. Twenty-four (43%) would be returned by non-popular election in 1985. Though the Green Paper had not included any option of popular election to the LegCo, the White Paper indicated that the LegCo would have popularly-elected members in 1988. It seems worthwhile to quote here:

> .... With few exceptions the bulk of public response from all sources suggested a cautious approach with a gradual start by introducing a very small number of directly elected members in 1988 and building up to a significant number of directly elected members by 1997. .... In summary, there was strong public support for the idea of direct elections but little support for such elections in the immediate future. (Hong Kong Government, 1984b:8)

With respect to the ExCo and the Governor, no timetable was provided to implement the Green Paper's proposals. Though a ministerial system had been raised before and during the consultation period, the White Paper stated that the issue would be addressed at a later stage because it "raises important constitutional question". Regarding the position of the Governor, the White Paper indicated that: "Any proposals for change in the position and role of the Governor will need to take into account the provisions of the Joint Declaration and these important issues will be considered at a later stage" (Hong Kong government, 1984b:11). Nevertheless, the White Paper had proposed to review the Governor's position as President of the LegCo in 1987. As a whole, it is strange to note that the far-reaching reforms outlined in the Green Paper had only been given a start but no definite schedule beyond 1985 in the subsequent White Paper.

China's Pressure to Converge

The optimists in Hong Kong seemed to believe that the coincidence of the timing of the release of the 1984 Green and White Papers, and the initialling of the Sino-British Joint Declaration in September 1984 indicated that London and Beijing had already arrived at certain consensus on political reforms and arrangements during the transitional period. This false hope was eventually shattered by the high profile the Beijing leaders adopted in the ensuing years of the transition.

The rather self-restrained gestures by Beijing leaders in late 1984 up to mid-1985 witnessed an about-turn in late 1985, from the one that emphasized British responsibility to administer Hong Kong up to 1997 to the one that actively spoke out about what Beijing would like or not like to see in the transitional period. As indicated in a previous section, the British pre-emptive move to reform aroused China's suspicion about the motive behind it. Hence, Xu Jiatun, the director of the NCNA's Hong Kong Branch, gave a warning in a press conference on 21 November 1985 that he "did not want to see major changes in the twelve years [to come], transforming the fundamental system in Hong Kong, and then no more changes in the following fifty years." He further remarked that if Hong Kong wanted to maintain stability and prosperity, it would be better for it to follow the text of the Joint Declaration. He warned that:

> Now we cannot help noticing a tendency of doing things deviating from the Joint Declaration. If there are unexpected changes, I think one should pay attention to question of this kind. (quoted in Cheng, 1987:278)

It was believed that Xu wanted to express Beijing's disapproval of the British attempt to introduce further political reforms in Hong Kong as well as to intimidate political activists who were lobbying for a faster pace of democratization. At that moment, the issue of popular election to the LegCo and the installation of a ministerial system were hotly debated in Hong Kong. Beijing seemed to worry that the pre-emptive political reforms would dictate the drafting of the Basic Law, which was to be promulgated in 1990, and thus lessen its command over the political changes in Hong Kong in the transitional period. Moreover, Beijing also regarded the move as a prelude to "transfer power to the Hong Kong people" rather than to China (Xu, 1993:168-73).

The sceptical attitude of Beijing towards the political reforms in Hong Kong was further reinforced by the existence of the Colonial Laws Validity Act 1865 (Sun, 1987:102-12). The Act stated that if a colonial legislature developed to have one-half of its members elected by the inhabitants of the colony, the said legislature would become a "representative legislature" which has the "full power to make laws respecting the constitution, powers, and procedure of such legislature".

Beijing alleged that London, in doing so, would transfer the power to local pro-British political forces. Instead, Beijing stressed that London was bound to restore sovereignty to the PRC's government, not the people of Hong Kong. Thus, any political reforms in the transitional period should have the approval of the Chinese government and must converge with the Basic Law (*FEER*, 12 December 1985). Ji Pengfei, the then Director of the State Council's HKMAO, revealed at the end of his visit to Hong Kong on 21 December 1985 that only small changes could be made in the transitional period and all proposed big changes must be discussed by China and Britain as the future HKSAR political system involved not just Hong Kong people but also China and its relations to Britain (*FEER*, 2 January 1986). He was also quoted as saying:

> The question of Hong Kong's political system after 1997 will be decided by the Basic Law. Reforms of Hong Kong's political system in the transitional period have to take into consideration convergence with the Basic Law. (*Liaowang*, 30 November 1985; quoted in Cheng, 1987:278)

In fact, he had already put through his message as early as 19 October 1985 when he received a visiting Hong Kong delegation of architects. On that occasion, he expressed Beijing's reservations at the fast pace of political reforms in Hong Kong and reportedly said the political system for the HKSAR would be decided by the Basic Law, the drafting of which had just started and which would be promulgated in 1990 (*FEER*, 31 October 1985). Furthermore, Beijing officials seemed to stop using the phrase "*gangren zhigang*" (Hong Kong people governing Hong Kong) any more as Lu Ping, the then Secretary-General of the HKMAO, had openly regarded the phrase as "unscientific" (*FEER*, 13 February 1986).

The above Chinese assertions stirred up the question of who was responsible for the Hong Kong administration in the transitional period. As mentioned before, Article 4 of the Joint Declaration stated that "the Government of the United Kingdom will be responsible for the administration of Hong Kong" during the transitional period and China "will give its cooperation in this connection". In refuting his deputy, Alan Scott, who reportedly said in a seminar on 3 October 1985 that the Hong Kong government will consult Beijing before taking any further political reforms, David Akers-Jones, the then Chief Secretary, had stated clearly that: "The Chinese Government has made it clear it is our responsibility to run Hongkong in the next 12 years. Therefore we don't have to consult them." He further said political reforms would not be a subject for discussion in the Joint Liaison Group (JLG), an organ set up to help effective implementation of the Joint Declaration (*FEER*, 17 October 1985).

But shortly after Xu's warning, London reportedly conceded to Beijing by promising to discuss the future political reforms in the second meeting of the JLG (*FEER*, 2 January 1986). On 30 December 1985, Akers-Jones revealed that the Hong Kong government would exchange views with Beijing before publishing any proposals for political reforms in 1987 review (*FEER*, 16 January 1986). Furthermore, Timothy Renton, the then British Foreign Minister with special responsibility for Hong Kong, after his visit to China on 24 January 1986, indicated his agreement with Beijing that political changes must "converge" with the Basic Law. Renton further elaborated his idea of convergence:

> We are creating a set of railway lines that lead up to 1997. The Chinese will be creating a set of railway lines that lead on from 1997. The need is to see that those two railway lines meet together at a crossing point.

In contrast to his former statement that London would not interfere with constitutional reforms in Hong Kong, he emphasized that Britain has overall responsibility for the administration of Hong Kong during the transitional period (*FEER*, 6 February 1986). Apparently, London had opted to cooperate with Beijing by informing the latter beforehand of any political reform plan in the future.

Being faced with China's constant stress on the convergence of political reform in Hong Kong with the Basic Law, on the return of sovereignty and administration to China but not the Hong Kong people, and on the maintenance of the status quo at the time of the conclusion of the Joint Declaration but not that of 1997, as well as with the constraints imposed by the responsibility of maintaining stability and prosperity as well as effective governing of Hong Kong, the British government seemed to lose enthusiasm for carrying out its "unfinished" political reform at that moment (Lau, 1987:33-40).

The Conflicting Ideas on the Pace of Democratization

The pressure to converge with the Basic Law being drafted called into question Britain's impartiality in reviewing the developments in representative government in 1987 and in implementing relevant reforms in Hong Kong. Although the public in Hong Kong had widely debated the relationships between the executive and the legislature, the 1987 Green Paper, released on 27 May 1987, opted neither to discuss it, nor to examine the overall role of the Governor at the moment. The 1987 Green Paper seemed to confine the review to the less controversial topics: the role and composition of the DBs and the relationship of the UrbCo and urban DBs, the size and committee structure of the UrbCo, the composition of the LegCo, the position of the Governor as President of the LegCo, and the issues concerning technical aspects of elections.

Nevertheless, the Hong Kong government had pledged to remain in a "neutral and open-minded position" in the review process and urged the public to offer their views on the matter. David Ford, the then Chief Secretary, had also told the LegCo when tabling the Green Paper that: "All of them are genuine options. There are no preconceived ideas on the part of the Government. There is no pre-determined outcome." In order to achieve this aim in the four-month long consultation period, a Survey Office had been set up to "collect, collate and report on the public response to the Green Paper". Though the government had tried to play down the most controversial issue of popular election, by stressing that the review was not completely concerned with that particular issue but the whole political landscape of Hong Kong, the issue of the day was still whether to introduce popular election to the LegCo in 1988.

Before the release of the 1987 Green Paper, Chinese officials had, in one way or another, made known their views on the political reform in general and the issue of popular election in particular. In February 1987, an unidentified Chinese official reportedly indicated that China was against the introduction of popular election in 1988, but would consider allowing it in 1991. The official also charged that the intention of the pro-popular-election group was to resist Communist China by promoting democracy in Hong Kong (*SCMP*, 6 February 1987). In an address to the Basic Law drafters in April 1987, Deng Xiaoping said:

> I don't believe that introducing direct election now will be good to Hong Kong. The first criterion of Hong Kong people governing Hong Kong is to elect those Hong Kong people who love China and Hong Kong. Does the one-person one-vote [method] elect such kind of people? It is not sure. . . . Introducing direct election in a gradual way [of doing it] is preferred. (Cheung, Yeung, Lo and Chan, 1991:109-10)

In an interview with the *Liaowang* (Overseas) published on 22 June, Li Hou, the then Deputy Director of the HKMAO and the Secretary-General of the Basic Law Drafting Committee (BLDC), was quoted as saying (but later denied) that popular election in 1988 "will naturally fail to converge with the Basic Law" and "would not be in accordance with the spirit of the Sino-British Joint Declaration" (*SCMP*, 19 and 24 June 1987). Later in July, Ke Zaishuo, Head of the Chinese side of the Joint Liaison Group, made clear that "we [China] have no significant view against direct election" (*SCMP*, 11 July 1987). Probably, Beijing had adjusted its position from the question of "if" to "when". Subsequently, NCNA's officials had reportedly promoted a "political swap plan" of having popular election in 1991 instead of 1988 (*Hong Kong Standard* (hereafter *HKS*), 18 September 1987).

The pro-popular-election activists and pressure group leaders (hereafter the democrats) criticized the Hong Kong government of not living up to its 1984 promise of furthering the developments in representative government. Ding Lik-kiu, a long-time democratic campaigner and the then chairman of the Christian Industrial Committee, said: "The 1987 Green Paper reflects the sober mood of these times while the 1984 Green and White Papers reflected the euphoria of those times." He further blamed the Green Paper of "souring of a dream that grew out of the Joint Declaration". Thomas Tam, the Chairman of the Hong Kong Policy Review, also criticized the government for escaping "from its responsibility in overseeing the development of a representative government in Hong Kong after China has indicated very clearly its strong objection to direct election" (*SCMP*, 28 May 1987).

On the contrary, the opponents of popular election (hereafter the conservatives[9]) in 1988 stressed the paramount importance of stability and prosperity, and any political reforms should be sure to have convergence with the Basic Law. Vincent Lo, the convener of the Business and Professional Group of the Basic Law Consultative Committee (BLCC), said: "Changes in 1988, if any, should only involve the fine-tuning of the existing system and direct election for 1988 would be a premature move as this [*sic*] will be a new development which may impinge on the Basic Law" (*SCMP*, 28 May 1987). Tsang Yok-sing[10] of the leftist Hong Kong Federation of Education had reportedly regarded popular election as a drastic constitutional change that would adversely affect the prosperity and stability of Hong Kong and thus was contrary to the Joint Declaration (*HKS*, 15 June 1987). Furthermore, chairman of a constituted union of the leftist Federation of Trade Unions (FTU) argued that "One-man one-vote

The Rise of the Centre-Periphery Cleavage 67

will not be the aim of democracy, but harmony among Hongkong's people and the promotion of an environment that attracts investments and which is conducive to stability and prosperity" and added that "To the workers, a meal is better than a vote" (*SCMP*, 22 June 1987).

The LegCo members were also divided over the issue of popular election. In the motion debate on the Green Paper on 15 and 16 July 1987, 18 LegCo members supported the introduction of popular election in 1988 and a similar number were against it. A similar pattern of opinion was also found in the RegCo and the DBs. In the case of the UrbCo, a majority of the speakers in the debate supported popular election in 1988 (Survey Office, 1987:53). On the other hand, most of the independent opinion polls had shown that respondents were more inclined to support popular election in 1988 than the opponents, ranging from two to one to three to one in favour of it (*SCMP*, 30 September 1987). Given that the officio and/or appointed member were in the majority in these councils, it is understandable why the council members were so divisive in demanding that popular election should be held in 1988.

The proponents and opponents were deeply engaged in the "war of public opinion". Each side wanted to have an edge over the other in the hope of tipping the balance in their favour in the Survey Office's opinion collection process. The democrats under the umbrella organization, the Joint Committee on the Promotion of Democratic Government, launched signature campaigns in supporting their cause. The broadcast during the campaign reads: "There is only 10 years to go before 1997, the future of Hongkong depends on our participation. If we have partial direct elections to the Legislative Council next year, we can participate more in central policy-making and will be in a better position to safeguard our livelihood in Hongkong" (*SCMP*, 7 September 1987). This appeal to protect people's rights and interests managed to collect more than 210,000 signatures. In addition, the Joint Committee also placed a political advertisement on 4 September 1987, in which 145 pressure groups, trade unions, and grass-roots organizations as well as 864 individuals had shown their support.

On the anti-popular-election side, the leftists made use of their organization networks in advancing their cause. The Bank of China and its 12 sister banks reportedly told their 10,000 employees to sign a petition to oppose popular election in 1988 (*SCMP*, 7 September 1987). The FTU urged their 170,000 members to sign an anti-popular-election position letter which would be directed to the Survey Office later on. In expressing their opposition to popular election in 1988, 84 business organizations and nearly 400 socio-economic elites advertised their stance in several local newspapers on 28 and 30 September, respectively.

The report of the Survey Office released in early November sparked off another wave of criticism towards the government about its mis-handling of public opinion. The bone of contention between the government and the democrats was focused on the design and result of the government-commissioned survey, and the classification of the pre-printed submissions and the signature campaigns. Contrary to all media-sponsored surveys, the Survey Office's survey had found that more respondents were against 1988 popular elections. Furthermore, the wording and ordering of option (4) in a question concerning popular election was called into question. It reads:

> If changes are desirable in 1988, it will be possible to make one or more of the following changes, e.g. increase slightly the number of Official Members, reduce the number of Appointed Members, increase the number of indirectly elected Members or have directly elected Members.

This clumsy and hard-to-understand option received criticism not only from the democrats but also from academics and private polling companies.

In addition, the Survey Office treated the pre-printed submissions as individual submissions but not the signature campaigns. Among the 95,835 individual submissions, 60,706 were against 1988 popular election, of which 50,175 were in pre-printed forms. But only 1,313 out of 35,129 submissions for 1988 popular elections were in pre-printed forms (*HKS*, 15 November 1987). On the other hand, the signature campaigns, which were overwhelmingly in favour of 1988 popular elections, had collected over 220,000 names of individuals and organizations. But only one signature campaign, which contained 295 names, was against 1988 popular election (Survey Office, 1987:57). On the whole, the views expressed at the establishment and organization levels were slightly more inclined to object to the introduction of popular elections in 1988, but there was a quite clear majority supporting 1988 popular elections at the individual level if the pre-printed forms and signature campaigns were treated equally.

As a result, the democrats accused the government of playing around with the figures so as to bow to Beijing pressure on popular elections. This accusation called into question the integrity and credibility of the government. In rebuffing the above allegation, David Ford, the then Chief Secretary, warned that: "Those who continue to make them in the misguided belief that they are dealing with a lame duck will learn that they have a tiger by the tail -- and not a paper tiger either" (*Hong Kong Hansard*, 11 November 1987; *SCMP*, 12 November 1987). Despite Ford's warning, the Joint Committee on the Promotion of Democratic Government dispatched delegations to London and Beijing to petition against alleged government manipulation of public opinion in the Survey Office report. In an open letter addressed to British Prime Minister Thatcher, Martin Lee[11], leader of the London delegation, wrote that:

> We submit that a decision not to hold direct election next year would be wholly unacceptable to the majority of the people of Hongkong. For the introduction of direct elections is no longer just a question of timing. To most people in Hongkong, it has become an indicator as to whether the British administration is credible and responsible to the people.
> We submit that time is of the utmost importance and time is not on our side. If we were to lose precious years just to please the Chinese Government, there is simply not enough time left to evolve progressively an effective democratic government before 1997. (*SCMP*, 16 December 1987)

Despite the last-minute effort of lobbying London and Beijing, the hope of the democrats was formally shattered by the release of the White Paper in February 1988. According to the White Paper, only ten popularly-elected LegCo seats would be introduced in 1991 to replace those presently filled by the electoral college of the DBs.[12] The fate of 1988 popular elections had already been sealed, but the political forces aimed at reforming the colonial structure shifted their attention to the drafting of the Basic Law and triggered off another round of intense competition among various political groups.

The Centre-Periphery Cleavage in the Making

With the British rule over Hong Kong not being extended beyond 1997, and the Chinese promise of "Hong Kong people governing Hong Kong" and "high degree of autonomy" for 50 years after 1997, there was a need to re-frame the constitutional and political system so as to reflect the corresponding change in Hong Kong's political status. Under such circumstances, the drafting of the Basic Law of the HKSAR was called into play. Because of its paramount importance in regulating the relationships between China and Hong Kong as well as the political life within the future HKSAR, the drafting of the Basic Law would inevitably be a political game in which various political forces would participate to shape the outcome in their favour.

For the democrats and their supporters, they had campaigned for democratic reforms since the mid-1970s, well before the surge of the 1997 issue. They regarded the Chinese promise of "Hong Kong people governing Hong Kong" in the early 1980s as a timely push to advance their cause. Thus, they viewed the establishment of representative government as a logical development of such promise. Furthermore, it also helped to safeguard their freedom and living style after 1997 and worked as an effective mechanism to ward off unnecessary intervention from China. Regarding the future political model, they advocated a popular and responsive political structure where the executive should be placed under the control of either the legislature or the electorate. In other words, they would like to have a legislature-centred political system.

For the conservatives, although they understood the importance of an open government and the rule of law, their intimate economic relationships with China had dictated their attitude towards the campaigns for setting up representative government. Once the Beijing government expressed its disapproval of major political reforms in the transitional period in late 1985, the conservatives had to follow suit. Moreover, their privileged and nearly exclusive access to the Establishment would be threatened if political reforms implemented. It was also logical for them to side with the Chinese government to counter the advance of the democrats by limiting the scope of democratic reforms, if not totally opposed. A fragmented legislature and an executive-centred political system were thus their ideal model to be fought for in the Basic Law drafting process. In other words, they tried to maintain some form of colonial system or elite rule after 1997.

For the British and Hong Kong governments, they always found themselves crosscut by the Chinese and the conservatives' pressure for limited, if not definitely no, reform, and the democrats' demand of full democracy. Governing in such a turbulent environment, like Hong Kong in the late 1980s, would not be an easy job. Furthermore, the British-Hong Kong government also suffered from the diminishing support from the socio-economic elites, the lack of will to govern from the departing senior bureaucrats and the rising welfare demands from the mass public. How to maintain the effective governing in the face of growing intervention from China in the transitional period would be the major question waiting to be resolved. To accommodate and cooperate with China in local affairs, and to open-up partially the political structure through popular elections would be two possible ways to restore the declining legitimacy. But given the incompatibility of these two measures, it was very difficult to maintain the right balance. Nevertheless, Britain seemed to adopt a co-operative attitude towards the transition of power, at least before the appointment of Christopher Patten as Governor in 1992. Percy Cradock wrote in his memoirs that "the policy of cooperation with China for the benefit of Hong Kong, if not the only conceivable policy, is the only one that will allow Britain to leave the stage knowing that it was done its best to fulfil its responsibilities to the six million people in its charge" (Cradock, 1994a:258). Regarding the future political model, the British government tried hard to convert the principles that it had stipulated in the Sino-British Joint Declaration into the operational details of implementation, i.e. a political system where the executive is accountable to the elected legislature.

Needless to say, China would be the host of the game with overwhelming power and influence in the drafting process. Acting as a referee or as an arbiter was all up to China's decision. With China acting as a referee, the political controversy over Hong Kong's electoral reforms might be confined to being a local issue and Beijing might then have a free hand to balance the conflicts between the democrats and the conservatives. But Beijing seemed to opt for the role of arbiter and to support the conservatives as reflected in the Basic Law drafting process. Thus, Beijing intervened in the local political contradictions of the democrats and the conservatives. There were two institutional barriers used to limit the influence of the democrats in the future HKSAR political system. One was to restrict the popularly-elected seats of the legislature to a minority in terms of both number and influence. That meant to institute a fractionized and fragmented legislature. The other was to insulate the executive and its agencies from effective checks by the legislature and the mass public. That meant to maintain the executive-centred political system. These basic calculations of Beijing and the conservatives had worked to frustrate the democrats' efforts and reinforced the contradictions between them. After intense mobilization efforts made by the concerned parties during the Basic Law drafting process and the subsequent polarization of political forces, the centre-periphery electoral cleavage emerged and played a significant role in the ensuing LegCo popular elections.

The Politics of Appointment

The drafting of the Basic Law would probably be the most pressing task in the transitional period. In his published memoirs, Xu Jiatun noted that there were two kinds of opinion within China as to whether Hong Kong people should be invited to join the BLDC. Xu was of the opinion that in order to have the widest support from the Hong Kong people, the BLDC should include a certain number of Hong Kong drafters (Xu, 1993:155-6). Chinese leaders seemed to accept what Xu had suggested. When Beijing released the appointment list of the BLDC in June 1985, 23 (out of 59) members were from Hong Kong. The numerical strength of the Chinese drafters reflects the fact that the ultimate decision power rested with the Chinese side (Scott, 1989:298-305; Cheng, 1987:275-6; Lane, 1990:119-26; Lau, 1988:90-104). Any piece of legislation would, then, need the approval of the Chinese drafters and in fact, they held the vetting power in their own hands.

Although Beijing pledged to take care of as many sectors of interest as possible, the appointed Hong Kong drafters were mainly recruited from the upper and middle-upper strata of businessmen and professionals. Only two members were from the trade unions: Tam Yiu-chung from the leftist FTU and Szeto Wah from the Hong Kong Professional Teachers' Unions (HKPTU). In response to comments that the grass-roots were under-represented in the BLDC, Xu made clear that in deciding who should be appointed to the BLDC, Hong Kong's historical background and reality had to be considered, and the guiding principle was to maintain Hong Kong's stability and prosperity (Cheung *et al*, 1991:38). That means those who had occupied the strategic locations in Hong Kong society would be the prior targets to be wooed. But Xu later in his memoirs admitted that he was originally planning to use the mainland drafters to counter-balance the businessmen's influence in the BLDC, but he found it unnecessary at the end of the day (Xu, 1993:156).

As revealed by several sources, Britain had participated informally in the whole drafting process of the Basic Law through diplomatic channels and the Hong Kong Basic Law drafters (Fifoot, 1991:301, n3; Xu, 1993:154-5; Cradock, 1994a:233). Xu claimed that the degree of British involvement in the drafting of the Basic Law was very deep, having examined every paragraph and even particular wording of the Basic Law (Xu, 1993:155). Percy Cradock had also indicated the involvement of Hong Kong government and the ExCo in the drafting process (Cradock, 1994a:233). In addition, Beijing had also invited, but failed to persuade, some pro-Hong Kong establishment and pro-Taiwan figures to join the BLCC.

Besides, two instances had worked to undermine the confidence of Hong Kong people towards the independence and operation of the BLCC which aimed to consult and collect public views on the Basic Law drafts. The first one concerned the sudden withdrawal of the leftist trade unions' support for Lau Chin-shek, the Director of the independent Hong Kong Christian Industrial Committee (HKCIC), to be one of the seven nominees representing labour in the BLCC. Lau was said to be militant in fighting for labour interests and thus had invited the dislike of the businessmen (*Pai Shing* 107, 1 November 1985:49-51; Lau, 1991:47-53). Xu admitted in his memoirs that it was he who put pressure on the leftist FTU not to support Lau (Xu, 1993:162-3).

The second one concerned the election of office bearers of the BLCC. The said election was held immediately after the election of the BLCC Standing Committee's members. Pao Yue-kong, a BLDC Vice-chairman, swiftly proposed seven names to fill the said posts. The seven were regarded as duly elected as nobody in the meeting had shown their objection at that time. Later, critics challenged the appropriateness of Pao to propose the candidates. The constitution of the BLCC had stipulated that the said posts "shall be elected from among members of the Standing Committee". That means Pao had no such right. A NCNA official defended the result by saying that consultation was the same as "election from among members". Nevertheless, public pressure brought a new round of election but with the same result (*Pai Shing* 110, 16 December 1985:6-8 & 58; Lau, 1988; Cheung *et al*, 1991:47-53). Though this was just a matter of procedure, harm had already been done to the image of and the people's faith towards the drafting process.

Threshold of Representation and Barriers of Entry

Accompanying the establishment of the BLDC and the BLCC was the Sino-British row over the further developments in representative government and the emergence of different interpretations of the Joint Declaration as more and more Beijing leaders put through their own version in the media, especially on the future political system. Their opinion seemed to set the parameter for the drafters.

In elaborating the "accountability" of the executive to the legislature, Mao Jun-nian, a NCNA official and a member of both the BLDC and the BLCC, reportedly said the present executive was already accountable to the legislature, in the sense that the LegCo had the right to question government policies and to vet government finance (*FEER*, 12 December 1985). In February 1986, Lu Ping indicated that the word "accountable" could mean "clarify, explain and consult" and did not imply that the HKSAR legislature would become the power centre. He further elaborated his idea later that the HKSAR executive and legislature should check and balance each other, and the latter should not be superior to the former or vice versa (*FEER*, 20 February 1986).

Li Hou, the then Deputy Director of the HKMAO and the Secretary-General of the BLDC, made further clarification in June that the executive should make periodic reports to, answer questions from, submit budgets to, and be impeached by, the legislature, but the two should be of equal status (*FEER*, 26 June 1986). Furthermore, Deng Xiaoping told the BLDC drafters on 16 April 1987 that he did not support either the installation of a check-and-balance mechanism among the three powers of government, or the immediate introduction of popular elections (Xu, 1993:152).

As mentioned before, the attitude of these Chinese leaders towards the political reforms in Hong Kong, in one way or another, coincided with those of the conservative leaders of the Hong Kong business community. The rather sudden and progressive introduction of universal suffrage and popular elections had given a shock to those political figures recruited by the appointment system. Their privileges and status would then be threatened. Consequently, they tended to oppose liberalization or democratization. Because of such propensity, it is not surprising to find the frequent mutual support between the Chinese and the conservative Hong Kong drafters during the drafting process.

For the emerging democrats, the unreformed colonial system did not provide a fair opportunity for them to compete for political power. Thus, they tended to support a quicker pace of democratization and tried to mobilize support from the under-privileged. The critical questions for their development before and after 1997 are: how far can they remove the institutional barrier of entry and how high the threshold of representation will be. Given the drafting exercise as an institution-building process, the democrats would try hard to remove the institutional barrier of entry and to lower the threshold of representation.

Immediately after the establishment of the BLDC and the BLCC, the political elites in Hong Kong had actively participated in the discussion on the future political model of the HKSAR. At one time, the Secretariat of the BLCC had noted that 41 models had already been proposed. These models were later being sorted into 5 alternatives for selecting the Chief

Executive (CE) and 4 alternatives for constituting the Legislature in the Draft Basic Law (for solicitation of opinions) released in April 1988. The differences among these alternatives were largely on the methods of nominating and electing the Chief Executive, and on the proportion of popularly-elected seats in the Legislature (Secretariat of the Consultative Committee for the Basic Law, 1989a:89-101).

Among the proposed models, the keen competition was between the Group of 190 and the Group of 89. The "190 Proposal" was put forward by the democrats. It suggested that the candidates for the CE should be nominated by the legislature and selected by territory-wide popular election on a one-person-one-vote basis; and the legislature should be made-up of no less than 50% popularly-elected members, no more than 25% members returned through electoral college, and no more than 25% members returned through functional bodies. Under this model, the legislature, with popularly-elected members as a majority, would have an edge over the CE as the former have the right to nominate the CE's candidates. As a variant of this legislature-led political system, the legislature would become the political centre of gravity. The low threshold of representation would allow more participation from the wider society and lessen the chance of manipulation.

In contrast, the "89 Proposal" drew its support largely from the conservative business community and professionals. It proposed that three candidates for the CE position should be nominated by a 20-member nomination committee of the 600-member electoral college and elected by a vote of the same electoral college; the legislature should be composed of 50% members returned through functional bodies, 25% members through popular election and the remaining 25% through the electoral college. Comparatively speaking, the institutional barrier of choosing the CE and the threshold of representation were quite high. By using the electoral college and functional elections, the eligible participants would be largely confined to the narrow strata of socio-economic elites and the bulk of the mass public would be screened out. The influence from the mass society would also be prevented from playing a role because of its sheer size and proportion (one-fourth of the total). Given the predominance of the socio-economic elites in the selection of the CE and in the legislature, and the coincidence of their interests, the legislature and the CE would then work hand-in-glove and thus contribute to an executive-led political system. The public would be prevented from effective participation.

Time was running short, as there had to be a BLDC-recommended draft political model incorporated into the draft Basic Law which would then be submitted to the Standing Committee of the NPC for approval as a piece of proposed legislation in early 1989. The political activists in Hong Kong had spared no effort in seeking such compromise but failed at the end of the day. Under such circumstances, Louis Cha, the co-convenor of the Subgroup on Political Structure of the BLDC, proposed the so-called "Mainstream Model" at the Subgroup meeting in Guangzhou on 19 November 1988. The revised form of the "Mainstream Model" passed and the subgroup meeting recommended: the CE shall be first elected by the electoral college and then a referendum shall be held during the third term of the CE to decide whether the CE shall be popularly elected from the next term onwards; the proportion of the popularly-elected seats in the HKSAR legislature for the first four terms are 27%, 38.5%, 50% and 50%, respectively, and then a referendum shall be held during the fourth term of the legislature to decide whether all its members shall be returned by popular election from the next term onwards.

According to this model, the earliest possible year for popular elections to the CE (five year term) and all the members of the legislature (four year term, except the first two year term) would be 2013 and 2012, respectively. Regarding the timing of introducing a full-fledged popularly-elected CE and legislature, this model might be considered as the most conservative of all the models proposed.

The "Mainstream Model" aroused a widespread outcry in Hong Kong. The democrats organized a series of protests, ranging from a marathon hunger strike to a mass rally in which the section on the HKSAR's political structure of the draft Basic Law was burned. A group of undergraduates also burned the *Ming Pao Daily News*'s editorials outside the *Ming Pao* Building to protest against Cha of taking advantage of his ownership of the newspaper to defend his political model. Although showing their dismay and frustration, their efforts were abortive because of the lack of institutional control of the Basic Law drafters. The effect was to prevent a true reflection of societal preferences in the drafting process. Coinciding with this was the inflexibility of China's Hong Kong policy and its apparent identification with the conservative businessmen's interests. The stage was set for the polarization of political forces both within and without Hong Kong. The democrats were fighting a no-win battle with the "unholy" alliance of the Beijing government and the conservatives.

In the midst of protests, criticism and calls for revision, the "Mainstream Model" was finally adopted by the eighth session of the BLDC in January 1989. Furthermore, Cha Chi-min, an influential but conservative businessman, had successfully sought a two-third majority backing in attaching four conditions to the introduction of a referendum in the session. Therefore, the referendum "shall only be held with the endorsement of the majority of members of the Legislature Council, the consent of the Chief Executive and the approval of the Standing Committee of the National People's Congress. The result of the referendum shall only be valid and effective with the affirmative vote of more than 30 per cent of the eligible voters" (Secretariat of the Consultative Committee for the Basic Law, 1989a:100; for the evolution of and comparison between the "mainstream" model and other models, see Secretariat of the Consultative Committee for the Basic Law, 1988).

The effect of the adoption of the most conservative "Cha-Cha formula" was the nearly endless delay in the implementation of full democracy. The four hurdles of getting a referendum to take place could not be regarded as a real progression path at all. Even if the crossing of the first three hurdles were secured, the threshold of the last hurdle was so high as to be unattainable. It was the matter of the adoption of the eligible voters as the basis to calculate the affirmative vote. The effect was that the higher the registration rate and the turnout rate in the referendum, the lower the threshold would be, or vice versa. For example, if there were 10,000 eligible votes, then the minimum vote of getting pass the threshold was 3,000+1 (more than 30% of the eligible voters); if 6,000 (60%) eligible voters got registered and 3,600 voters cast their votes (60%), then the referendum will only be passed if about 83.4% of voters were in favour of it.

The "Cha-Cha formula" might be regarded as another blow to the democrats after the 1987 political review. To those who hoped for the more democratic and open government that was promised, though vaguely, in the Joint Declaration, their hearts were really not at ease. Although Chinese officials had repeatedly said that there would be a chance to revise the conservative "Cha-Cha" political model, harm had already been done to the confidence and trust of the general public and the pro-democrat supporters. As one academic wrote, "by winning a blatantly unfair and political costly battle in the first round of the Basic Law drafting process over the trampled aspiration of the local democratic elements, the PRC unintentionally, but irrevocably, lost the hearts and minds of the great majority of the Hong Kong people" (Chan, 1991:16).

Demand for Democracy from Below: The Tiananmen Effect

The "tug of war" between conservatives and democrats did not end with the inclusion of the "Cha-Cha" formula in the draft Basic Law. At first, the Hong Kong people at large and the political activists in particular seemed to have lost their momentum in further discussing the Basic Law in the second round of the consultation process. But the democratic movement in Beijing and the subsequent tragedy in the Tiananmen Square in June 1989 brushed the political low pressure aside and sparked off another round of political rows over the HKSAR political structure.

The political situation was transformed. The "apolitical" Hong Kong people changed overnight by actively participating in mass rallies to show their support and hope for a democratic China and Hong Kong. It was reported that one million people participated in one mass rally, which was a record-breaking event in the political history of Hong Kong. Leaders of the democrats, now under the umbrella organization of Hong Kong Alliance in Support of the Patriotic Democratic Movement in China led by two LegCo members and BLDC's drafters, Martin Lee and Szeto Wah, were deeply involved in the movement. The whole society was scared by the event and demanded a speeding up in the pace of democratic reform. Not only the democrats but also the conservatives and establishment politicians joined hands to work for it.

The ExCo and the LegCo non-official members, in May 1989, had put forward the "OMELCO Consensus Model", which recommended that the legislature shall have 33.3%, 50%, 66.6% and 100% popularly-elected seats in 1991, 1995, 1999 and 2003, respectively; and the CE shall be popularly elected no later than 2003 (Office of Members of the Executive and Legislative Councils, 1989:23). The Joint Committee for Promotion of Democratic Government, the flagship of the democrats, also revised the "190 Proposal" and suggested that half of the LegCo seats should be returned by popular election in 1991 and then all in 1995; the CE to be popularly elected in 1997 (Secretariat of the Consultative Committee for the Basic Law, 1989b:123-4).

The reaction of the Beijing government was tough. By labelling Hong Kong as a "subversive" base aiming to topple the communist Chinese government with the aid of global anti-Chinese and anti-communist forces, Beijing's leaders had reinforced their negative image towards the democrats and thus, tightened its Hong Kong policy. As Percy Cradock observed:

[The] Tiananmen [Incident] revived all Beijing's neuroses about British duplicity and the external threats to the socialist system. . . . It became a more obvious Chinese goal to extend a dominant influence over the territory as rapidly as possible, whatever the undertakings that British rule would continue undisturbed until 1997. . . . Democracy in Hong Kong . . . became a neuralgic issue. (1994a:223)

As mentioned above, the business community was more vulnerable and prone to Beijing's pressure. The conservative business figures also took advantage of Beijing's tough policy to counter the advance of the democratic forces in the future political system. Because of such considerations, the conservative New Hong Kong Alliance (NHKA), led by former ExCo and LegCo member Lo Tak-shing, proposed a controversial "Bicameral Model" or "One-Council Two-Chamber Model" in which there should be a Functional Chamber comprising mainly non-popular returned members of functional constituencies, and a District Chamber comprising at least 50% popularly-elected members and the remaining members returned by district organizations. Both chambers would have equal legislative powers and equal number of members. In regard to the selection of the CE, the first two terms would be elected by an election committee and the third term by popular election (Cradock, 1994a:124-7). In the name of ensuring the equal participation of all walks of life, the "Bicameral Model" in fact had sought to limit the proportion of popularly-elected seats in the HKSAR legislature. But the actual effect was to decrease the chance of a consolidated democratic force in the legislature by limiting their strength and influence in one of the chambers. With the apparent blessing of China, Lo and the NHKA leaders sold the model vigorously.

The release of the "Bicameral Model" was regarded as a move to counter-balance the "OMELCO Consensus Model" which was considered by China as a British plot to exploit and lead public opinion in Hong Kong in Britain's own interests. Though criticized by many political leaders and media comments, the "Bicameral Model" managed to generate support from some political figures, like ExCo and LegCo member Maria Tam, LegCo members Peter Wong Hong-yuen and James Tien Pei-chun (*HKS*, 1 September 1989), and the leftist FTU (*HKS* and *SCMP*, 29 October 1989).

Meanwhile, the moderates had also taken an initiative to bring the conservatives and the democrats to a compromise.[13] With the common objective of defeating the "Bicameral Model", the concerned parties decided to enter into negotiation in the hope of seeking a compromise political model in early October 1989. After nearly a month of bargaining, they came out with a "New Compromise Model" or "4-4-2 Model" which recommended that the first legislature (1997) should be made up of: 40% from popular election, 40% from functional constituency election, and 20% from election through an election committee. The second legislature (2001) would have 60% popularly-elected seats and 40% functional constituency seats; the composition of the third legislature (2005) and whether all the members shall be elected through popular election would be reviewed and decided by the second legislature. Regarding the selection of the CE, the Model suggested that the CE for the first two terms would be elected by an election committee comprising 50% members selected from functional constituencies and the remainder from the UrbCo, the RegCo and the DBs; the third CE to be elected by popular election (Secretariat of the Consultative Committee for the Basic Law, 1989b:139-41).

Although there was some dissent among the moderates and the democrats, the "New Compromise Model" could be regarded as a great success in producing a common demand on the HKSAR political structure after a four-year-long rivalry and "war of words". The consensus shown by the three camps of moderates, conservatives, and democrats seemed to receive a cool reception by the Chinese officials. These officials had reportedly regarded the compromise exercise as a British plot to manipulate the future political system, and seemed to favour the "Bicameral Model" because "business interests would be protected" (*HKS*, 20 September 1989). In response to the question of whether the BLDC would accept the "New Compromise Model", Xu Jiatun declined to give a straight answer, but stated that "Any models will have to take the long-term interest of the territory into account. If there's no stability, can there be prosperity and advancement?" (*SCMP*, 29 September 1989) It was understood that China would not accept the "New Compromise Model" because Beijing has often regarded the swift introduction of popular election as detrimental to the stability and prosperity of Hong Kong.

Among the models floated at the time, the "Bicameral Model", the "OMELCO Consensus Model", and the "New Compromise Model" were the most discussed within Hong Kong, and the latter two models seemed to have had more support than the first. In anticipation of Beijing's likely rejection of the "OMELCO Consensus Model" and the "New Compromise Model", some members of the Group of 89, like Philip Kwok and Hu Fa-kuang, proposed the "Assorted Model" in mid-November 1989. This model tried to integrate the "Bicameral Model" with the "New Compromise Model" by proposing to install a "separate vote counting" mechanism under which a simple majority of both groups of members from the functional constituencies, and of members from popular election and the election committee should be sought for the passage of those motions and bills, or amendments to government bills introduced by individual legislative members. The model also proposed that the first three legislatures should have 65 members; 25 from the functional constituency, 25 from popular election, and the remaining 15 from the election committee. It seemed that separate vote counting would have the effect of keeping the popularly-elected members at bay.

Although a handful of models had been floated, even fewer had a hearing at the meeting of the BLDC's Subgroup on Political Structure. At its last meeting held on 20 January 1990 in Guangzhou, the Subgroup adopted a rather conservative "New Mainstream Model" which was proposed by a mainland drafter and recommended that the first legislature should have 30 seats (50%) from functional constituencies, 18 seats (30%) from popular election and 12 seats (20%) from the election committee; and separate vote counting be installed.

Immediately after the passage of the said model in the meeting, four Hong Kong drafters, namely Raymond Wu, Maria Tam, Wong Po-yan and Cha Chi-man, called a press conference to express their discontent at the passage of the "New Mainstream Model". They claimed that no Hong Kong drafters had given their consent and only one Hong Kong drafter had supported separate vote counting. This gave an impression that all Hong Kong drafters had fought against the slow pace of introducing popular election. Raymond Wu also claimed that the rather high-handed manner on the Chinese side in putting through the "New Mainstream Model" made the Hong Kong drafters act as rubber stamps. But later it was reportedly disclosed that Hong Kong drafters had tabled three models at the meeting, of which two models suggested the same number of popularly-elected seats as the "New Mainstream Model" and the remaining one proposed even fewer popularly-elected seats in the second and third legislature than the "New Mainstream Model". Instead, their opposition seemed to target separate vote counting, which was a variant form of the "Bicameral Model" proposed by the NHKA (Cheung *et al*, 1991:190).

As mentioned before, Britain agreed to be involved in the drafting of the Basic Law because this could help to smooth the transfer of power and to ensure the faithful implementation of the Sino-British Joint Declaration. Given such arrangements, both governments had to sort out the electoral arrangements for the 1991 and 1995 elections and the "through train" method of transferring power in 1997. Beijing and London engaged in behind-the-scene-bargaining in early 1990. According to the seven diplomatic documents disclosed by both London and Beijing on 28 October 1992, the two governments discussed and exchanged views on the proportion of popularly-elected seats, the composition of the electoral committee, the introduction of separate vote counting, the restriction of foreign nationals serving in the legislature and so on.[14] In regard to the number of popularly-elected seats, London had asked for 24 (40%) in 1995 by preparing to limit it to 18 in 1991. But Beijing had insisted that there would be 20 (30%) popularly-elected seats in 1997 (1995), 24 (40%) in 1999 and 30 (50%) in 2003. London had agreed subsequently to Beijing's counter-proposal. In explaining his judgement on the deal, Percy Cradock wrote:

> ... more democracy was not, as increasingly claimed, an infallible protection against Chinese pressure if Chinese were bent on that course. To be of real worth, our arrangements had to stick after 1997; that required Chinese acquiescence. . . . I saw little chance of extracting agreement for 20 directly elected seats in 1991 from Beijing in its ugly mood at the time. . . . (1994a:228)

The ninth plenary session of the BLDC held in mid-February 1990 had sealed the fate of the nearly five-year-long row over the political structure of the HKSAR. The "New Mainstream Model" passed at the subgroup meeting in January was adopted with the following amendments: there were to be 20, instead of 18, popularly-elected seats in 1997; separate vote counting would be applied only to those bills, motions, and amendments to government bills introduced by individual LegCo members; and the limit of foreign nationals in the HKSAR legislature was set at 20%, instead of 15%, of its total.

The Price to Pay

The Chinese promise of "Hong Kong people governing Hong Kong" under the roof of "one country, two systems" had fascinated most of the Hong Kong people in the early 1980s. For some Hong Kong people, the pledge seemed to be a safeguard against Communist rule after 1997. For others, it offered an opportunity to develop democracy.

But subsequent developments have disappointed Hong Kong people, especially during the drafting of and consultation on the Basic Law--the future mini-constitution of the HKSAR. China seemed to have no faith in the political reforms that had been "engineered" by the British-Hong Kong government, fearing knock-on effects in China. This attitude may well be reflected by its conservative attitude towards the pace of democratic reform in the transitional period and the political structure of the future HKSAR. On the one hand, China, supported by the conservatives, tried to contain the budding democratic forces by limiting the number of political posts returned by universal franchise. Out of 60 members of the HKSAR legislature, only 20 in 1997, 24 in 1999 and 30 in 2007 would be elected by geographical constituency, the rest would be returned by functional constituency and/or election committee. On the other hand, China followed more or less the colonial structure of concentrating power in the HKSAR executive, which is hardly checked by the legislature. Moreover, through the use of the election committee, China would probably exert a tremendous influence on choosing the HKSAR executive head. The Basic Law stipulates the process of selecting the Chief Executive as follows: nominations will only be made among the members of the Election Committee that is selected mainly from the businessmen, professionals, and local political figures; upon nomination, only those members on the Committee have the right to vote; finally, the appointment of the executive head will be confirmed only by the Chinese government.

The clash of the democrats and their potential supporters with the Chinese government was further intensified as the first two took a different view on the nature of the democratic movement in China in 1989. After regaining its control of the capital, the Chinese government openly criticized those who supported the democratic movement; it also regarded Hong Kong as a subversive base working to undermine communist rule in China. Given such negative feelings towards both the representative government and the democrats in Hong Kong, China tried in every way to shape the political reform in its favour and to contain the growing influence of the democrats.

From China's point of view, Hong Kong had better develop its economic potential, but not "bourgeois" democracy. If Hong Kong becomes a democratic polity, China would not only find it harder to control the development of Hong Kong, but also feel the pressure of change from within China.

The decision-makers in Beijing, thus, come under cross-pressures of economic prosperity, autonomous government and possible models of unification on the one hand, and loss of control over Hong Kong as well as threat of domestic "peaceful evolution" on the other. In such a situation, China opts to play safe by establishing a political structure that may allow the conservative businessmen and local figures to counter-balance the emerging democratic forces.

For the democrats and their potential supporters, the mis-handling of the Tiananmen Incident and the adoption of the not-so-popular political model in the Basic Law by the Chinese government seemed to serve as a basis of political mobilization. Coupled with the widespread distrust of the communist Chinese government among the Hong Kong people, the centre-periphery cleavage would then find mass electoral support and may be transformed to become part of the electoral cleavage system, where the periphery (the democrats) has emphasized local autonomy and quicker pace of democratization while the centre (the conservatives and the leftists) stressed compromise with the central Chinese government and nationalist feeling.

Notes

1 See Article 3 and Annex I of the *Joint Declaration of the Government of the People's Republic of China and the Government of the United Kingdom of Great Britain and Northern Ireland on the Question of Hong Kong* (hereafter the Joint Declaration); and the *Basic Law of the Hong Kong Special Administrative Region of the People's Republic of China* (hereafter the Basic Law).

2 The Hong Kong people are being defined as "people who have lived in Hong Kong for seven years, accept Hong Kong as part of China and accept that China is the only legitimate Chinese government." Quoted in Lane (1990:94); also understood as "patriotic compatriots" whom "China would not require all to favour China's socialist system but who must love the motherland as well as Hong Kong". Quoted in Duncanson (1988:34).

3 See the interview of Denis C. Bray, the then Secretary for Home Affairs, Hong Kong Government, in *The Nineties Monthly* 180 (January 1985):26; Cheng, 1984:219, 231-2; H.K. Lamb, 1985:29-33; Harris, 1986:48, n10.

4 Edward Youde passed away in office during a trip to Beijing in late 1986.

5 The term *"gangren zhigang"* is believed to be coined by Liao Chengzhi, the then Director of the Hong Kong and Macau Affairs Office of China's State Council, in January 1983 when receiving a visiting group of Hong Kong New Territories village leaders. Before that day, the concept was widely floated in Hong Kong, but the exact wording had not been fixed.

6 For the role of the new middle class in the Hong Kong urban movements, see So and Kwitko (1992); for a collection of criticisms written by one of the active pressure groups, see Hong Kong Observers (1981); for the attitude of the Hong Kong government and its treatment towards the pressure groups in the late 1970s, see Campbell (1980).

7 *The Further Development of Representative Government in Hong Kong*, Address by the Governor Sir Edward Youde, GCMG, MBE, to the Legislative Council on 18 July 1984, p. 5.

8   Geoffrey Howe revealed this before the Foreign Affairs Committee, *see Foreign Affairs Committee, Volume II, Minutes of Evidence*, p. 24; cited by Miners (1991:25 & 30, n20).
9   The term "conservative" is denoted those who favour as little change in the status quo as possible. The various proposals put forward during the drafting of the Basic Law are summarized in Mushkat (1990:33-53).
10 Tsang Yok-sing is currently the Chairman of the Democratic Alliance for the Betterment of Hong Kong (formed in 1992), one of the leading pro-welfare political parties in Hong Kong, with a close relationship with the Beijing government.
11 Martin Lee was a Basic Law drafter but later withdrew from the post because of his support of the Chinese democratic movement in June 1989. He was also the Chairman of the United Democrats of Hong Kong which was merged with the Meeting Point in 1994 to form the Democratic Party. Lee is at present the Chairman of the Democratic Party.
12 The popularly-elected seats were later adjusted to have 18 in 1991 and 20 in 1995 because Beijing and London were pressurized to quicker the pace of democratization in Hong Kong after the Tiananmen Incident in 1989.
13 The moderates are comprised of the following political groups: the Tritolaire Academy, the University Graduates' Association of Hong Kong, the Association for Democracy of Hong Kong, the Hong Kong Chinese Civil Servants' Association, the Progressive Society of Hong Kong, the Hong Kong People's Association and the New Hong Kong Society. The conservatives were represented by the Business and Professional Group of BLCC led by Vincent Lo. The democrats were represented by the Joint Committee for Promotion of Democratic Government led by Martin Lee and Szeto Wah.
14 These diplomatic documents were released in the midst of intense conflict between London and Beijing over the political reform proposals initiated by the new Governor Chris Patten in his first annual address to the LegCo.

4 State Expansion and Consumption Cleavage

This chapter will discuss and analyse the trend of state expansion and development in Hong Kong since 1945, the rise of privatization politics, and the emergence of the collective consumption cleavage, focusing on the development of both the state and the society itself as well as their dynamic relationship. First of all, the phases of the development of the colonial administration and its relations with the society of Hong Kong since the post-war period will be traced and examined. Second, contrary to the generally accepted view of "positive non-interventionism", the expansion of the Hong Kong state in terms of both structural and functional aspects will be probed empirically. Third, the reasons for and impact of privatization of the social service programmes on the state-society relations as a whole and on electoral politics in particular will be investigated.

Development of the Hong Kong State

Hong Kong retained its colonial status for over 150 years. In general, its governmental structure experienced no significant transformation, nevertheless the Hong Kong government adapted to the ever-changing foreign and domestic environments by adjusting its relationships with the society of Hong Kong and its neighbouring country, China. As will be discussed in the following sections, the China factor has been the most influential one in shaping the postwar political development of Hong Kong. For illustrative purposes, three phases could be identified to examine this process of adjustment.

The First Phase, 1945-67

The period from 1945 to 1967 could be classified as the first phase of development. In this period, the nature and the composition of the society underwent significant changes. What made this period different from the pre-1945 period, as examined in Chapter 2, was the growing significance of the external factors: the establishment of the PRC in 1949 and the coming of the Cold War in the late 1940s. Several impacts could then be identified. First of all, the influx of hundreds of thousands of refugees from Mainland China had made Hong Kong into a "refugee society". Second, some of them came from Shanghai with their capital, skills and machinery which proved to be indispensable for the later industrial development of Hong Kong. Third, the imposition of the United Nations' embargo against the PRC after the outbreak of the Korean War in 1950 forced Hong Kong to replace its declining entrepot trade with industrial development, especially in the manufacturing industry. Taking advantage of the abundance of cheap labour and the world market situation, Hong Kong succeeded in its export-led economic growth. Fourth, the victory of the CCP in the late 1940s and the possible spill-over of the Chinese civil war into Hong Kong had contributed partly to the dropping of Governor Mark Young's proposal for post-war democratic reforms.

The worsening of living standards and social order caused by the influx of refugees had alerted the Hong Kong government to take active measures to alleviate the growing social problems. How to house the ever-growing refugee population was the most pressing problem remaining to be solved in the early 1950s. The Hong Kong government allowed the refugees to build their temporary huts elsewhere in the first instance. But a fire in Shek Kip Mei in December 1953 forced the government to engage in providing housing in resettlement estates. As shown in Table 4.1, the population of the multi-storey resettlement estates went rapidly up, from around 8,000 in 1954 to nearly 1.2 million in 1973. There were several reasons advanced to account for government intervention in housing (Caetells, Goh and Kwok, 1990:18), but one of the reasons would be that the political status of Hong Kong became clear in the mid-1950s as the PRC, the then newly established regime in China, had made no plan to take over Hong Kong in the near future. As a result, the British-Hong Kong government could continue its governing over Hong Kong and thus could afford to undertake long-term planning. This massive resettlement scheme proved to be decisive for the subsequent social stability and economic development of Hong Kong.

Table 4.1 The Authorized Population of Cottage Resettlement Areas and Multi-storey Resettlement Estates, 1954-73

Year	Cottage Resettlement Areas	Multi-Storey Resettlement Estates
1954	45906	8653
1955	58224	66598
1956	70393	105404
1957	73704	139797
1958	77546	158662
1959	81640	196958
1960	82482	246821
1961	87519	292371
1962	79656	373274
1963	73377	462582
1964	82899	544156
1965	74729	681134
1966	74702	770869
1967	72484	861213
1968	72986	967184
1969	68058	1030022
1970	57585	1077094
1971	55825	1100277
1972	50293	1154792
1973	49907	1183677

Source: Commissioner for Resettlement, *Annual Department Report 1972-73*, appendix 5.

These societal changes had coincided with an adjustment in the Hong Kong government, though a minor and not a structural one. Originally, pushed by the British Labour government and echoing the international climate of decolonization, the Hong Kong government attempted to reform its own government structure by proposing to set up an elected municipal council. The idea was put forward by the then Governor Mark Young in 1946 (the Young Plan) and the Municipal Council Ordinance 1949 was also gazetted on 3 June 1949. But subsequent developments within and without the society seemed to work against the plan. First of all, the continued British rule over Hong Kong was called into question by the founding of the PRC in 1949. The uncertainty was whether the new

Chinese government would allow the colonial status of Hong Kong to continue as it was. Second, the influx of large numbers of refugees from China had made Hong Kong into a "refugee society" where the lack of citizenship and sense of belonging among the refugees would prove to be detrimental to the successful operation of representative government. Third, the arrival of the Cold War in Asia in the early 1950s and the ensuing United Nations' embargo against China had re-ordered the priority of government concerns from political reforms to those of security and economic issues. Fourth, the possible spill-over of the struggle between the CCP and the KMT into Hong Kong electoral politics would undermine the security of Hong Kong. Last but not least, the resistance of the non-official LegCo members to the Young Plan and the unenthusiastic attitude of Young's successor, Alexander Grantham, meant the reform plan lacked institutional support. Because of such developments, the plan was shelved at the end of the day (Tsang, 1988). The UrbCo did reintroduce its elected members in 1952 (two out of total 13), but the elections carried little significance and consequence because of that Council's limited jurisdiction.

Meanwhile, the Hong Kong government expanded its activities for the sake of people's welfare, social stability and economic development. As mentioned above, the Hong Kong government took a more active role after the political status of Hong Kong became clear in the mid-1950s. Amid the rapid economic growth, the government seemed to accelerate its capacities to facilitate further economic development and at the same time to handle the contradictions that had been aroused by the rapid economic and social changes. The expansion of government activities can be viewed as an expanding network of organization in which more and more people as well as resources were being included and involved in these activities (Strath and Torstendahl, 1992:12-37).

The process of state expansion can be traced back to the late 1940s. Judging from the record of the official reports and papers released since then, a pattern of state expansion could be unearthed. But it should be pointed out here that the official reports or papers are used to show the concern of the government in that particular area and period of time, and may not imply that the corresponding government efforts or commitments would then be followed. From the late 1940s up to 1968, the government engaged in creating the right infrastructure for economic development by initiating some sort of planning and regulation. Starting from the postwar overall planning and reorganization of the administration in the late 1940s and early 1950s (Hong Kong Government, 1949), the Hong Kong government began to solve the pressing problems of housing and education (for education: Abercrombie, [1948]; Fisher, 1951; Hong Kong Government, 1952, 1953a, 1963a, 1963b, 1965c; for housing: Hong Kong Government, 1953b, 1958b, 1963f, 1964b, 1964d). Public works on infrastructure had also been planned, like the expansion of the Kai Tak Airport and the construction plan for a cross-harbour tunnel (Hong Kong Government, 1954, 1956a). Moreover, the government provided a more active role in economic development by coordinating a federation of industries and despatching trade missions overseas (Hong Kong Government, 1958a, 1961a, 1963d, 1963e, 1964f, 1965f, [1966]b; Commerce and Industry Department, 1958, 1960). In the early 1960s, the government expanded its activities in the economic sphere by carrying out an export credit insurance scheme and planning to set up a central export development council (Hong Kong Government, 1963c, 1965a; Freeman, 1964). Meanwhile, efforts were also devoted to reforming the banking system and measures adopted to increase its productivity (Tomkins, 1962; Hong Kong Government, 1964e). The government also expanded the scope of its social and medical services (Hong Kong Government, [1963]g, 1964a, 1966a, 1967b; Council of Social Services, 1958; Gill, 1966).

The government's regulative capacities over the society has also extended as more corruption, drug addicts and criminal offences were reported (Hong Kong Government, 1959, [1961]b, 1965b, 1965d). Its activities seemed to cover more than before, but its penetration and integration capacity into/with the society have still lagged behind the pace of economic and social development. The failure to alleviate the widespread social frustration caused by corruption and relative deprivation had irritated the public and had paved the way for developing social unrest (Lee, 1981; Lethbridge, 1985; Harris, 1988: chapter 6).

After the dropping of the Young Plan, the Hong Kong government underwent some minor adjustment in this phase, for example, the granting of financial autonomy by Britain in 1958 and the increase of LegCo's non-official members from 8 to 13 in 1964.[1] The pre-war political institutions and the socio-economic composition of members largely remained unchanged. The non-official seats in the ExCo and the LegCo were so often occupied by the "Princely Hong", the wealthy families, and the like. Although a working party was set up in April 1966 to "explore and advise on practicable alternatives for the development of an effective and convenient system of local administration in Hong Kong", its proposals were not adopted at the time (Hong Kong Government, 1966c).

Communication with society still relied on the narrow strata of social elites whose reach and understanding of the grass-roots was arguably minimal. For the Chinese community, the Hong Kong government relied on the traditional Chinese organizations, like the Tung Wah (voluntary organization comprised solely of prominent Chinese elites), the Po Leung Kuk (the Society for the Protection of Women and Girls) and the Kaifongs (neighbourhood organizations), to enlist support and thus, enhance its efficiency of governing. But this system was later proved not to be effective in channelling contacts between the government and society, especially at a time of rapid social and economic transformation. Although there was demand for political reform in the colony, the response from the then Minister of State for Colonial Affairs, Lord Perth, was that:

> Her Majesty's Government consider it undesirable that there should be any radical or major change in the present constitutional position in Hong Kong. . . . This does not, however, preclude the possibility of minor modifications, within the framework of existing principles, in the composition of the Legislative Council or the Urban Council. (*SCMP*, 30 October 1960; quoted in Endacott, 1964:200)

It was a fact that there was seldom strong demand for political reform in terms of either scope or intensity, but it does not follow that the population was fully satisfied with what was going on in the society. The widespread corruption in the government, especially in the Police Forces, the economic exploitation which was bound to happen in the process of capitalist development, the unbearably congested living environment and the sense of relative deprivation were some of the reasons which contributed to social frustration and resentment, especially among the low-income groups. Although this state of affairs could be tolerated by many ex-refugees who fled the communist rule in China, the local-born Hong Kong people were finding it more difficult to accept it as normal.

Given that the population was largely apolitical and without effective organization, its grievances needed to be reflected by the social elites whose critical position in the government structure was so vital in channelling communications between the government and the society. Unfortunately, they were mostly insulated from the public. Because of such an institutional barrier, the discontent seemed to be redressed only by extra-constitutional means, as when the Star Ferries proposed a 5 cents (Hong Kong currency) fare increase in 1965. After hot public debate on the issue, riots broke out in April 1966. The 1966 riot came quickly to an end, but the ensuing 1967 riot disrupted the societal order totally. Although the latter was inspired by the Cultural Revolution in mainland China and led by the local communists, domestic problems had a role to play in these two riots. The time had come to make some reform or adjustment in both the structure and policy of the Hong Kong government.

The Second Phase, 1968-81

The Hong Kong government, having learned from the two riots in the 1960s, had taken actions to improve the situation by carrying out local administrative reforms as well as embarking on intervention in both the production and the collective consumption processes. A study to reform the local administration had already been carried out before the outbreak of the riots in 1966 and 1967 (Hong Kong Government, 1966c, 1967c). But the touch-and-go situation at that time made it hard to hold back any longer. After the two riots, a City District Officer Scheme (CDO) was swiftly implemented and an office was established in each of the administrative districts in 1968 (Secretariat for Chinese Affairs, 1969). The principal aim of this scheme was, to quote the directive to City District Officers in 1968, "to provide the public with a local manifestation of the Government in your person" (Secretariat for Chinese Affairs, 1969:cover page). Afterward, several local institutions were also established. The City District Committees and Area Committees were set up in 1972, and the District Management Committee (consisting only of representatives from various government departments) in Kwun Tong in the early 1970s. Mutual Aid Committees which developed at the block level were also established in 1973, and gradually replaced the role played by the traditional Kaifong associations (Wong, 1972). With the development and growth of new towns in the New Territories, there was an urgency to set up a new local administration. As a result, the District Advisory Boards were set up in 1977 and the Town Management Committee was also established in the New Territories in the late 1970s.

Furthermore, after the release of the McKinsey Report in 1973, the reorganization of the central administration was launched to enhance its efficiency and effectiveness in policy planning (Hong Kong Government, 1973c). The Independent Commission Against Corruption (ICAC) was established in 1974 in order to fight against the widespread corruption within and without the government. Moreover, adjustments in the LegCo were noted: the elimination of the informal practice of appointing two elected nominees from the non-official Justices of the Peace and the Hong Kong General Chamber of Commerce in 1974, the introduction of a *de facto* non-official majority in the LegCo in 1976, and the reorganization of the Office of the Unofficial Members of the Executive and Legislative Council (UMELCO)[2] in 1970 so as to deal with public complaints more effectively instead of establishing the publicly-advocated Ombudsman office (Miners, 1991:129, n1 & 151-2; Tsang, 1989:70).

At the same time, the Hong Kong government began to put more emphasis on labour legislation in order to regulate the tense relationships between employers and employees. Attempts were also made to improve the living quality of the mass public. With the appointment of the new Governor, Murray MacLehose, in 1971, Hong Kong had entered the so-called "MacLehose era" that was characterized by massive government intervention in the collective consumption process of housing, education, and health care. The promise was to provide adequate low-rent public housing, nearly free medical care, free nine-year education, and so on (Hong Kong Government, 1973a, 1973b, 1974a, 1974c, 1977a, 1977b, 1977c, 1977d, 1978, 1979b, 1981b).[3] Thus, the state expansion in the provision of social service programmes had the effect of integrating the public with the government policy.

The significant economic growth and the massive provision of social services had contributed to the improvement of living standards. Nevertheless, several social movements took place in this phase. They were the Movement for Defending Diaoyu Islands, the Campaign for Demanding Chinese as an Official Language, the Golden Jubilee Affairs, and so on (Hong Kong Federation of Students, 1983). The activists in these movements mostly came from university students, social workers and teaching sectors. Other young professionals also began to criticize the colonial structure and some of its policies (Hong Kong Observers, 1981). Furthermore, the number of social conflicts in the mid- and late 1970s was rising as the government increased its regulative activities in the society, especially in the land resumption process (Cheung and Louie, 1991).

As the state expanded its activities in terms of both scope and intensity, the demand from the newly emerging professionals to participate in the governing process was also growing. The elected members of the then only partially-elected UrbCo put forward their proposals for reforming the UrbCo and the representation system in 1969 and 1979 (Urban Council, 1969; Bernacchi, 1979). The government responded to the former demand only by adjusting minimally the balance of the elected and appointed members (abolishment of the 6 ex-officio seats), and by granting the council's financial autonomy in 1973 (Colonial Secretariat, 1971). But the nature and the scope of power remained unchanged. The latter demand had to wait until the mid-1980s for its partial adoption by the Hong Kong government. The demands by the elected members of the UrbCo in 1979 were to phase out the appointed members in the UrbCo, to introduce universal franchise, to extend UrbCo's jurisdiction and to replace LegCo's appointed members with elected ones, or institute a fully elected municipal council. They ended their petition with the following lines:

> Unless the Urban Council is reformed, and that urgently, this only public body with elected representatives of some of the people will die a natural death. The bureaucracy will then take over, policies will be passed and put into effect without opposition of any kind, and the stage will be set for the next round of disturbances caused by frustration. The people are being blatantly exploited by Government business-policy-makers and big business and monopoly concerns of private origin. No Community can continue indefinitely if it ignores the interests of the silent majority of its citizens. (Bernacchi et al, 1979:12)

In regard to constitutional reform, the British-Hong Kong government seemed to be constrained by the Chinese attitude towards the status of Hong Kong. As mentioned in Chapter 3, China regarded Hong Kong as part of China. This was reflected in its prompt declaration, when admitted to the United Nations in 1972, that Hong Kong and Macau were not colonies but part of China, and its request to have them removed from the list of colonies. That meant no self-determination would be possible and that was understood to limit the potential for democratic reforms.

The Third Phase, 1982-97

This phase was quite different from the previous one in the sense of the growing direct influence of the PRC in the domestic development of Hong Kong. When the then Governor MacLehose visited Beijing in 1979, he was told by Deng Xiaoping that China would resume the sovereignty of Hong Kong in 1997, when the lease of the New Territories expired. The emergence of the 1997 question forced the British government to enter negotiations with the PRC over the future of Hong Kong. Subsequently, the Sino-British Joint Declaration was agreed in 1984, and the drafting of the Basic Law, which was promulgated in 1990, began in 1985. Both documents set the parameters and basic principles of the political and social life in both the transitional period and for the 50 years after 1997.

The coming to the stage of China constrained the will and policy options of the Hong Kong government in the transitional period. On the one hand, the British-Hong Kong government has the legitimate right to exercise its own rule by judging what measures needed to be adopted in maintaining the "stability and prosperity" of Hong Kong. On the other hand, the British-Hong Kong government had to work closely with China to sort out the detailed plan of power transfer. Given the sensitivity and complexity of the matter, it was not difficult to imagine that the right balance was hard, if not impossible, to hold.

The Hong Kong government continued its unfinished political reforms in the 1980s by publishing a series of Green and White Papers concerning the development of district administration and representative government.[4] The establishment of the partially elected DBs (1982) and RegCo (1986), while the injection of non-popularly and popularly-elected members into the LegCo in 1985 and 1991 enlarged the scope for political participation. As indicated in Chapter 3, this development was unwelcome to Beijing and the conservative business community in Hong Kong. On the one hand, the introduction of elections in the LegCo received opposition and criticism from Beijing. Beijing seemed to believe that the British and Hong Kong governments had engaged in a conspiracy of transferring power to pro-British Hong Kong people, rather than to China. The retention of some forms of political influence after 1997 through the institution of representative government was said to be the British motivation behind the conspiracy. On the other hand, the conservative business community did not like greater democracy because it undermined their privileged access to the government structure, and would lead to high taxes resulting from the pressure of the popularly-elected elements for greater spending on social welfare. Moreover, their intimate economic ties and interests with China also dictated their attitudes towards political reform.

Two events in this period had proved to be detrimental to the confidence of Hong Kong people, the anti-nuclear movement in 1986 and the suppression of the democratic movement in China in 1989. The former issue arose with China's decision to build a nuclear plant in Daya Bay, which is only fifty kilometres away from Hong Kong, provoking fierce opposition from the Hong Kong public (Yee and Wong, 1987:617-30). Even though one million people signed petitions objecting to the nuclear plant project, China nevertheless proceeded with the project. The other was the Tiananmen Incident of 1989. The suppression of the democratic movement in China had given a serious shock to the Hong Kong people. It was reported that about one million Hong Kong people had taken to the streets to show their dismay and disapproval of what the Beijing government had done in the Tiananmen Incident. Their confidence in the imaginative "one country, two systems" formula and their faith in the promise of "high degree of autonomy" were shattered. Furthermore, the non-responsive attitude towards Hong Kong's public demands in the former event and the high-handed suppression of the popular democratic movement in the latter had, in one way or another, deepened the tensions in the already strained Sino-Hong Kong relations and the polarization of the political forces within Hong Kong. The details of the alignment of Hong Kong political forces will be examined in Chapter 5.

At this juncture, different political groups within Hong Kong had reached a consensus on speedy democratic reform. The original 10 popularly-elected seats in LegCo in 1991 were expanded to 18. This was contradictory to the Chinese arrangement that was stipulated in the then draft Basic Law. For Beijing, the claim of conspiracy appeared to be further substantiated by the following moves of the Hong Kong government: the introduction of the Bill of Rights, the British Nationality Selection Scheme, and the announcement of the new port and airport building programme. For the British and Hong Kong governments, these measures were aimed at restoring the confidence of the Hong Kong people and the business community after the Tiananmen Incident. The "brain drain" issue well reflected the loss of confidence among the Hong Kong people and it was estimated by the government that 62,000 people emigrated overseas in 1990 (Skeldon, 1991:235). The mistrust between China and Britain seemed to have reached a point of no return.

After decades of socio-economic development in Hong Kong, a significant demographic transformation in both composition and quality was evident. The local-born population in Hong Kong had steadily increased over the years. The respective figures of local born population for 1961 and 1996 were 47.7% and 60.3% (Census and Statistics Department, 1969:22; 1997a:19, Table 8). The education qualifications of the population were also improving to a large extent. The percentage of population aged 15 or above and finished degree education was 2.6% in 1971 and 10.4% in 1996 (Census and Statistics Department, 1992b:199, Table 15.1; 1997a:24, Table 13). The percentage of managers, administrators, professionals and associate professionals among working population was growing rapidly, from 7.7% in 1976 to 29.2% in 1996 (Census and Statistics Department, 1987:38, Table 34; 1997a:31, Table 19). The GDP per capita had grown from less than HK$2,350 in 1961 to over HK$188,800 in 1996 in current market prices (Census and Statistics Department, 1999:13, Table 1).

Since the mid-1980s, the Hong Kong government has tried to privatize some of its social services programmes like housing. As will be discussed in the following section, the heavy reliance on land revenue and the fluctuation of land prices accounted for the privatization drive. The timing of privatization coincided with the structural transformation of the Hong Kong economy, from a manufacturing to a service-based economy. Furthermore, there was a trend by Hong Kong manufacturing industry to relocate its production lines to the Pearl River delta where abundant cheap labour could be hired to increase their products' competitiveness in the world market. The decision of the Hong Kong government to import foreign labour also frustrated the already suffering workers. The above changes hit the workers quite seriously, because most of them were living in public housing estates and were lacking the necessary quality to find jobs in the growing tertiary sectors. These developments mobilized the grass-roots for participation and thus set the stage for the rise of local activists in the embryonic electoral politics, which will be discussed in Chapters 5 and 6. Now, we turn to the empirical examination of the expansion of the Hong Kong government.

Empirical Analysis of State Expansion

In examining the role of the state in France, Britain, West Germany, Canada and the United States, Anthony King (1973:291-313, 409-23) found that the latter was "strikingly different" from the rest in providing public services. He contended that:

> the pattern of American policy is what it is, not because America is dominated by an elite (though it may be); not because the demands made on government are different from those made on governments in other countries; not because American interest groups have greater resources than those in other countries; not because American institutions are more resistant to change than those in other countries (though they probably are); but rather because Americans believe things that other people do not believe and make assumptions that other people do not make. More precisely, elites, demands, interest groups and institutions constitute neither necessary nor sufficient conditions of the American policy pattern; ideas, we contend, constitute both a necessary condition and a sufficient one. (1973:423)

The American idea that King referred to was *"the State plays a more limited role in America than elsewhere because Americans, more than other people, want it to play a limited role*" (italics in original). He further summarized the American beliefs and assumptions about government as follows:

> free enterprise is more efficient than government; government should concentrate on encouraging private initiative and free competition; government is wasteful; governments should not provide people with things they can provide for themselves; too much government endangers liberty; and so on. (1973: 418)

What the Americans thought about the appropriate role of government might conceivably be the same as in Hong Kong. One could not fail to find the readiness of the Hong Kong mass public to accept the official ideology of "laissez faire" and later "positive non-interventionism" (Haddon-Cave, 1984:xiii-xx).[5] It was true that the Hong Kong government restrained itself to a minimal role in most aspects of economic activities. Its basic role was to maintain a system that could ensure and facilitate fair economic exchange and transactions. But these official ideologies disappeared, in one way or another, when Hong Kong entered the "take-off" stage of economic development in the 1960s.

There are plenty of theories advanced to account for the state expansion (Tilly, 1975b; Cameron, 1978; Larkey, Stolp and Winer, 1981; Flora and Alber, 1981; Lehner and Widmaier, 1983; Peter and Heisler, 1983; Rueschemeyer and Evans, 1985; Hall, 1986; Lee, 1988; Hanneman and Hollingsworth, 1992). Modern state-building and the corresponding capitalist economic development seemed to contribute to the state expansion. In this period of expansion, the government involved itself deeply in constructing a system that would facilitate economic development. Later on, the government intervened in the consumption process by introducing massive social services programmes so as to deflate the social conflicts that had been aroused in the capital accumulation process. Furthermore, for late developing countries like Hong Kong, the demand for government intervention in the economic sphere has an additional feature: to have "independent" rather than "dependent" economic development. Following this line of thinking, the sections below will describe and discuss the process and the consequences of state expansion in Hong Kong, in terms of both structural and functional aspects, since the 1950s.

The Structural Expansion of the Hong Kong State

The structural expansion of the Hong Kong state could be detected from the growing number of government organs since the 1950s. Starting from the central level was the growth of both the Secretaries in the Government (Colonial) Secretariat and implementation departments (see Table 4.2). The number of Secretaries in the Secretariat grew from 6 in 1970 to 15 in 1974 after the reorganization in that year, then expanded to 24 in 1991. The growth of the Secretaries could be seen as showing the increased regulating capacity of the Hong Kong government. The growth of departments was also significant, from 39 in 1970 to 60 in 1991. The decline of the figures in Department in and after 1997 was only due to the regrouping of relevant data.

Table 4.2 The Number of Senior Posts in the Government Secretariat and Department Level 1970-98

Year	Government Secretariat	Departments
1970	6	39
1974	15	39
1980	16	42
1987	21	50
1991	24	60
1996	22	64
1997	24	35
1998	24	36

Notes:
1. Figures include those which have the equivalent status.
2. Starting from 1997, the figures in the Government Secretariat and Department reflect those of the "Posts of Principal Officials / Director of Bureaux" and "Posts of Directorate Grade 6 Rank and above (and equivalent)", respectively.

Source: Government Secretariat, *Civil and Miscellaneous List*, various years.

Given the nature of the Hong Kong government and the stress on government by consultation, the representation system did not change much up till the early 1980s. The higher the council was located in the power hierarchy, the less the change in its nature and composition (see Table 4.3). Although the non-official members in the ExCo outnumbered the official members after 1966, recruitment still relied solely on appointment by the Governor. Constitutionally speaking, it is at the governor's pleasure to recommend whoever he wishes to appoint. People from wealthy families, big business firms and the like were so often appointed up till the late 1970s.

The LegCo non-official majority appeared in 1964 (exclusive of the Governor) and in 1976 (inclusive of the Governor). The LegCo seemed more ready for adjustment than the ExCo. Simply put, the location of the LegCo in the power hierarchy is less important than that of the ExCo because the latter is part of the executive. As a result, the institutional barrier in the LegCo to reform was smaller than that of the ExCo. Unlike the ExCo, the number of LegCo official and non-official members grew from 15 (exclusive of the Governor) in 1947 to 60 in 1991. Moreover, the method and the pool of recruitment were similar to those of the ExCo. Constitutional change had been introduced to the LegCo when twenty-four members were opened to elections on the basis of the functional constituency and electoral college in 1985, and the number increased to twenty-six in 1988. The popularly-elected seats of the LegCo were only instituted in 1991. Originally, the government had indicated in the 1984 White Paper that there might be popular elections in the LegCo in 1988. But the 1988 White Paper concluded that although the introduction of popular election into the LegCo "would be a logical and desirable" step, the timing would be more suitable in 1991 rather than 1988, "given that opinions in the community on this issue are so clearly divided" (p.9). The decision had understandably invited vigorous protest from the democrats. By 1995, all the LegCo members were returned by some kind of elections. Because of the Sino-British rift after the arrival of Patten in 1992, the "through train" arrangement was derailed. As a result, the Provisional Legislative Council (Provisional LegCo) was established and its members were elected by the Selection Committee which was not empowered to have that function in the Basic Law. Details of this development will be taken up in Chapter 5.

Table 4.3 Changes in Composition of the Executive Council and the Legislative Council, 1947-98

Year	A	B	C	D	E	F	G
1947	6	6	8	7	-	-	-
1952	6	6	9	8	-	-	-
1964	6	6	12	13	-	-	-
1966	6	8	12	13	-	-	-
1972	6	8	14	15	-	-	-
1976	6	8	19	22	-	-	-
1977	6	8	20	24	-	-	-
1978	6	9	20	24	-	-	-
1980	6	9	22	26	-	-	-
1981	6	9	22	27	-	-	-
1983	6	11	18	29	-	-	-
1984	6	10	16	30	-	-	-
1985	6	8	10	22	12	12	-
1986	6	10	10	22	12	12	-
1987	5	9	10	22	12	12	-
1988	5	9	10	20	14	12	-
1989	5	10	10	20	14	12	-
1991	5	9	3	18	21	-	18
1992	7	9	3	18	21	-	18
1993	4	9	3	18	21	-	18
1995	4	9	-	-	30	10	20
1996	3	8	-	-	30	10	20
1997	3	11	*	*	*	*	*
1998	3	11	-	-	30	10	20

Notes:
A = ExCo Official Members (inclusive of ex-officio members)
B = ExCo Non-official (Appointed) Members
C = LegCo Official Members (inclusive of ex-officio members)
D = LegCo Non-official (Appointed) Members
E = LegCo Elected Members through Functional Constituency
F = LegCo Elected Members through Electoral College
G = LegCo Elected Members through Popular Election
* = 60 Provisional LegCo members were elected by the Selection Committee which is not empowered to have that function in the Basic Law. This was an extra-ordinary measure as the "through train" arrangement was derailed because of the Sino-British rift in the late transitional period.

Source: *Hong Kong Annual Report*, various years.

Before the introduction of some forms of election in the LegCo in 1985, the UrbCo had had its popularly-elected members before the Second World War. But its limited jurisdictions--mostly confined to public health, recreational and cultural affairs--had rendered the UrbCo's election insignificant. The UrbCo held its first post-war election in 1952 with two popularly-elected members and since then the number has risen steadily from 4 in 1953, 8 in 1956, 10 in 1965, 12 in 1973, 15 in 1983 and finally 32 in 1995 (see Table 4.4). This increase was counter-balanced by the corresponding increase in the number of appointed members in the Council (except 1995). The 1973 reform resulted in the withdrawal of the official members, and the seats in the council were equally assigned between the appointed and elected members, each side having twelve seats (fifteen in 1983).

The UrbCo's elected members had continually sought reform of the political system since the 1950s, especially those of the Reform Club's members. When the pressure for reform had built up to a certain level, the Hong Kong government responded to it by marginally adjusting the number of elected seats and the function of the Council. For example, starting from the mid-1960s, there was consistent push to have a Great Hong Kong City Council with wider franchise and powers than the then UrbCo. Two reports had been published in 1966 and 1969 (Hong Kong Government, 1966c; Urban Council, 1969). The government made some concessions to the demand in 1971 by granting the UrbCo financial autonomy and the right to levy rates (Colonial Secretariat, 1971). Some minor functions were added, but its powers and its relationship with the central government remained unchanged as a whole.

And only in 1989 would there be a chance to have a non-appointed majority when ten representatives from the DBs were being introduced. In 1995, with the implementation of the Patten reform, the UrbCo, for the first time in its history, comprised of elected members, who were elected either by popular elections or by the DBs. With the establishment of the Provisional UrbCo in 1997, another 9 appointed members were added to the serving members who were elected in 1995.

The RegCo was set up in 1985 when the new towns in the New Territories flourished. Its functions and powers are similar to those of the UrbCo and mainly confined to public health, recreational and cultural affairs. The administration of the New Territories was different from that of the urban area because of the different legal basis of British rule between the ceded territory of Hong Kong Island and Kowloon, and the leased New Territories. After the lease of the New Territories to Britain in

1898 for 99 years, the Hong Kong government adopted an almost noninterventionist policy towards the newly leased territory (Endacott, 1964:126-34). By setting up minimal government institutions there, the government relied very heavily on the village elders in running the rural area. But the situation changed rapidly as the government started to develop the New Territories in the 1960s. The then District Officer's jurisdiction was gradually shared with those central government departments involved in development. The Heung Yee Kuk had played a significant role in communicating with the government and the native residents. But given the Heung Yee Kuk's role as a statutory representative body for the native residents, the new immigrants from the urban area had little chance to participate if they wished to do so.

The emerging new communities in the New Territories thus highlighted the need to reform the local administration system there. As a result, a local administration reform was initiated and implemented: the creation of the DBs in 1982 and the RegCo in 1985. Since then, the three-tier legislature has evolved, but the destination was not clear as there was scarcely any consensus among Britain, China and the local political forces on the timing as well as the procedure to arrive at the widely accepted goal of democratization. In 1991, the RegCo was made up of 12 appointed and 12 popularly-elected members, 9 representatives from the DBs, and 3 ex-officio members from the Chairman and Vice-Chairmen of the Heung Yee Kuk (see Table 4.4). Like the UrbCo, the RegCo's appointed members were abolished in 1995, but they were re-introduced when the Provisional RegCo was established in July 1997.

Regarding the DBs, there were eighteen (nineteen in 1985-1994) DBs and 346 DB members in 1994. The percentage of popularly-elected members increased from 27% (132 out of 490) in 1982 to 92.8% (346 out of 373) in 1994. Like the Provisional UrbCo and Provisional RegCo, there were 96 appointed members added to the serving DB members to form the Provisional DBs in July 1997 (see Table 4.5).

In contrast to the development of representative government or local administration, the growth in consultation networks was spectacular. From thirty-one in 1947, the number of advisory bodies and committees increased to 386 in 1998, more than twelve times those of 1947 (see Table 4.6). But there were variations in the growth rate among different types of advisory body. From 1970 to 1980, the annual growth rate for "the statutory bodies", "the permanent non-statutory bodies with official and unofficial members", "the permanent non-statutory bodies with official members only", were 4.1%, 7.5%, and 1.1%, respectively. In the period

1980-90, the growth rates for the non-statutory ones with official and unofficial members declined. In contrast, the non-statutory ones with official members only increased. The respective figures were 4.0%, 4.1%, and 4.8%. But the trend was slightly different during the period 1990-98. The first two kinds of bodies (the statutory bodies, and the permanent non-statutory bodies with official and unofficial members) increased and had a 5.5% and 5.7% growth rate, respectively. The official non-statutory bodies experienced a zero growth rate. The details of these ups and downs in the growth rate are beyond the scope of this study, but one point that should be stressed is that the government had reinforced its incorporation (absorption) capacity in the 1980s and 1990s.

Table 4.4 The Composition of the Urban Council and the Regional Council, 1947-91

Year	A	B	C	D	E	F	G	H
1947	5	6	-	-	-	-	-	-
1952	5	6	2	-	-	-	-	-
1953	5	6	4	-	-	-	-	-
1955	6	6	4	-	-	-	-	-
1956	6	8	8	-	-	-	-	-
1965	6	10	10	-	-	-	-	-
1973	-	12	12	-	-	-	-	-
1983	-	15	15	-	-	-	-	-
1985	-	15	15	-	12	-	9	3
1986	-	15	15	-	12	12	9	3
1989	-	15	15	10	12	12	9	3
1995	-	-	32	9	-	27	9	3
1997	-	9	32	9	11	27	9	3

Notes:
A = UrbCo Ex-officio Members
B = UrbCo Appointed Members
C = UrbCo Elected Members through Popular Election
D = UrbCo Representatives from District Boards
E = RegCo Appointed Members
F = RegCo Elected Members through Popular Election
G = RegCo Representatives from District Boards
H = RegCo Ex-officio Members (the Heung Yee Kuk)

State Expansion and Consumption Cleavage 105

Notes:
1. The number of UrbCo's ex-officio members are inclusive of the Chairman before 1973. Since 1973, Chairman and Vice-chairman are elected among members.
2. In July 1997, the Provisional UrbCo and RegCo were established and its memberships comprised the respective serving members, and another 9 and 11 appointed members, respectively.

Sources:
1. For 1956 and before, Colonial Secretariat, *Civil Service List*, various years;
2. For 1965 and after, *Hong Kong Annual Report*, various years.

Table 4.5   The Composition of the District Boards, 1982-97

Year	A	B	C	D	E	F
1982	167	134	132	27	30	490
1985	-	132	237	27	30	426
1988	-	141	264	27	-*	432*
					(30)*	(462)*
1991	-	140	274	27	-	441
1994	-	-	346	27	-	373
1997	-	96	346	27	-	469

Notes:
A = Appointed Official Members
B = Appointed Unofficial Members
C = Elected Members
D = Rural Committee Chairmen
E = Urban Council Members
F = Total
* = From 1 April 1989 to 31 March 1991, 30 UrbCo members were no longer the District Boards' members.

Sources:
1. Updated from Li (1995b:60);
2. Supplied by the City and New Territories Administration on 22 July 1993 and the Home Affairs Department on 18 July 1995;
3. *Ming Pao*, 17 June 1997, p. A2.

The Hong Kong government regarded this consultation system as an effective one, and it was believed by many others that it could avoid the "unnecessary" debates and confrontations found in Western democracy. The members of all these bodies were nominally appointed by the Governor. In fact, some boards' and committees' members were first elected among the concerned parties and then recommended to the Governor for appointment. Some were ex-officio members because of their positions in relevant activities. Through this particular channel, the Hong Kong government could co-opt most, if not all, of the socio-economic elites into its consultation networks. The government granted them social status as well as the power of influence in anticipation of their support in the governing process. In return, the social elites were willing to cooperate as long as the government could provide what they wanted. As a result, the legitimacy and efficiency of the Hong Kong government would then be enhanced. The growth of this network had facilitated the penetration of the government into society and the integration of the social elites with the government. But once again, like other political appointments, the less organized and under-privileged sectors in the society were so often left out of the membership. More important was the fact that many government policies, whether welcomed or not by the public, were based on the recommendation of or consultation with the advisory bodies concerned. In fact, this could enhance the transparency of the government as well as enable it to avoid taking direct responsibility in certain controversial and sensitive policy areas.

Let us take the Transport Advisory Committee as an example, when the application for a fare increase by the franchised transportation company is first considered by the Committee and then recommendation made to the Transportation Bureau of the Government Secretariats and later the ExCo for adoption. If the recommendation and its subsequent adoption go against the opinion of the public, the Committee's members might more or less lose their credibility, and their roles might be doubted by the public. The government can, therefore, avoid direct conflict with the mass public. Moreover, the issue of conflict of interests has long been the focal point of public discussion because many committee members are coming from the business sector. Thus, the neutrality of the committee's recommendation might be questioned by the public. Maria Tam's scandal is a case in hand (details in Chapter 5).

Table 4.6 The Number of Government Advisory Bodies, Selected Years

Year	A	B	C	D
1947	-	-	-	31
1948	-	-	-	43
1954	-	-	-	50
1957	-	-	-	60
1970	71	34	17	122
1975	79	46	17	142
1980	103	62	19	184
1985	120	68	22	210
1990	148	90	29	267
1995	192	92	24	308
1996	208	126	27	361
1997	213	140	29	382
1998	221	136	29	386

Notes:
A = Statutory Bodies
B = Permanent Non-Statutory Bodies with Official and Non-official Members
C = Permanent Non-Statutory Bodies with Official Members Only
D = Total Number of A, B and C

Sources:
1. For 1958 or before, Colonial Secretariat, *Civil Service List*, various years;
2. For 1970 or after, Government Secretariat, *Civil and Miscellaneous List*, various years.

The Functional Expansion of the Colonial State

Accompanying the growth of the state structure was the expansion of the number of public employees. The study of public employment has often faced the problem of availability of data. This has also been the case in Hong Kong. Conceptually, there is a different coverage to the following two terms: "public employees" and "civil servants". The former were those who were directly or indirectly employed by the government, but the latter only involved those who were directly hired by the government. That means the employees in the voluntary or quasi-official organizations which received government funding or subvention were regarded as public employees. Ideally, the data on public employees, rather than that of the civil servants, are more suitable to measure the size and the growth rate of the public sector. This was especially true in Hong Kong as some of the social services were delivered by non-governmental agencies with annual financial support from the government, e.g. member agencies of the Council of Social Service. Others were former government but now privatized programmes which had been granted capital investment by the government, e.g. the Housing Authority. Still others were those which were funded by the government but had their own personnel policy, e.g. the Tourist Association (Miners, 1991:101-6). But so often, there was a lack of accurate figures for that kind of public employee other than the civil servants. Nevertheless, the number of civil servants might be regarded as the fundamental one that could shed some light on the growth of the government employment.

As shown in Table 4.7, the strength of the civil servants grew from about 53,000 in 1963 to a little less than 180,000 in 1995. A gain of about 3.4 times the figure of 1963. Once again, the growth rate varied in different periods. The average annual growth rates for the period 1964-73, 1974-84 and 1985-95 were 6.9%, 6.0% and 0.5% respectively. Moreover, the growth rates among different function areas were not the same. In the period 1964-73, there were four function areas with two-digit annual growth rate. The order of annual growth rates was: government secretariat (17.3%), social welfare (15.9%), inland revenue and treasury (13.2%) and housing (10.1%). In the period 1974-84, the growth rate slowed down except for the disciplinary forces (from 6.8% for the period 1964-73 to 8.6% for the period 1974-84). However, those function areas which had enjoyed two-digit annual growth rate in the period 1964-73 had still maintained more than 6% (the average growth rate of the total civil servants for the period 1974-84) annual growth rate. The growth rate further declined in the period 1985-95 with education (–3.4%) and housing (–0.4%) experienced even annual minus growth rate. If we further subdivided the period 1985-95, the trend of minus growth was clearer in the period 1992-95 with a range from –0.6% (government secretariat) to –16.4% (health). The low growth rate experienced in the 1985-95 period was probably due to the fact that the Hong Kong government came across financial constraints caused by the public work projects and social investments on the one hand, and the unstable government revenue imposed by the uncertainty of the future of the territory on the other.

In general, the growth of revenue and the growth of expenditure of Hong Kong in the post-war period was remarkable but with some variation. First of all, the growth of revenue and expenditure in 1997, at the current market price (constant prices are not available in the said annual report), was more than 2117 and 1774 times the figures for 1947 respectively (see Table 4.8). For the whole period of 1947-97, the average annual growth rate of revenue and expenditure was 17.1% and 17.9% respectively; but there was a wide variation in terms of comparison yearly and periodically. The respective ranges of revenue and expenditure growth were −18.1% (1954) and 100.1% (1948) for the former, and −13.7% (1954) and 70.1% (1981) for the latter.

The revenue growth rates for the periods of 1948-67, 1968-74, 1974-84, 1985-92 and 1992-97 were 18.7%, 16.8%, 20.0%, 16.4% and 13.5% respectively with an average of 17.9% for the whole period of 1948-97. Meanwhile, the respective expenditure growth rates were 17.3%, 17.1%, 21.9%, 14.3% and 10.9% with an average of 17.1% for the whole period of 1948-97. There were only a few occasions of a minus growth rate of revenue and expenditure: 3 for the former (in 1954, 1983 and 1984) and 5 for the latter (in 1954, 1968, 1976, 1984 and 1997). The Hong Kong government adhered to a conservative fiscal policy of balanced budgeting and thus accumulated an enormous surplus of HK$121,950.3 million (equivalent to GBP9,834.7 million, if GBP1 = HK$12.4) up to 1997 (at current market price) (Lo Cheng, 1990:66-79). Only on nine occasions (1947, 1960, 1966, 1975, 1983, 1984, 1985, 1991 and 1996) had there resulted a negative balance at the end of the financial years.

The government's extracting capacity improved steadily over the post-war period, especially during the 1980s. As shown in Table 4.9, the percentage of the actual revenue in term of the gross domestic product was on the rise, from 12.4% in the period 1974-80 to 15.2% in the period 1981-90. This meant that the growth of revenue was faster than that of the GDP, and more and more resources were extracted from the society and placed at the disposal of the government. But the growth rate slowed down in the 1990s. This aggregated growth rate did not necessarily imply that the same amount would go to individual revenue sources. Some components of revenue would contribute more than others to the course of development, or vice versa. Furthermore, different growth rates among revenue sources indicated that one or more sectors in the society had been drilled more than the rest. As shown in Table 4.10, the land revenue (excluding property tax and estate duty) contributed about 20.9% on average during the period 1947-97, with the range from 6.9% in 1993 to 48.4% in 1981. The period

1974-84 recorded an average contribution of 28.6%, but the ensuing period 1985-91 decreased more than half of that in 1973-84 and took up only 12.8% of the total actual revenue. The respective figure even came down to 8.8% in the period 1992-97.

Table 4.7 The Growth of the Civil Servants (Actual Strength) by Selected Function Areas, Selected Years

Year	A	B	C	D	E	F	G	Total
1963	6770	4636	2504	12000	790	491	352	52955
1964	7527	5006	3099	13194	848	581	375	57809
1965	8266	5217	3609	13805	906	608	455	60181
1967	9033	5478	4329	16660	1115	748	768	69150
1968	9523	5447	4781	17225	1235	833	778	72936
1969	9711	5586	4769	17990	1386	952	645	75444
1971	10661	5596	5072	19240	1794	1254	967	81438
1972	11103	5789	5269	19229	1985	1424	1146	84495
1973	11981	5784	5279	20106	2085	1573	1024	89941
1974	12605	5763	6180	21283	2199	1833	1254	95284
1975	13407	5829	6536	25039	2393	2087	1035	104291
1976	13956	5736	5789	25758	2631	2063	1245	104157
1977	14712	5548	5621	28109	2743	2159	1386	108385
1978	15314	5630	6046	31007	2882	2271	1532	115674
1979	15857	5715	6560	32887	3240	2560	1689	122838
1980	16421	5484	7200	35374	3558	2532	1875	129217
1981	17595	5661	8101	37299	4093	2676	1808	139252
1982	18977	6148	10373	40157	4552	2817	2462	154034
1983	20398	6760	11198	47154	4781	3073	2605	166569
1984	21884	6976	11364	49282	4809	3073	2429	170051
1985	23604	7062	11049	50536	4819	3139	2818	172641
1986	24500	7048	11065	51696	4877	3070	2847	174946
1987	25642	7193	11564	53033	5038	3247	3057	179053
1988	26587	7292	11943	54293	5194	3512	3275	182843
1989	26852	7354	12176	55710	5061	3751	3507	186054
1990	27888	7432	12554	56323	4901	3856	3255	188393

State Expansion and Consumption Cleavage 111

1991	28744	7483	12580	56041	5074	3883	3318	190448
1992	23408	6835	12782	56478	5089	3861	3526	185685
1993	19503	6811	12755	56873	5019	3886	3574	182099
1994	16774	6856	13037	57677	4992	4030	3372	180695
1995	14035	6671	13204	58132	4823	4224	3229	179972

Annual average growth rate:

1964-95	2.8	1.3	6.0	5.5	6.5	7.7	9.0	4.2
1964-73	7.4	2.8	10.1	6.8	13.2	15.9	17.3	6.9
1974-84	5.6	1.8	7.7	8.6	8.0	6.4	9.1	6.0
1985-95	−3.4	−0.4	1.4	1.5	0.1	3.0	2.8	0.5
1992-95	−16.4	−2.8	1.2	0.9	−1.3	2.2	−0.6	−1.4

Notes:
A = Health
B = Education
C = Housing
D = Police, Fire, Custom and Excise, Immigration, and Correctional Service
E = Inland Revenue and Treasury
F = Social Welfare
G = Government Secretariat

Sources: Compiled and calculated from Government Secretariat, Civil Service Branch, *Civil Service Personnel Statistics*, and Colonial Secretariat, Establishment Branch, *Personnel Statistics*, various years; figures are as April for 1975-95, as January for 1963-74.

112 *Hong Kong from Britain to China*

Table 4.8 The Actual Revenue and Expenditure of Hong Kong, 1947-97 (At Current Market Prices)

Financial Year Ended	Expenditure (HK$ million)	(%)	Revenue (HK$ million)	(%)	Balance
1947	85.6	--	82.1	--	−3.5
1948	127.7	49.2	164.3	100.1	36.6
1949	160.0	25.3	194.9	18.6	34.9
1950	182.1	13.8	264.3	35.6	82.2
1951	251.7	38.2	291.7	10.4	40.0
1952	275.9	9.6	308.6	5.8	32.7
1953	411.8	49.3	484.6	57.0	72.8
1954	355.4	−13.7	396.9	−18.1	41.5
1955	373.3	5.0	434.5	9.5	61.2
1956	402.5	7.8	454.7	4.6	52.2
1957	469.5	16.6	509.7	12.1	40.2
1958	532.7	13.5	584.2	14.6	51.5
1959	590.0	10.8	629.3	7.7	39.3
1960	710.0	20.3	664.6	5.6	−45.4
1961	845.3	19.1	859.2	29.3	13.9
1962	953.2	12.8	1030.5	19.9	77.3
1963	1113.3	16.8	1253.1	21.6	139.8
1964	1295.4	16.4	1393.9	11.2	98.5
1965	1440.5	11.2	1518.3	8.9	77.8
1966	1769.1	22.8	1631.7	7.5	−137.4
1967	1806.1	2.1	1817.8	11.4	11.7
1968	1766.0	−2.2	1899.5	4.5	133.5
1969	1873.0	6.1	2081.1	9.6	208.1
1970	2032.2	8.5	2480.7	19.2	448.5
1971	2452.2	20.7	3070.9	23.8	618.7
1972	2901.4	18.3	3541.3	15.3	639.9
1973	4299.6	48.2	4936.3	39.4	636.7
1974	5169.2	20.2	5240.8	6.2	71.6
1975	6255.2	21.0	5875.3	12.1	−379.9
1976	6032.2	−3.6	6519.3	11.0	487.1
1977	6590.9	9.3	6898.5	5.8	307.6
1978	8996.9	36.5	9534.5	38.2	537.6

1979	11090.1	23.3	11766.0	23.4	675.9
1980	13872.3	25.1	15905.6	35.2	2033.3
1981	23593.5	70.1	29124.3	83.1	5530.8
1982	27778.2	17.7	32916.2	13.0	5138.0
1983	34597.8	24.6	31097.6	−5.5	−3500.2
1984	33393.1	−3.5	30399.7	−2.2	−2993.4
1985	36901.8	10.5	36342.5	19.5	−559.3
1986	39798.2	7.8	41241.0	13.5	1442.8
1987	39927.7	0.3	43869.6	6.4	3941.9
1988	44022.0	10.3	55641.4	26.8	11619.4
1989	48952.6	11.2	65780.6	18.2	16828.0
1990	69661.6	42.3	74365.2	13.1	4703.6
1991	82837.2	18.9	82674.5	11.2	−162.7
1992	93401.1	12.8	101456.4	22.7	8055.3
1993	102024.5	9.2	120780.8	19.0	18756.3
1994	121040.3	18.6	143899.8	19.1	22859.5
1995	147260.9	21.7	151052.3	5.0	3791.4
1996	155856.9	5.8	153194.3	1.4	−2662.6
1997	151932.3	−2.5	173857.4	13.5	21925.1

TOTAL NET BALANCE   121950.3

Annual Growth Rate For:
1948-97	17.1	17.9
1948-67	17.3	18.7
1968-74	17.1	16.8
1974-84	21.9	20.0
1985-92	14.3	16.4
1992-97	10.9	13.5

Note: The actual revenue and expenditure may be slightly different from those of the Reports due to the rounding of each item of revenue and expenditure.

Sources:
1. For 1975-1992, *Annual Report of the Director of Accounting Services*, various years;
2. For 1947-1974, *Annual Report of the Accounting General*, various years.

Table 4.9 The Actual Revenue and the GDP, 1974-97 (At Current Market Prices)

Financial Year Ended	Revenue (HK$ million)	GDP (HK$ million)	Revenue/ GDP (%)
1974	5240.8	43014	12.2
1975	5875.3	47137	12.5
1976	6519.3	52217	12.5
1977	6898.5	65323	10.6
1978	9534.5	75552	12.6
1979	11766.0	89688	13.1
1980	15905.6	118467	13.4
1981	29124.3	149121	19.5
1982	32916.2	176938	18.6
1983	31097.6	194600	16.0
1984	30399.7	223284	13.6
1985	36342.5	264666	13.7
1986	41241.0	274625	15.0
1987	43869.6	327710	13.4
1988	55641.4	400323	13.9
1989	65780.6	472813	13.9
1990	74365.2	536263	13.9
1991	82674.5	599671	13.8
1992	101456.4	695525	14.6
1993	120780.8	807353	15.0
1994	143899.8	927290	15.5
1995	151052.3	1027929	14.7
1996	153194.3	1097343*	14.0
1997	173857.4	1229069*	14.1

Annual Growth Rate For:
1974-80	12.4
1981-90	15.2
1991-97	14.5

* Estimated figures

Sources:
1. For GDP, Census and Statistics Department. *Estimates of Gross Domestic Product 1961 to 1998*, (Hong Kong: Printing Department, 1999), pp. 48-53, Table 10(a);
2. For revenue, *Annual Report of the Accounting General*, and *Annual Report of the Director of Accounting Services*, various years.

Why was this so? The rapid decline in the yield from land sales seemed to be one of the most promising reasons (see column 2 in Table 4.10). The share of land sales reached its peak in the early 1980s (37% in 1981 and 29.4% in 1982) and then fell rapidly from the mid-1980s, with an average share of 3.6% and 0.3% in the period 1985-91 and 1992-97, respectively. The sudden and swift fall of land sale shares since the early 1980s might be attributed partly to the political uncertainty in the early 1980s and partly to the sharing of the land sale revenue with the Chinese government since the coming into force of the Sino-British Joint Declaration in May 1985. Annex III of the Joint Declaration laid down the details of land leases arrangements during the transitional period of 1984-1997. Article 6 of the Annex III stipulated that:

> From the entry into force of the Joint Declaration until 30 June 1997, premium income obtained by the British Hong Kong Government from land transaction shall, after deduction of the average cost of land production, be shared equally between the British Hong Kong Government and the future Hong Kong Special Administrative Region Government. All the income obtained by the British Hong Kong Government, including the amount of the above mentioned deduction, shall be put into the Capital Works Reserve Fund for the financing of land development and public works in Hong Kong. The Hong Kong Special Administrative Region Government's share of the premium income shall be deposited in banks incorporated in Hong Kong and shall not be drawn on except for the financing of land development and public works in Hong Kong . . . .

The revenue from land sale for the period 1986-1997, which was credited into the Capital Works Reserve Fund, amounted to HK$133,155.1 million and represented a drain of average 9.3% of the actual revenue in the said period (see Table 4.11). This was very likely to have a financial consequence on the government fiscal system.[6] Although the Hong Kong government could still be the one to decide how to spend its own share, the programmes which were financed should be of a public works nature. That meant the Hong Kong government lost the flexibility of using this sum of money to finance other general expenses and thus had to tighten its budget and expenditure or cut back some social commitments.

Table 4.10   The Main Components of Actual Revenue, 1947-97 (%)

Year	A	B	C	D	E
1947	0.2	3.0	8.3	11.5	14.8
1948	5.5	2.2	6.1	13.8	23.6
1949	3.0	2.7	7.7	13.4	36.2
1950	1.8	2.9	7.3	12.0	27.5
1951	2.0	4.5	9.3	15.8	29.3
1952	1.5	5.5	9.7	16.7	32.4
1953	1.1	3.9	7.0	12.0	33.3
1954	1.5	5.7	9.5	16.7	40.4
1955	2.7	5.8	9.1	17.7	38.7
1956	3.0	6.9	10.9	20.9	33.9
1957	2.9	7.3	11.1	21.4	32.3
1958	4.5	7.3	11.2	22.9	31.6
1959	4.9	7.9	11.9	24.7	31.0
1960	3.4	7.7	12.8	23.9	29.1
1961	7.3	7.2	11.7	26.2	27.6
1962	8.8	6.9	11.3	27.0	31.0
1963	16.6	7.0	10.3	33.8	27.8
1964	14.0	7.7	10.4	32.1	30.0
1965	8.8	8.3	11.0	28.1	32.4
1966	4.5	9.8	13.7	28.0	32.3
1967	2.7	8.7	13.6	25.0	33.3
1968	2.2	9.0	14.8	26.0	33.1
1969	1.9	9.3	14.3	25.5	33.8
1970	4.9	9.5	12.7	27.1	33.7
1971	8.8	9.4	10.9	29.2	34.1
1972	7.6	10.1	10.4	28.0	36.9
1973	13.6	8.5	7.9	29.9	39.2
1974	6.1	7.7	7.0	20.8	43.3
1975	4.9	8.2	6.9	20.1	44.3
1976	5.3	6.3	8.2	19.8	44.4
1977	8.1	4.7	9.0	21.7	51.4
1978	19.2	3.9	7.6	30.7	45.9
1979	17.1	5.3	6.9	29.2	47.6
1980	17.9	8.4	5.6	31.9	48.0
1981	37.0	8.0	3.4	48.4	38.6

1982	29.4	11.1	3.2	43.6	43.2
1983	16.2	9.5	2.2	28.0	47.6
1984	7.5	8.7	3.8	19.9	49.0
1985	11.7	6.6	3.4	21.7	49.2
1986	9.4	4.0	4.3	17.7	53.8
1987	1.7	4.1	2.7	8.5	59.6
1988	0.8	3.8	2.5	7.1	62.9
1989	0.6	8.3	2.3	11.2	61.6
1990	0.3	9.8	2.2	12.3	61.3
1991	0.3	7.1	3.7	11.0	60.6
1992	0.4	4.5	3.4	8.3	63.0
1993	0.2	3.0	3.7	6.9	65.5
1994	0.2	5.7	3.1	9.0	67.2
1995	0.3	5.5	3.4	9.2	65.5
1996	0.3	5.7	3.8	9.8	66.7
1997	0.3	5.4	3.6	9.3	69.0
Annual Average For:					
1947-97	6.6	6.7	7.7	20.9	42.5
1947-73	5.2	6.8	10.6	22.6	31.8
1974-84	15.3	7.4	5.8	28.6	45.7
1985-91	3.6	6.2	3.0	12.8	58.4
1992-97	0.3	5.0	3.5	8.8	66.2

Notes:
A = % of Land Sale
B = % of Land, Rents, Property and Investment
C = % of Rates
D = % of Total Land Revenue (exclusive of property tax and estate duty)
E = % of Internal (Inland) Revenue

Sources: Calculated from *Annual Report of the Accountant General*, and *Annual Report of the Director of Accounting Services*, various years.

Table 4.11   Capital Works Reserve Fund and the Actual Revenue, 1986-97 (HK$ million)

Year	CWRF	Revenue	CWRF/ Revenue (%)
1986	586.4	41241.0	1.4
1987	2330.9	43869.6	5.3
1988	3513.4	55641.4	6.3
1989	6393.0	65780.6	9.7
1990	7457.8	74365.2	10.0
1991	4002.5	82674.5	4.8
1992	9074.4	101456.4	8.9
1993	8957.3	120780.8	7.4
1994	19111.8	143899.8	13.3
1995	20192.6	151052.3	13.4
1996	22478.0	153194.3	14.7
1997	29057.0	173857.4	16.7
TOTAL	133155.1	1207813.3	
AVERAGE			9.3

Notes:
1. CWRF = Capital Works Reserve Fund (Works Account)
2. The figure of revenue in the Annual Digest of Statistics is different from that of the Annual Report of the Director of Accounting Services. The revenue's figure here is followed the latter.

Sources:
1. For CWRF, Census and Statistics Department, *Hong Kong Annual Digest of Statistics*, 1992 Edition, p. 119; 1995 Edition, p. 149; and 1998 Edition, p. 168;
2. For revenue, *Annual Report of the Director of Accounting Services*, various years.

In ensuring the availability of the necessary funding for other expenditures, the revenue from other taxing sources had to yield more. As shown in Table 4.10, the share of internal revenue climbed significantly from 31.8% in the period 1947-73 to 66.2% in 1992-97. Among the items within the heading of internal revenue, as shown in Table 4.12, the share of salaries tax grew at a rapid rate. The salaries tax contributed only 9% in average in 1955-73, and steadily rose to 15.6% in 1973-84, 23.8% in 1984-91 and finally reached 24.6% in 1992-98. The share of stamp duty decreased more than 4% in average from 1973-84 to 1984-91 and grew more than 5% from 1984-91 to 1992-98. The share of property tax was declined from 8.8% in 1955-73 to 1.5% in 1992-98. The contribution from profits tax grew from 44.7% in 1955-73 to 49% in 1973-84, but eventually dropped to 42.5% in 1992-98.

As shown in Table 4.13, the net of salaries tax had extended widely with a significant growth of total taxpayers from little more than 255,500 in 1982 to 1,351,808 in 1998. That meant, on average, more than 68,500 persons were being drawn into the net yearly in the said period. Furthermore, a differential growth of the standard rate taxpayers, in terms of both number and share of final tax contribution, can be noted. The annual average of standard rate taxpayers increased from 48,345 (6.3% of the total taxpayers) in 1986/87-1989/90 to 129,599 (9.6%) in 1990/91-1994/95, and then declined to 75,567 (5.5%) in 1995/96-1997/98, the share of final tax for the respective period were 49.5%, 55.7% and 43.75%. As the figure revealed, only about 7.5% of the total taxpayers accounted for 50.6% of the final tax in the period 1986/87-1997/98.

As a whole, the growing number of standard rate taxpayers seemingly imply that more and more individuals and families (mostly middle or lower-middle income groups) that were not liable to pay the standard tax rate before had to pay more tax then, especially in the period of 1990/91-94/95. Though one would argue that the expanding population of taxpayers was the result of the real growth of income, the fact remained that salaries and related tax allowances were not growing at the same pace as the inflation rate. As shown in Table 4.14, Column G, only on eight occasions (1981/82, 1982/83, 1983/84, 1984/85, 1994/95, 1995/96, 1996/97 and 1997/98) did the amounts of salaries tax allowances (with additional allowance) catch up with the inflation rate during the period 1973/74-1997/98. The effect of the untimely adjustment of salaries tax allowances was the expanding of the tax net to include more and more working class taxpayers, especially during the period 1985/86-1993/94.

Table 4.12 Selected Components of the Inland Revenue, 1955-98 (%)

Year	A	B	C	D
1955	6.0	11.8	7.5	51.7
1956	6.5	14.4	9.6	45.3
1957	6.1	13.1	10.0	35.5
1958	8.1	14.1	10.1	39.3
1959	7.0	12.2	6.9	44.4
1960	7.5	14.5	7.8	43.6
1961	8.1	16.7	7.3	45.1
1962	7.4	17.7	11.8	40.4
1963	7.9	15.8	9.8	40.9
1964	8.1	15.5	9.6	43.6
1965	7.8	15.8	8.6	45.8
1966	8.8	12.1	11.0	46.9
1967	9.6	10.7	11.0	47.2
1968	12.3	8.2	10.9	47.2
1969	12.8	10.0	9.2	47.5
1970	12.4	11.8	8.2	48.9
1971	12.2	12.6	6.8	50.1
1972	12.7	16.9	6.1	48.6
1973	9.5	36.9	4.4	38.1
1974	12.5	20.4	6.2	50.9
1975	15.9	11.6	5.7	54.2
1976	16.1	13.2	5.1	51.5
1977	16.8	12.1	7.1	48.3
1978	17.1	11.2	5.6	50.3
1979	18.1	13.6	4.3	47.3
1980	16.7	12.2	3.9	50.2
1981	13.3	18.3	2.9	48.9
1982	11.9	15.2	5.4	48.5
1983	15.9	9.4	5.2	52.9
1984	23.0	7.4	4.1	47.0
1985	23.7	6.6	4.9	47.5
1986	24.8	7.8	3.2	46.8
1987	25.5	11.9	3.5	42.2

1988	22.8	15.2	2.6	44.7
1989	21.4	12.8	2.2	48.6
1990	23.2	12.1	2.1	47.1
1991	26.4	12.0	2.3	42.8
1992	27.6	15.2	1.9	39.9
1993	25.8	17.1	1.7	41.2
1994	23.5	18.8	1.6	41.6
1995	23.7	12.8	1.5	47.6
1996	25.6	10.9	1.6	45.5
1997	23.9	17.0	1.3	41.7
1998	21.9	21.2	1.2	40.2
Annual Average For:				
1955-98	15.6	14.0	5.8	45.9
1955-73	9.0	14.8	8.8	44.7
1973-84	15.6	15.1	5.0	49.0
1984-91	23.8	10.7	3.1	45.8
1992-98	24.6	16.1	1.5	42.5

Notes:
A = Salaries Tax
B = Stamp Duty
C = Property Tax
D = Profits Tax (Corporations and Unincorporated Businesses)

Source: Calculated from Commissioner of Inland Revenue, *Annual Departmental Report*, various years.

Table 4.13   Statistics of Salaries Tax, Selected Years

Year*	Standard Rate Taxpayers	% of Total Taxpayers	Share of Final Tax (%)
1986/87	33771	4.9	45.5
1987/88	43429	5.6	47.5
1988/89	53209	7.0	50.6
1989/90	62973	7.7	54.4
1990/91	100170	9.4	55.0
1991/92	112485	8.8	54.0
1992/93	138917	9.8	55.8
1993/94	156678	10.5	56.4
1994/95	139747	9.4	57.3
1995/96	71570	5.3	43.3
1996/97	77129	5.5	43.4
1997/98	78002	5.8	44.4
Annual Average For:			
1986/87-1997/98	89006.7	7.5	50.6
1986/87-1989/90	48345.5	6.3	49.5
1990/91-1994/95	129599.4	9.6	55.7
1995/96-1997/98	75567.0	5.5	43.7

*Year refers to the reporting year.

Source: Commissioner of Inland Revenue, *Annual Departmental Report* (1986/7-1990/1); *Annual Review* (1991/2-1994/5); *Annual Report* (1995/6-1997/8).

Table 4.14   Salaries Tax Allowances and Inflation, 1973/74-1997/98

Year	A	B	C	D	E	F	G
1973/74	10,000	-	-	10,000	11.5	-	-	-
1974/75	10,000	-	-	10,000	5.0	11,500	1,500	1,500
1975/76	10,000	-	-	10,000	9.5	12,075	2,075	2,075

	A		B	C	D	E	F	G
1976/77	10,000	-	-	10,000	3.7	13,222	3,222	3,222
1977/78	10,000	(2,500)	15	10,000	8.0	13,711	3,711	3,711
1978/79	10,000	(2,500)	15	10,000	17.5	14,808	4,808	4,808
1979/80	10,000	(2,500)	10	10,000	15.4	17,400	7,400	7,400
1980/81	12,500	(2,500)	0	15,000	10.3	20,079	7,579	5,079
1981/82	15,000	(7,500)	0	22,500	9.7	22,147	7,147	−353
1982/83	20,500	(7,500)	0	28,000	4.5	24,296	3,796	−3,704
1983/84	20,500	(7,500)	0	28,000	9.7	25,389	4,889	−2,611
1984/85	20,500	(7,500)	0	28,000	5.4	27,852	7,352	−148
1985/86	20,500	(7,500)	0	28,000	3.9	29,356	8,856	1,356
1986/87	20,500	(8,500)	0	29,000	8.9	30,501	10,001	1,501
1987/88	29,000	(5,000)	10	29,000	9.5	33,215	4,215	4,215
1988/89	29,000	(7,000)	10	29,000	12.3	36,371	7,371	7,371
1989/90	32,000	(7,000)	10	32,000	7.5	40,844	8,844	8,844
1990/91	32,000	(7,000)	0	39,000	9.2	43,908	11,908	4,908
1991/92	34,000	(7,000)	0	41,000	9.7	47,947	13,947	6,947
1992/93	39,000	(7,000)	0	46,000	8.5	52,598	13,598	6,598
1993/94	49,000	(7,000)	0	56,000	6.9	57,069	8,069	1,069
1994/95	65,000	(7,000)	0	72,000	2.5	61,006	−3,994	−10,994
1995/96	72,000	(7,000)	0	79,000	5.9	62,532	−9,468	−16,468
1996/97	83,000	(7,000)	0	90,000	7.2	66,221	−16,779	−23,779
1997/98	100,000	-	0	100,000	1.1	70,989	−29,011	−29,011

Notes:
A = Basic Allowances with Additional Allowance in Bracket
B = Percentage that Additional Allowance Subject to Clawback
C = Basic and Additional Allowances
D = Inflation Rates (as measured by the GDP deflator)
E = Amounts of the Sum of Salaries Allowances X (1 + Annual Inflation Rate); 1973/74 serves as the base year
F = E minus A
G = E minus C

Sources:
1. For tax allowance in and before 1992/93, Tang Shu-hung, *The Public Finance of Hong Kong in the Late-Transitional Period* (Hong Kong: Joint Publishing, 1992), pp. 58-9. (in Chinese); in and after 1993/94: Inland Revenue Department, *Notes on Computation of Salaries Tax/Personal Assessment*, various years;
2. For inflation rates for the period 1973/74-1997/98, Census and Statistics Department, *Estimated of Gross Domestic Product 1961 to 1998* (Hong Kong: Printing Department, 1999), p. 18, Table 2.

State Contraction and the Consumption Cleavage

Accompanying the growing extractive capacity of the Hong Kong state was its expansive and exclusive role in providing most of the social and economic services. The growing government expenditure on social services programmes carried with it the redistributive effect. For example, the provision of free nine-year education could reduce parents' financial burden and thus increase the share of bring-home money. The same logic would also apply to other fields of government provisions. For example, the public works projects of the transportation system could facilitate the internal movement of goods and services, and thus lowered the cost of economic activities. James O'Connor (1973:5-10) differentiated the former type of government provisions as social consumption, the latter as social investment. Manuel Castells (1978: chapter 2) termed the former as collective consumption. Patrick Dunleavy (1979:418) highlighted the difference between the collective and individualized forms of consumption in the following three "politically significant ways":

(a) Collective consumption in advanced capitalist societies is typically concerned with services provided by the state apparatus, . . .
(b) . . . individuals' location in these consumption processes is no longer directly determined by market forces. . . .
(c) Collective consumption processes create an inter-subjective basis for the development of political action. . . .

Following Dunleavy's and Castells' framework, this section will only deal with the collective consumption aspect of the expenditure as it was the fundamental factor in politicizing the grass-roots since the mid-1980s in the context of Hong Kong. The spending capacity of the post-war Hong Kong government witnessed a steady growth and at a rate faster than that of the GDP, especially during the 1980s. We can see from Table 4.15 that there was an average of about 2% growth from 1974-80 to 1981-90.

The steady growth of the government expenditure appeared to be related to the expanding role of government in the collective consumption processes. As shown in Table 4.16, the average aggregated social services expenditures were 41.3% in 1971-80, 43.8% in 1981-90 and 48.3% in 1991-99, with a overall average of 44.3% in the whole period of 1971-99. Only on 3 occasions (1973, 1974 and 1982) did the figure fall below 40% of the total actual expenditure. The figure has even gone up to more than half of the total actual expenditure in 1998. The components of the social services expenditure had all more or less experienced some sorts of growth, with higher growth rates in social welfare.

Table 4.15   Actual Expenditure and the GDP, 1974-97 (At Current Market Prices)

Financial Year Ended	Expenditure (HK$ million)	GDP (HK$ million)	Expenditure/ GDP (%)
1974	5169.2	43014	12.0
1975	6255.2	47137	13.3
1976	6032.2	52217	11.6
1977	6590.9	65323	10.1
1978	8996.9	75552	11.9
1979	11090.1	89688	12.4
1980	13872.3	118467	11.7
1981	23593.5	149121	15.8
1982	27778.2	176938	15.7
1983	34597.8	194600	17.8
1984	33393.1	223284	15.0
1985	36901.8	264666	13.9
1986	39798.2	274625	14.5
1987	39927.7	327710	12.2
1988	44022.0	400323	11.0
1989	48952.6	472813	10.4
1990	69661.6	536263	13.0
1991	82837.2	599671	13.8
1992	93401.1	695525	13.4
1993	102024.5	809301	12.6
1994	121040.3	927297	13.1
1995	147260.9	1027929	14.3
1996	155856.9	1097343*	14.2
1997	151932.3	1229069*	12.4
Annual Growth Rate For:			
1974-80			11.8
1981-90			13.9
1991-97			13.4

* Estimated figures

Sources:
1. For GDP, Census and Statistics Department. *Estimates of Gross Domestic Product 1961 to 1998*, (Hong Kong: Printing Department, 1999), pp. 48-53, Table 10(a);
2. For expenditure, *Annual Report of the Accounting General*, and *Annual Report of the Director of Accounting Services*, various years.

As shown in Table 4.17, more than one-fifth (22%) of the total expenditure was spent on the subvention of social services in the period 1973-98. Besides, there was a trend of growing proportion of subvention since the mid-1980s. The average percentage of social service subvention for the periods 1973-80, 1981-90, and 1991-98 were 19.3%, 19.6% and 27.6%, respectively. The year 1998 reached the highest with more than 33.2% of the total expenditure being dispersed through subvention. A lion's share (about three-fourths) of the subvention was taken up by the heading under education which included subvention of the Universities and Polytechnic, and the Vocational Training Council. The subvention under the heading health increased significantly from an annual average of 2.6% in both periods of 1973-80 and 1981-90 to that of 9% in the period 1991-98. The social welfare subvention only took up an average of 1% of the total expenditure in the whole period of 1973-98.

Table 4.16   Public Expenditure by Policy Area Group, 1971-99 (%)

Year	A	B	C	D	E	F
1971	1.6	10.1	20.4	8.4	0.3	40.8
1972	2.0	10.3	20.2	7.4	0.3	40.2
1973	2.3	9.8	18.3	6.4	0.3	37.1
1974	3.0	9.0	20.0	6.7	0.3	39.0
1975	4.1	8.4	17.4	10.1	0.2	40.2
1976	5.5	8.5	19.6	10.1	0.3	44.0
1977	5.0	8.8	19.5	8.4	0.3	42.0
1978	4.4	8.2	18.0	11.2	0.3	42.1
1979	4.5	7.9	16.2	14.2	0.3	43.1
1980	4.6	7.9	15.9	15.6	0.2	44.2
1981	4.0	7.6	15.3	16.8	0.4	44.1
1982	4.2	7.3	14.2	13.3	0.3	39.3

Year	A	B	C	D	E	F
1983	4.8	7.4	14.3	13.8	0.3	40.6
1984	5.0	7.7	14.9	14.5	0.3	42.4
1985	5.6	8.3	17.4	13.3	0.3	44.9
1986	5.7	8.7	17.4	12.7	0.3	44.8
1987	5.8	9.1	17.5	12.1	0.3	44.8
1988	5.9	9.3	17.1	13.1	-	45.4
1989	5.9	8.8	17.5	15.1	-	47.3
1990	5.8	8.9	15.9	14.1	-	44.7
1991	6.1	9.8	16.9	13.0	-	45.8
1992	5.8	10.0	18.0	11.6	-	45.4
1993	6.0	11.0	17.9	10.5	-	45.4
1994	5.9	11.9	16.4	10.7	-	44.9
1995	6.6	11.6	17.4	11.9	-	47.5
1996	7.4	12.7	17.6	10.0	-	47.7
1997	8.5	11.9	17.9	11.5	-	49.8
1998*	9.1	11.6	19.9	12.3	-	52.9
1999**	9.1	10.9	18.4	16.9	-	55.3
Annual Average For:						
1971-99	5.3	9.4	17.5	11.9	0.2	44.3
1971-80	3.7	8.9	18.6	9.9	0.3	41.3
1981-90	5.3	8.3	16.2	13.9	0.2	43.8
1991-99	7.2	11.3	17.8	12.0	0.0	48.3

Notes:
A = Social Welfare
B = Health
C = Education
D = Housing
E = Labour
F = Total Social Services
* = Revised estimate
** = Draft estimate

Source: *The Budget: Speech by the Financial Secretary*, various years; figures for the period 1971-80 are adjusted by the Government.

This picture is not complete because housing had not been included in the above-mentioned figures. Due to the lack of comparable data, the government contribution to public housing (as reported in the balance sheet of the Housing Authority's Annual Report) was used as an estimation of its share of subvention of the total actual expenditure. As shown in Table 4.18, the share was more than 11% in average in 1978-94. As a result, it was estimated that about one-third of the total expenditure was delivered through the statutory bodies or other social organizations.

Although claiming not to be a welfare state, the Hong Kong government, in fact, provided some basic social services which were indispensable to the stability and the economic development of Hong Kong, as well as to the betterment of the material life of the Hong Kong people. In other words, the government had intervened in the individual consumption process so as to provide a sector of the population with some protection against the usual logic of market forces. In so doing, a favourable environment for investment and economic production would be maintained and enhanced. Having this strategic thinking in mind, the Hong Kong government set the priority for intervention. Different from the Western experience of the welfare state, the prior target of intervention was the social services but not the social security programmes (Flora and Heidenheimer, 1981).

Table 4.17   Subventions of Selected Social Services Programmes (Recurrent and Capital Expenditure) (%)

Year	Total Subvention/ Expenditure	Education/ Expenditure	Health/ Expenditure	Social Welfare/ Expenditure
1973	16.7	12.8	2.6	0.5
1974	19.4	15.4	2.6	0.5
1975	18.8	14.5	2.7	0.6
1976	21.6	17.1	2.8	0.8
1977	22.0	17.3	2.8	0.8
1978	19.0	14.6	2.7	0.8
1979	18.4	14.2	2.6	0.8
1980	18.6	14.5	2.5	0.8
1981	15.2	11.8	2.0	0.6
1982	15.7	11.8	2.3	0.7
1983	17.0	12.9	2.4	0.8
1984	18.1	13.6	2.6	0.9
1985	21.3	16.2	2.8	1.1

Year				
1986	20.9	15.9	2.7	1.1
1987	23.1	17.7	3.0	1.2
1988	22.6	17.1	2.9	1.3
1989	21.4	15.9	2.7	1.4
1990	20.2	14.8	2.5	1.4
1991	21.2	15.2	2.7	1.5
1992	25.6	16.3	6.1	1.7
1993	28.8	15.5	10.0	1.6
1994	25.8	13.8	9.2	1.4
1995	26.7	14.3	9.6	1.4
1996	27.8	14.7	10.2	1.5
1997	31.9	16.4	11.6	1.8
1998	33.2	16.9	12.4	2.4

Annual Growth Rate For:

Period				
1973-98	22.0	15.0	4.6	1.1
1973-80	19.3	15.0	2.6	0.7
1981-90	19.6	14.8	2.6	1.0
1991-98	27.6	15.4	9.0	1.6

Sources: Calculated from Census and Statistics Department, *Hong Kong Annual Digest of Statistics*, 1983 Edition, p. 111, Table 8.3; 1992 Edition, p. 120, Table 8.3; 1995 Edition, p. 150, Table 8.3; and 1998 Edition, p. 169, Table 9.3.

The government intervention in the individual consumption processes of medical care, housing and education had the effect of turning the original private goods and services into public or collective ones. The direct effects of these measures were the stabilization of wages and price systems, and the suppression of the inflation rate. In so doing, the pressure to ask for a salary increase from the workers would effectively lessen, and thus, part of their consumption could be insulated from the influence of the market. That means their living would be hit only slightly compared with others by the rising living standard and inflation rate, which usually prove to be the normal phenomenon of a rapid developing economy. As long as the government could manage stable supply funding, the above-mentioned effects would be maintained. But the ups and downs of the economic growth rate or the financial stringency provoked by the fluctuation of land price and the competing programmes of spending, worked to erode the government's fiscal power. Consequently, budget-cutting or privatization might be logical solutions.

Table 4.18 Government Contribution to Public Housing and Total Actual Expenditure, 1978-94 (HK$ million)

Year	A	B	C
1978	418.0	8996.9	4.6
1979	591.2	11090.1	5.3
1980	1749.0	13872.3	12.6
1981	786.4	23593.5	3.3
1982	832.1	27778.2	3.0
1983	2247.8	34597.8	6.5
1984	2748.2	33393.1	8.2
1985	6884.6	36901.8	18.7
1986	5552.5	39798.2	14.0
1987	5213.2	39927.7	13.1
1988	5254.5	44022.0	11.9
1989	7175.4	48952.6	14.7
1990	10887.4	69661.6	15.6
1991	12110.3	82837.2	14.6
1992	9756.5	93401.1	10.4
1993	13377.3	102024.5	13.1
1994	26434.9	121040.3	21.8
Annual Growth Rate For: 1978-94			11.3

Notes:
A = Government Contribution to Domestic Housing (Housing Authority's figures only)
B = Total Actual Expenditure
C = % of A/B

Sources: Calculated from *Housing Authority Annual Report*, various years; and *Annual Report of the Accountant General*, and *Annual Report of Director of Accounting Services*, various years.

The Logic of Privatization

In explaining the trend of privatization in Hong Kong, Anthony B.L. Cheung (1991:12-4; 1995:59-61) put forward the "government off-loading" thesis. This thesis regarded privatization as a move the Hong Kong government adopted in reaction to its growing incapabilities in the face of increasing Chinese intervention in the transitional period as well as in meeting the demands from its restless population. Besides this political explanation, this author would argue that the fiscal crisis resulting from the high reliance of government revenue on land sales and the constraints on the use of such revenue by the Sino-British Joint Declaration would also be responsible for the privatization drive.

The trend of privatization is well reflected in the publication of a discussion paper entitled *Public Sector Reform* released by the Finance Branch of the Hong Kong government in February 1989. The government sought "a change in the attitude and approach to the spending of public money in order to improve efficiency and give a better service to the public . . . by adapting and developing the structures and procedures that already exist" (quoted in Cheung, 1991:1). The paper proposed a pricing system on government services. As a result, some government services were classified as "support" or "commercial" services and subject to partial or full cost recovery (Finance Branch, 1989; reproduced in Lee and Cheung, 1995:Appendix A, pp. 260-3).

As mentioned before, the Hong Kong government experienced the expected financial stringency caused by the designated use of the revenue from land sale and the slowing down of the growth of the GDP from the mid-1980s. The situation grew worse when the government committed itself to the expensive port and airport plan, the massive expansion of the education programme, and other measures in 1989.

As a result, one can easily distinguish a trend of privatization of some collective consumption programmes. Housing, medical and health services, and education have, in one way or another, embarked on the road of privatization since the mid-1980s. Among the list, housing appeared to be the most controversial one as housing might be regarded as more basic in the sense of its recurrent nature and the sums of money involved. It was reported that the household expenditure on housing ranged from 19% for the lowest income groups to 36.5% for the highest income groups in 1989-90 of their respective monthly income, and the average was 25.6% (Census and Statistics Department, 1992b:141, Table 10.5). Furthermore, it was estimated that nearly half of the population were living in public housing estates. Given the scale and its importance in urban politics, we now turn to discuss the privatization process of public housing.

Public Housing and Privatization Drive

The Housing Authority has been solely responsible for the provision of low-rented public housing since the launching of the Ten-Year Housing Programme in the early 1970s by the then Governor Murray MacLehose. Since then, more and more public housing estates have been constructed to house the low income families. Through the Public Works Department, public housing estates were constructed and then handed to the Housing Authority when finished. The cost of construction was largely shouldered by the government through its general revenue account, but the Housing Authority had to pay the interest and amortisation of the capital expenditure to the government as well as to take up all the management and maintenance cost. In fact, the government often absorbed the deficits when they were presented at the end of each financial year. Because of such special financial arrangements, the Housing Authority could manage to maintain the low rent policy. According to one study, it was estimated that the amounts of government subsidy which the public housing residents received was HK$840 million in 1976 and HK$6,528 million (in real terms) in 1981 (Li and Yu, 1990:249-60). The impact on the household's consumption patterns was said to be "substantial" and estimated to increase; "on the average, housing consumption by 120 percent and non-housing consumption by 17 percent" with the welfare cost of about 25 percent in 1979 (Yu and Li, 1985:138-9). Rents in public housing had been very stable up to 1981. The respective rent per square metre for the former resettlement estates, the Housing Authority blocks, and a tenement floor in the private market was HK$3.31, HK$6.14 and HK$18.84 in 1976; but the corresponding figures were HK$4.36, HK$6.6 and HK$55.9 in 1981.

The growing government expenditure and subsidy in social services could only be continued provided that the necessary revenue was in place. But the high economic growth rate in the 1970s slowed down in the 1980s and the future of Hong Kong was put into doubt as the 1997 question emerged in 1979. Thus, the fiscal condition of the Hong Kong government also encountered the same problem of uncertainty. As mentioned before, the uncertainty about the political future in the early 1980s had plagued both the property market and land sales. A decrease in revenue from the land-related sources followed. Under such circumstances, the continuation of massive social services programmes was not possible. Furthermore, as mentioned before, the Hong Kong government was restrained by the land arrangements stipulated in the Sino-British Joint Declaration which came into effect in 1985.

Even before the reorganization of the Housing Authority in 1988 which made it into a self-financed statutory body with government capital investment, some measures of privatization were already planned and put into practice (Hong Kong Government, 1984c, 1985, 1986a, 1986b). First of all, the rent policy underwent significant changes after the centralisation of housing management into the hands of the Housing Authority in 1973. Before that date, rents for government Low-Cost Housing estates and resettlement estates were based on "historic costs" (Morris, 1978:69). That means "rents were fixed by Government to cover land and building costs amortized over 40 years as well as management and maintenance costs" (*Housing Authority Annual Report* 1973-74:10). In 1973, rents for all public housing had to be reviewed biennially and no more than 10% increase could be allowed. In the early 1980s, rents were charged, on average, at 5-7% of the household income of the tenants. But in 1987, rents were fixed at no more than 15% of the median household income of the tenants, and the percentage soared to 18.5% for new buildings after 1992. In addition, the tenants in the redeveloped resettlement estates were liable to pay the new rents which were several times higher than before.

Second, the adoption of double-rent policy in 1987 for those tenants whose income exceeded twice the Waiting List Income Limit (the maximum income limit for applicants for public housing flats) and had already been living there for more than 10 years. In its first year of application, 22% of the target tenants (N=41,000) were required to pay double rent.

Third, tenants and potential tenants of public housing have been offered favourable terms in purchasing flats from the Home Ownership Scheme (HOS) and the Private Sector Participation Scheme (PSPS). These included the low interest rate, high mortgage limit (90% of the purchase price, and later up to 95%), long repayment period (15 years at first and later 20 years), no income limit and restriction of property ownership. Later on, in 1988, an interest-free loan (the Home Purchase Loan Scheme) was introduced to help the tenants to purchase flats in the private sector with the condition that they have to evacuate from their public housing flats. Meanwhile, the prices for the HOS's and PSPS's flats have been pegged with the private market prices and usually at a discount of 30-40% of the latter. As the prices of private property skyrocketed, so did those of the HOS's and PSPS's flats. In 1993, the Sandwich Class Housing Scheme was introduced "to help families living in private rented accommodation . . . to buy their own homes" (Housing Branch, 1997:19). Furthermore, the Tenants Purchase Scheme was adopted in late 1997 to sell rental flats to the sitting tenants of public housing estates at the replacement cost of the concerned flats.

The decision to undertake privatization sparked off waves of tenants' protests and thus, to a certain extent, helped to politicize the grass-roots. According to one study, 169 cases of social conflicts (19.2% of the total, N=882) were of a housing nature during the period 1975-86, of which 36 cases were related to public housing rent (Cheung and Louie 1991:13-4, Tables 3 & 5). Regarding the modes of action, housing conflict stood out as the most "violent" one because it took the form of protests and mass rallies more often than other social conflicts (Cheung and Louie 1991:29, Table 19). This is very important to urban politics as the universal franchise had only just been introduced into the Hong Kong political system. The newly-born politicians have taken advantage of the privatization issue (not only housing) and rallied considerable constituency support in the course of election campaigns. The details of the election appeals by the various political groups will be discussed in Chapter 6.

Notes

1. It was the first time for the LegCo to have its non-official members in a majority (if the Governor was excluded).
2. Renamed as the Office of Members of the Executive and Legislative Councils (OMELCO) in 1986.
3. For MacLehose's policy statement, see his annual speech to the LegCo on October 18th 1972.
4. These are: *Green Paper: A Pattern of District Administration in Hong Kong* (June 1980); *White Paper: District Administration in Hong Kong* (January 1981); *Green Paper: The Further Development of Representative Government in Hong Kong* (July 1984); *White Paper: The Further Development of Representative Government in Hong Kong* (November 1984); *Green Paper: The 1987 Review of Developments in Representative Government* (May 1987); *White Paper: The Development of Representative Government: The Way Forward* (February 1988).
5. The phrase "positive non-interventionism" was coined by Philip Haddon-Cave, the former Financial Secretary from 1971 to 1981.
6. Before 1982, revenue from land sales had been set aside for fiscal reserves. But the then Financial Secretary John Bremridge, successor of Philip Haddon-Cave, used it for expenditure. See Sung (1986:130).

5 Development and Alignment of Political Forces

This chapter examines the development and nature of various political forces and their alignment and realignment since the 1970s so as to understand the orientation of political groups emerging in the early 1990s and their respective positioning in the budding party market in the ensuing LegCo popular elections. First of all, the background prior to the 1970s will be examined so as to put the subsequent development of political groups into context. Second, the emergence of pressure groups in the 1970s will be analysed against the rapidly changing socio-economic developments. Third, the alignment of political forces and the rise of electoral parties by stages resulting from the political reforms in the 1980s will be studied. Fourth, the budding party system in the 1990s will be charted.

Political Groups Before the 1970s

Two kinds of political groups could be differentiated during the period from the end of the Second World War to the early 1970s. One was the exogenous, ideological political parties of the KMT and the CCP. The other was the endogenous, electoral-oriented political groups of the Reform Club of Hong Kong (RCHK) established in 1949 and the Hong Kong Civic Association (HKCA) formed in 1954. Basically, these two kinds of political groups differed in their priority political concerns. The first two were mostly concerned with Chinese national politics, while the last two mostly concentrated on Hong Kong local politics. Needless to say, their influence on Hong Kong would not be the same as the KMT and the CCP, which have, at one time or another, been the ruling parties of China; while the RCHK and the HKCA had only managed to have several of their members sitting in the local LegCo and UrbCo.

The Kuomintang (KMT) and The Chinese Communist Party (CCP)

The presence of the KMT and the CCP in Hong Kong has long been considered a sensitive issue. If both of these two parties adopted a high profile attitude towards Hong Kong affairs, the British-Hong Kong government would find it very hard to govern. Thus, the Hong Kong government wanted to avoid the presence of two power centres at one time within Hong Kong. Because of such considerations, the KMT and the CCP were not allowed to have open and legal existence in the territory, except for the former in the brief period of 1945-1949.

On the contrary, the KMT and the CCP have used Hong Kong as a stepping stone to support their respective activities on mainland China or on Taiwan and they seldom showed keen interest in local politics. Thus, the presence of these two parties may not be regarded as a "direct challenge" to the British-Hong Kong government, but rather a "potential threat". Given the overwhelming population of Chinese, the British-Hong Kong government would feel a great security pressure as these two parties could easily mobilize the Hong Kong Chinese to drive away the alien British-Hong Kong government. In addition, the rivalry between these two parties within the territory would give rise to serious internal security problems (Tsang, 1988:136-8). This was especially the case in the early 1950s when the retreated Nationalist Army organized subversive activities against the newly established CCP's regime from within Hong Kong, and when conflicts between the core supporters of these two parties broke out in 1956. Furthermore, the rivalry of these two parties had indeed entailed diplomatic embarrassment for the British and Hong Kong governments. For example, the handling of an aeroplane explosion by the British-Hong Kong government in 1955 had been criticized fiercely by the Communists; in this case a bomb was planted by KMT agents on a plane which Zhou Enlai, the then Chinese Prime Minister, was supposed to be using (Wong Man-fong, *Eastweek*, 20 July 1994:161-4).

The victory over Japan in the Second World War was accompanied by the rising influence and prestige of the KMT in the territory. Many of the mass media, labour unions, local schools and Chinese community organizations came under the influence of the KMT. But the KMT's membership did not match with its rising status. In 1947, a drive to recruit 50,000 members was kicked off but subsequently only attracted 8,000 to 10,000 to join (Tsang, 1988:52). By the late 1940s the influence of the KMT was declining rapidly as the CCP marched to win the Chinese civil war.

Nevertheless, the KMT maintained a certain level of support up to the early 1970s, because the population at that period comprised mostly refugees and the first generation in Hong Kong, who tended to have negative feelings towards the communist Chinese government and a more accommodative attitude towards the Nationalist government in Taiwan. Against this background, many schools, "Kaifong" associations and local community organizations were dominated by these people. During the 1967 riots, the KMT's supporters (the rightists[1]) helped the British-Hong Kong government to counteract the advance of the leftists by providing protection to those workers who opted not to take part in the local CCP's inspired strikes. However, the influence of the rightists declined thereafter. The aging of the leadership, the emergence of the local-born Hong Kong Chinese, and the diplomatic breakthrough by Communist China (which joined the United Nations in 1971 and established full diplomatic ties with the United States in 1979) contributed to the decline of KMT influence.

Before 1949, the chief task of the CCP in Hong Kong was, more or less, the same as that of the KMT after 1949, which was "to support their struggle for power in China without overtly breaking the laws of the colony" (Tsang, 1988:85). Like the KMT, the CCP did not involve itself deeply in local politics and has been described as adopting an appeasement policy towards the Hong Kong government before 1949. After becoming the governing party in China in 1949, the CCP's activities in Hong Kong were still very low-key, though there was a propaganda campaign against the British-Hong Kong government in early 1952 (Tsang, 1988:175-82). Although there were still other conflicts between Britain and Mainland China in this period, no significant mobilization of national feeling against the Hong Kong government by the CCP was recorded. This can be attributed to the CCP's pragmatic policy which allowed the status of Hong Kong to remain as it was. As mentioned in Chapter 3, the basic policy towards Hong Kong has been "Make long-term plan, utilize to the full." Besides, the CCP also appeared to adopt a low profile in recruiting members in Hong Kong and was estimated to have only 5,000 members in Hong Kong in the early 1990s (Central Intelligence Agency, 1993:150).

Nevertheless, this policy had come under challenge in the mid-1960s when the Cultural Revolution in China spilled over into Hong Kong leading to a series of riots and bomb attacks. After the 1967 riots, the CCP suffered from the loss of support from its "compatriots" in Hong Kong and the uncovering of the underground network there (Xu, 1993:144-5). The drastic drop in the readership of the CCP- and PRC-sponsored "patriotic" newspapers could be used to illustrate their unpopularity in Hong Kong after the 1967 riots. According to Kam Yiu-yu, the former NCNA's party secretary for the press front and editor-in-chief of the communist *Wei Wen Pao*, the total sales of the six "patriotic" newspapers amounted to about 500,000 and occupied half of the market before the 1967 riots, but declined significantly afterwards. He indicated that the total sales of three of these "patriotic" newspapers had dropped from around 120,000 to 10,000-20,000 after the 1967 riots (Kam, 1992:88).

The Reform Club of Hong Kong and the Hong Kong Civic Association

During the period from 1950 until 1982, there were two prominent political groups participating in the electoral contest for the UrbCo elected seats: the RCHK and the HKCA. A lion's share of the candidates in the pre-1982 UrbCo election was fielded by these two traditional political groups. According to one study, the two political groups had put up 33 of the 37 successful candidates between 1955 and 1967 (Hoadley, 1973:607).

Regarding the membership of these two groups, the Reform Club claimed to have over 40,000 in 1974 and the Civic Association was quoted to have about 10,000 in 1973 (Reform Club of Hong Kong, 1974; Hoadley, 1973:607). These groups had managed to attract citizens to join, especially the RCHK. Brook Bernacchi, the RCHK's chairman, revealed that his club had 35,000 members in 1969, of which 11,000 were workers, 7,700 hawkers, 7,400 businessmen, 3,200 fishermen, 3,100 farmers and 1,200 drivers (Bernacchi, [1989]:3). Unfortunately, not all their members were entitled to vote in the UrbCo elections because of the restricted franchise. Thus, it is interesting to note that the numbers of voters in each of the UrbCo elections in the late 1960s and early 1970s only amounted to around 10,000.

In response to the plea made by the then Governor, Mark Young, to carry out political reforms in the late 1940s, the RCHK was formed mainly by a group of British and Chinese professionals aiming at pushing for a quicker pace of democratization. The RCHK had regarded itself as "an unofficial opposition incessantly putting up constructive criticisms on the side of the Hong Kong citizens thereby prodding Government into action or quicker action for social and political reforms" (Reform Club of Hong Kong, 1974). The RCHK had repeatedly proposed not only to reform the UrbCo by expanding its scope and power, and introducing a wholly elected Municipal Council, but also to institute a certain number of elected seats in the LegCo. In March 1953, the RCHK had gathered 12,000 signatures demanding the introduction of two elected seats to the LegCo (Reform Club of Hong Kong, 1953, 1959).

Unlike the RCHK, the HKCA took a rather moderate approach to Hong Kong politics. Formed mainly by Chinese professionals and school teachers, it stressed social and economic reforms that brought about "Stability and Progress", and placed political stability higher than that of "radical progress" (Hong Kong Civic Association, 1974:4). The Chair of the HKCA confessed that:

> ... we advocate that Government should be more open to the suggestions of the people, that the Urban Council should be given greater responsibility ... and that there should be elected membership in the higher Government councils. . . . This does not mean in any sense that we in the Civic Association advocate self-government or independence. We do not wish to interrupt the tranquility and peace that we at present enjoy in Hong Kong, and we do not dream of taking over the central power in government. (Wong, 1970-71:9)

The HKCA further regarded the Hong Kong government as a "Benevolent Dictatorship", who "always made laws and regulations to suit its own immediate purpose without carefully examining its later possible consequences" (Hong Kong Civic Association, 1974:2).

Accompanying the failed attempt to secure political reforms at the central level and the new challenge of the HKCA's moderate appeal was the RCHK's failure to enlist substantial social support for its own reform plan. The RCHK, thus, reacted by deflating its demands and by developing a political coalition with the HKCA. In 1960, the RCHK and the HKCA jointly dispatched a delegation to London to discuss the constitutional reform of Hong Kong. According to Hilton Cheong-leen, the HKCA's chairman and a member of the delegation, the joint delegation had asked for an increased number of UrbCo elected seats, the institution of elected representation to the LegCo, the establishment of a convention which would require the Governor to appoint a certain proportion of the LegCo elected members to the ExCo, and the gradual relaxation of the highly restricted franchise (Cheong-leen, 1962:19 & 25).

The unfavourable response from London was anticipated. There were several reasons for this. First of all, the domestic order in Hong Kong in the 1950s was still not so secure, as the KMT and the CCP were still engaged with each other and confrontations between their supporters periodically exploded. The riots, as stirred up by the rightists, in Tsuen Wan and Kowloon areas in 1956 were a typical example. The deterioration of domestic order could invite Beijing intervention and the subsequent possible Chinese take-over. Second, as demonstrated in the abortion of the Young Plan in early 1950s, the established elites, including the non-official members of the LegCo, were not in favour of any reform. For them, any reform would mean an influx of keen competitors to the political game and thus erode away their exclusive access to political power. Third, the lack of widespread demand and support from the mass public led the Hong Kong government to see no urgency to introduce such reforms. Most of the population were still struggling to make both ends meet and their immediate concerns were thus mostly of an economic nature. Demands for political reforms were still limited to the small circle of professionals.

Later in January 1961, in response to London's refusal to carry out reforms, the RCHK and the HKCA signed a coalition agreement for four years to press for the realization of the said reforms. Though having a consensus on constitutional reforms, the cooperation between the two was not a smooth one and later in 1965 the coalition formally broke down. According to the RCHK's allegation, it was partly the insincere HKCA's move to support their opponents in the 1964 UrbCo election that contributed to the dissolution of the coalition (Reform Club of Hong Kong, 1974).

The resistance of the British-Hongkong government to reform of the UrbCo and to the introduction of elected members to the LegCo had not only worked to discredit the UrbCo as an effective mechanism to redress social grievances but also to discourage the social elites from participation. Although the government had recommended the relaxation of the franchise restriction in 1965 and finally reformed the UrbCo in 1973, the powers of the reformed UrbCo were still limited, only taking care of public recreation and amenities, cultural affairs, and some minor regulating power, such as the licensing of hawkers (Colonial Secretariat, 1971).

Before 1965, the franchise was largely confined to those who knew enough English and who were teachers, taxpayers, jurors, and members of the defence force or the auxiliary services. But, there were altogether 23 categories of persons, mostly professionals, recommended to be added to the franchise lists in 1965.[2] It was reported that in deciding which category of persons would be eligible for the franchise, the following criteria had been used:

(a) that the category should be one which makes a valuable contribution to Hong Kong through
   (i) service to the community; or
   (ii) professional knowledge and skill; or
   (iii) educational standard;
(b) that a person's claim to belong to that category should be relatively easy to establish and check. (Hong Kong Government, 1965g:3)

After the expansion of the franchise, it was estimated to have a 200,000 potential electorate Only 13% (N=26,275) and 17% (N=34,392) of the potential electorate went to register in 1967 and 1969, respectively. Furthermore, as indicated in Table 5.1, the electorate in 1952 only amounted to 9,000 and increased very slowly to about 34,000 in 1981, representing less than 1% of the population.

After studying electoral participation in the UrbCo elections, one observer suggested that the low rate of participation was, in some senses, quasi-rational and concluded that:

> With politics separated from economics, the pay-off schedule of the political "game" is such that it remains a pastime, a hobby for those who have the time, energy, and inclination to engage in it. Its rewards may be gratifying to some, but they are modest and non-material. It is politics without power, a sanitized and safety-inspected simulacrum of the real thing, completely divorced from the dynamism of Hong Kong's economy. (Hoadley, 1973:616)

Another scholar (Wong, 1970-71:20) attributed the political indifference of the Hong Kong people not to the cultural factor, but to the electoral system adopted:

> ... the political indifference of the local Chinese cannot be understood as some residue of a traditional preference for a paternalistic form of government. Instead I have argued that the political apathy of the local population must be explained within the context of the present [1970] electoral system, i.e. the part the local people are allowed to play in the political scene.

Table 5.1 The Electorate of the UrbCo and Population of Hong Kong, 1952-81

Year	Electorate	Population	%
1952	9,000	-	-
1953	8,000	-	-
1954	13,700	-	-
1955	14,583	-	-
1956	15,638	-	-
1957	19,305	-	-
1959	23,584	-	-
1961	26,039	3,129,648	0.83%
1963	25,932	-	-
1965	29,529	-	-
1967	26,275	3,708,920*	0.71%
1969	34,392	-	-
1971	37,788	3,936,630	0.96%
1973	31,284	-	-
1975	34,078	-	-
1977	37,174	4,402,990**	0.84%
1979	31,481	-	-
1981	34,381	5,109,812	0.67%

Notes:
* = 1966 By-Census's figure
** = 1976 By-Census's figure

Sources:
1. For electorate's figure: compiled from the data supplied by the Registration and Electoral Office, Constitutional Affairs Branch, Government Secretariat, Hong Kong Government;
2. For the population of Hong Kong, see *Hong Kong Annual Digest of Statistics*, 1992 ed., p. 11, Table 2.1.

The Period of Pressure Group Politics

Since the late 1960s, a handful of pressure groups have come into play in Hong Kong and they have largely championed the cause of the underprivileged. As mentioned in the previous chapter, the government adopted a more active attitude towards the society from the 1960s. Thus, the conflict between the government and the society over the distribution of social resources grew significantly as the latter was becoming more and more affected by government decisions and policies. Given the closed nature of the political structure and the predominant business influence in it, a communication gap existed between the government policy-makers and the affected citizens.

According to one study, the number of urban social conflicts had risen from 6 in 1950-59 and 31 in 1960-69, to 188 in 1970-79 (Lui and Kung, 1985:63). These conflicts were at first largely concerned about the clearance of slum areas and its compensation, and the inadequacy of community facilities, but later they also kept an eye on some high-level policy issues, such as the overall distribution of housing resources, the issue of rent-fixing for public housing flats, the monitoring mechanism of public utilities, and so on. Although the pressure groups' activities were usually small in scope and weak in intensity, the social activists had gradually built-up their images as well as secured a certain amount of social support. This kind of asset later proved to be indispensable when electoral politics came into play.

The rise of pressure group politics not only transformed the political landscape of Hong Kong but also prompted the government to set up a "new and secret body" called the Standing Committee on Pressure Groups (SCOPG), which reportedly aimed to coordinate "government surveillance of any protest or campaigning group and of mounting counter-attacks" and to "undermine, co-opt or coerce" such groups (Campbell, 1980:8). The Hong Kong government seemed to care most about the infiltration of the Chinese government and the CCP. In addition, the social climate of the 1970s had mobilized people to identify with China because the latter had made a breakthrough on the international stage. The acquisition of the China's seat in the United Nations by the PRC and its rapprochement with the United States in the early 1970s had boosted up its acceptability in Hong Kong. The growing identification with China in the society and the rise of an anti-colonial mood had made it more difficult for the Hong Kong government to govern. Understandably, the security issue gained prominence on the agenda of the Hong Kong government. Under the circumstances, it was logical for the Hong Kong government to adopt measures to cope with the problem. Unfortunately, the growing pro-China sentiments had coincided with expanding conflicts between the government and the society as the result of the expansion of state activities since the late 1960s. Any challenge from the political activists would, more or less, be interpreted as an advancement by the communists. This was reflected in the rather harsh comments made in the SCOPG's reports. This unfortunate coincidence had proved to be detrimental for the development of an "independent" political force within Hong Kong.

Among the 11 pressure or community groups mentioned in the SCOPG's confidential reports, the Hong Kong Christian Industrial Committee (HKCIC), the Hong Kong Professional Teachers' Union (HKPTU), the Society for Community Organisation (SoCO) and the Hong Kong Observers (HKO) have enjoyed popularity in the media and in their respective community.

The HKCIC was formed in 1967 to "enhance the workers' movements" in Hong Kong and represented the emergence of an independent force in the labour movement.[3] By organising seminars, demonstrations, press conferences and petitions, the HKCIC has been deeply engaged in the fight to protect workers' interests and has earned the reputation of the "Robin Hood of labour". Moreover, the HKCIC regarded its role as "to set ways and means to make distributive justice a permanent feature of our [Hong Kong] society" (*HKS*, 21 March 1981; Leung and Chiu, 1991:55-8). Thus, its engagement in other sorts of campaigns was just a logical development, such as the Coalition Against Bus Fare Increase and the Committee fighting for raising personal tax allowances in 1981. The SCOPG's report said the CIC's activities were "biased and counter-productive" and commented that:

> The CIC's intervention in trade disputes not only usurps the role of the Labour Department but complicates issues, feed erroneous ideas into workers' minds, and render them less amenable to conciliation. Their criticism has always been destructive. (Campbell, 1980:9; *HKS*, 28 January 1981)

The HKPTU is one of the most active trade unions in Hong Kong. Its former chairman, Szeto Wah, had succeeded in fighting with the government for a reasonable salary scheme for the Certificate Masters in early 1970s and in supporting the sacked teachers who protested against the alleged corruption of the Golden Jubilee School's Principal in 1977. These events had earned him and the HKPTU a reputation in the teaching profession. In the 1970s, the HKPTU had been regarded as a "radical" trade union for it tended to use the "uncommon" methods of strike, petition and sit-in as its campaign instruments. Szeto has also been considered as a leftist because of his uncompromising attitude in challenging the government authority and his alleged link with the NCNA's Hong Kong Branch.[4] Moreover, Xu Jiatun revealed in his memoirs in 1993 that Szeto had asked to join the CCP, but without Xu supplying details (Xu, 1993:149-50). In reacting to this allegation, Szeto has denied it squarely (*Hong Kong United Daily News*, 14 June 1993:2). Because of such uncompromising attitudes and the alleged close relations with the NCNA, the SCOPG's report had labelled the HKPTU as "a Chinese communist united front target and several of its official [*sic*] ... have had contact with leading communist educationalists [*sic*]" and had seen "long-term danger of communist infiltration" (*HKS*, 28 January 1981). We can not comment on whether the HKPTU or Szeto has any connection with the CCP or the Chinese government because of the lack of information. But one sure thing is that in a highly de-politicized society like Hong Kong, any move to challenge the existing political order will be labelled as a "radical" and "leftist" whatever the cause one is fighting for. Nevertheless, when the LegCo functional elections were first introduced in 1985, Szeto was supported by the HKPTU and finally was elected with an overwhelming majority.

Besides, the SoCO was well-known for its skills in organising residents and its confrontational attitude, at least according to the government, in protesting against the inadequacy of government policies. The SoCO gave help to the under-privileged and marginal communities by organising them to fight for their own cause. As Fung Ho-lap, the then Director of the SoCO, claimed: "[the] SoCO seldom speaks on behalf of the people. In fact, we help them to speak on their own with dignity and confidence. Pressure comes from the people, not from the pressure groups" (*HKS*, 9 June 1982). Fung also attributed the formation of the SoCO in 1971 to the inspiration of the three main world-wide movements at the time, which were welfare rights movement, secularisation of religion, and community development movement; it aimed to enhance the sense of community of the Hong Kong people and to consolidate residents' forces through organization and action to fight for their own rights (*Hong Kong Economic Journal Monthly* 52, July 1981:29-30). The SCOPG's report had made it known that the SoCO had "no subversive motive", but that there was a real danger "that [the] SoCO may be able to start organising people to achieve certain objectives, but it may turn out that the group so organized may eventually do something completely beyond the control of [the] SoCO" (*HKS*, 28 January 1981).

The HKO was formed in 1975 by a handful of Chinese professionals and its stated objectives included: to press for more government response to the needs of Hongkong residents and to organize research on issues of public interest (Hong Kong Observers, 1983:211.). By publishing articles in both English and Chinese newspapers, they made their views known to the general public and the concerned government departments. Though they were vocal in criticizing government policies and maltreatment, they are not an action-oriented group. In fact, to quote a term from the Home Affairs Department's report, the HKO is "an intelligentsia representative group" (Hong Kong Observers, 1983:214). In the SCOPG's report, the HKO was being assessed as having great potential for "infiltration among the educated young" and thus "can be dangerous if the HKO should assume a biased attitude one-tracked mind in their interpretation of social issues" (*HKS*, 28 January 1981). But the political situation has changed since the arrival of Christopher Patten in 1992 as the new Governor of Hong Kong. Two former active members of this group have been appointed as LegCo members in late 1992.[5]

Other active pressure groups at the time also included: the Hong Kong People's Council on Public Housing Policy (HKPCPHP) and the Social Workers' General Union (SWGU). The HKPCPHP was formed in 1978 with the help of the SoCO and other social organizations which aimed to reflect the will of the public housing residents and to monitor the works of the governmental Housing Authority (Hong Kong People's Council on Public Housing Policy, 1988:7). The SWGU was formed in 1980 with a membership of over 700, one-fourth of the total social workers in Hong Kong. Many of the SWGU's leaders were active participants of the social and residents' movements in the 1970s.

The mushrooming of the community groups indicated that the conflicts between the government and the society had grown to a point where some sort of coordination would be desirable because of the adverse impact the government policies would have. As shown in Chapter 4, as the government administered more aspects of society and the economy in the 1970s, any dissatisfaction with the policies and their implications would necessarily take a political form, especially as the government had established new institutions to reflect its new interventionism. The urban redevelopment programmes, the land resumption plan, and related compensation schemes had had, in a sense, a destabilising effect on the then rather harmonious political order. Because of such developments, the mass public were more prone to political mobilization when their interests were at stake. Although small in size and weak in mobilization power, these community groups had been providing a training ground for the social activists who were then equipped with the necessary skills in organising the masses and the psychological readiness to confront the authority during their fights with the government in the 1970s.

Political Alignments in the 1980s and 1990s

The emergence of the 1997 issue and the subsequent Sino-British negotiations over the future of Hong Kong served to provide a new direction for political change in Hong Kong. The commitment to providing a "high degree of autonomy" and the promise of "Hong Kong people governing Hong Kong" by Beijing after 1997, and London's decision to open up partially the colonial political system by instituting a representative government there, created a wave of political group formation in Hong Kong. As explained in Chapter 4, the society in the 1980s had also transformed itself as Hong Kong advanced into being an international financial and business centre. Coupled with this were the improvements in living standard and education opportunity, the growing proportion of the local-born population, and the emergence of the new middle-class of professionals.

The "induced" expectation and aspiration of the "Hong Kong people governing Hong Kong through democratic means" at first ran high, but later diminished as Beijing's subsequent negative response to the political reform initiated by Britain, aiming at the institution of an independent and open legislature in the transitional period, became clear. Nevertheless, once the competitive elections have been put in place, whatever the proportion of seats returned by universal suffrage, the rules of the political game would be forced to change in the long run. Based upon the "supply" of institutional change in various political reform packages, there would be a "demand" on the existing political forces to adjust. The more power was released through competitive elections, the easier for the barrier of entry to be removed and the lower the threshold of representation would be possible, and thus, the stronger the pressure on the political forces to develop mass-oriented parties, or vice versa. Although the opportunity was there for the development of political groups or parties, the sudden introduction of the universal franchise and related political reforms had given no time for the pressure groups to penetrate deeply into society and to build-up their organizational strength. The condition was even worse because more and more middle-class professionals decided to emigrate, especially after the Tiananmen Incident in 1989. The middle-class professionals played the leadership role in the democratic movement elsewhere, but, in the case of Hong Kong, their participation was minimal. Even for those who participated actively, some of them were lacking the will to fight in the face of tremendous Chinese pressure. Added to this was the inexperience of the political activists that led to internal divisions and the adoption of a flawed strategy (So and Kwitko, 1990:388-94).

The development of political parties in Hong Kong was prone to China's and Britain's influence and pressure. As mentioned before, the sceptical attitude of Beijing leaders towards political reforms since the mid-1980s imposed hurdles on the road of democratization; they also intervened in local politics by siding with the conservatives in Hong Kong. The strategic move to side with the conservatives was dictated by their promise of "one country, two systems" and "Hong Kong people governing Hong Kong". Under these circumstances, any move to mobilize the local communists or the leftists openly would be interpreted as a move to shatter the promise of "Hong Kong people governing Hong Kong"; and any move that would put the privileges of the established elites at risk would drive away the business tycoons whose contributions were very vital to the economic prosperity of Hong Kong. It was logical for the Beijing leaders to seek a trustworthy alliance that would be under their reach and prone to their pressure in the transitional period. As illustrated in Chapter 3, the Chinese government at first adopted a more positive attitude towards democratization before the conclusion of the Sino-British Joint Declaration in late 1984 so as to soften the resistance of Hong Kong people, but changed gradually to a tougher one and later even sided with the conservatives. Being supported by the Chinese government, the conservatives mobilized themselves to form political groups in order to counter the emergence of the grass-roots democrats. Nevertheless, the conservatives were not a homogenous force in terms of status and location in the political establishment, let alone in their conflicting economic interests. Thus, the conservatives failed to produce a unified political group in the period under study, as demonstrated later in this section.

On the British side, its traditional co-opted partners in Hong Kong were those who came from the big business firms and the wealthy families. This state of affairs was challenged by the rise of the new middle-class in the 1970s and the 1997 issue in the 1980s. The established elites were firstly on good terms with the British-Hong Kong government before 1985, but later distanced themselves gradually from it because China would become the boss after the reversion of sovereignty in 1997. This was especially the case when Britain was at odds with China. In order to boost its legitimacy in the transitional period, Britain had to co-opt those who could represent the mass public through the introduction of popular elections. The pace of such reforms would not be so bold so as to alienate the established elites and not to overload the government when the demands from society grew significantly once the popular elections were in place. To strike the delicate balance was not an easy job, especially in the turbulent environment of the late transitional period. So, the British and Hong Kong governments were torn by the conflicting demands from the established elites and the democrats, as seen in the 1987 review, let alone the pressure from China. Thus, the prime concern of the British and Hong Kong governments was to ensure the smooth transfer of power.

In the context of the 1980s, three stages of party development could be differentiated. First, the political groups formed between 1982-85 appeared to respond to the upsurge of the 1997 issue as well as the introduction of universal suffrage to the newly formed consultative DBs. Given the uncertainty of Hong Kong's political future and the limited power enjoyed by the DB members, the incentives to form political groups were, thus, not large enough. As recorded in the following section, the political groups formed in this period were largely organized by social activists, who played an active role in the pressure group politics of the 1970s. Little effort to organize from the established elites was recorded. Election coalitions also appeared, but they only enjoyed a very short life span.

Second, in anticipation of the reform of the central government as the result of the Sino-British Joint Declaration and the subsequent political row over the pace and direction of democratization in the 1987 Review and the drafting of the Basic Law, the established elites had begun to mobilize. Furthermore, the revision of the Beijing's negative attitude towards party politics to a more positive one had given a push to group formation and mobilization. As mentioned before, some groups formed in this period appeared to have blessings from Britain and China, like the Progressive Hong Kong Society (PHKS). Besides, the political groups formed by social campaigners in the previous stage had consolidated by merging with each other.

Third, from 1989 onwards, political events outside Hong Kong gave a further push to party formation. The Tiananmen Incident in 1989 served as a mobilizer, with the Hong Kong public reacting to seek a faster pace of democratization. Before the incident, most of the mobilization efforts by the concerned political groups relied heavily on personal networks and thus their penetration into the society was very limited. The outburst of emotional feeling during the Tiananmen Incident had provided an opportunity for the concerned political forces, especially the democrats, to extend their networks of mobilization on a bigger scale. In addition, the political structure of the future HKSAR was finalized as the Basic Law was promulgated in early 1990 and the increase in popularly-elected seats from 10 to 18 in the 1991 LegCo elections. The arrival of Christopher Patten as the Governor of Hong Kong in 1992 and his political reform package gave a further push for democratization and politicization of the Hong Kong society. All these developments, in one way or another, provided the social and political impetus for consolidating the existing political groups.

The Pre-Mobilization Stage, 1982-85

During the period 1982-85, numerous political groups declared their formation. Shortly after the visit of Margaret Thatcher to Beijing in late 1982, two "political discussion groups"[6] had come into being--the New Hong Kong Society (NHKS) and the Meeting Point (MP). Probably, these two groups were the first to accept the return of Hong Kong to China and the idea of "Hong Kong people governing Hong Kong through democratic means" after 1997. The NHKS, comprising mainly young graduates who had recently graduated in the early 1980s, offered a detailed plan to implement the idea of "Hong Kong people governing Hong Kong" in early 1983 and had discussed it with the officials of the State Council's Hong Kong and Macau Affairs Office. The NHKS's stance towards the future of Hong Kong might be summarized as: "reunion, self-rule, democracy, and reform" (New Hong Kong Society, 1983:2).

Although declaring "the identification with the Chinese nation not equivalent to the identification with any existing regime or political party", the MP had still failed to escape the "pro-Beijing" label as it strongly supported Beijing's cause in restoring Hong Kong sovereignty after 1997. Their stance was not in line with the political mood of the time when the Sino-British negotiation had just started in late 1982. Not only championing the value of reunion with China, the MP had also demanded a reform of the colonial political system so as to pave the way for subsequent democratic self-rule after 1997. In addition, the MP also advocated social reform. According to Yeung Sum,[7] the then vice-chairman of the MP, "The present [social] situation in Hongkong is unequal and unreasonable. That's why we cannot accept that the status quo should remain" (*SCMP*, 19 October 1982). And he later also argued that: "the aspirations of this generation is not going to be met by the existing system which has been accepted in the past" (*HKS*, 10 February 1983). The group's faith and principles rested on the New Three Principles of the People, that is nationalism, democracy, and people's livelihood.[8] This group comprised mainly of young academics and social workers who graduated from local universities in the 1970s; many of them had been student activists during their university years.

The Hong Kong Affairs Society (HKAS) was formed in February 1984 and mainly comprised of professionals and academics who graduated in the late 1960s and early 1970s. The HKAS had highlighted its role of "think tank" by focusing its activities on research and study of government and social policies which, in return, could enhance citizens' political awareness and provide an analytical framework for policy judgement. In addition, the HKAS had also organized public seminars and invited speakers of different viewpoints to exchange ideas and to share their views. Though it had facilitated the flow of ideas and narrowed the misunderstanding among different walks of life, this kind of approach was criticized as too academic (Yip, 1984:42; *Pai Shing*, 84, 16 November 1984:7).

Quite contrary to the research-oriented HKAS, the Hong Kong People's Association, formed in November 1984, had openly declared that "we shall encourage Hongkong people to participate in public affairs and exercise their right to vote" and "we shall support able men and women to stand for election". The group felt that discussion in an age of rapid political transformation was not enough and they, therefore, stressed the importance of participation. Although stressing active participation, the Hong Kong People's Association did not regard itself as a political party. The initial proposers of the group had included many respected people, like Lo King-man, the vice-president of the Hong Kong Polytechnic; Anthony Neoh, a barrister; Luk Yan-lung, an historian; Wong Siu-lun and Lee Ming-kwan, both of them sociologists; Vincent Ko, District Board member; and so on (*SCMP*, 4 December 1984; Yip, 1984:40-1).

The social composition of the above-mentioned political groups was quite homogenous in the sense that they were mainly came from the middle-class strata and had received university education elsewhere. The NHKS and the MP were more inclined to uphold the principle of nationalism and regarded the reunion with China as compatible with the development of democratic government in Hong Kong. Their romantic nationalist feeling led them to minimize the incompatibility of an authoritarian communist state and democratic government. As for the HKAS and the Hong Kong People's Association, they tended to be concerned more with practical social problems and emphasized the importance of participation. Comparatively speaking, the members of the HKAS and the Hong Kong People's Association were more "establishment" than those of the MP and the NHKS.

In this period, there was no effort made by the established or business elites to get organized. One possible explanation for this condition could be the uncertainty of how much political power would be devolved and the pace of that devolution, and their privileged access anyway to the government structure. The opportunity cost of forming political groups was, thus, very high. Understandably, they would adopt a wait-and-see attitude until the dust settled, i.e. the political settlement of Hong Kong by the then on-going Sino-British negotiations.

This low profile attitude also applied to the leftists, but for different reasons (Ng, 1985:46-8). Their cautious approach reflected the sensitive situation of Hong Kong. First, Hong Kong people had still not accepted the ways the leftists employed in the struggle with the British-Hong Kong government during the 1967 riots. Any active mobilization of the leftists had, in one way or another, stirred up the fear of the local community and impaired their confidence. Second, the promise of "Hong Kong people governing Hong Kong" seemed to inhibit the leftists from engaging actively and openly in forming political groups. Otherwise, the offer of self-government by the Hong Kong people after 1997 would be self-defeating.

Nevertheless, the leftist Federation of Trade Unions (FTU) had encouraged its members to register and vote in the 1985 DBs elections (*SCMP*, 24 May 1984). Later, the member unions of the FTU had publicly supported 10 candidates to run in the 1985 DBs elections (*Sing Tao Jih Pao*, 14 February 1985). Five were elected; but, according to Albert C.C. Lam, the then Deputy Regional Secretary (Hong Kong and Kowloon), there were another 45 elected candidates (out of total 237) with a pro-Beijing background or stance (Leung, 1985:4; Cheung, 1985:21).

Moreover, an umbrella organization called the New Territories Association of Societies (NTAS) had been formed in April 1985. The group was headed by a local NPC member, Lee Lin-sang, and its member organizations were comprised primarily of rural community groups. Influential Heung Yee Kuk members and prominent rural leaders, such as

Lau Wong-fat, Chan Yat-sun and Wong Yuen-cheung, were invited to serve as honorary presidents. The group declared that it would not nominate candidates in future elections, but would rather give support to individual members (*SCMP*, 19 April 1985).

As indicated before, the rightists had in the past been a significant player in Hong Kong politics, but then declined significantly. Nevertheless, the Nationalist government has maintained a certain level of political involvement in local politics. In the 1985 District Board elections, the Taipei authority had claimed that 53 "liberal anti-communist" persons had been elected; but according to Hong Kong government sources, only 5 elected DB members had a pro-Taipei background (Cheung, 1985:20; Leung, 1985:4). Nevertheless, the rightists managed to return one LegCo member in the functional constituency of labour in the period of 1985-1995.

Election coalitions had appeared just shortly before the 1985 District Board elections. The "Group of 12" in the Central and Western District had aimed to take all the elected seats in the relevant constituency. This group had involved members from the HKO, the HKAS, the Hong Kong People's Association and the MP; but they claimed that their involvement was in an individual capacity. This might be interpreted as a lack of consensus within each of these political groups over their respective role and positioning in the ever-changing political system. Also in the list of members was Carl Tong, the then appointed LegCo member (*SCMP*, 29 December 1984 and 15 February 1985).

Another ad hoc election coalition was formed in the Eastern District with 12 serving DB members and an appointed LegCo member, Chan Ying-lun. This group seemed to gain support from the North Point Kaifong Association, mutual aid committees and owners' corporations (*HKS*, 3 January 1985). Quite contrary to the above coalitions that were based on a single district, a group of 17 young people had grouped together to seek election in different districts. This coalition had drawn its members from political groups, like the NHKS and the Public Policy Research Centre, and local concerned groups on people's livelihood. And they pledged to play a role in the democratization process during the transitional period (*SCMP*, 2 January 1985).

By the time of the 1985 DBs elections, most of the above-mentioned political groups and coalitions had, in one way or another, supported or nominated their members to run in the elections. As shown in Table 5.2, the success rate of candidates with group backing was quite high. Except those of the RCHK and the HKCA, the rate ranged from 80% to 100%.

The rather good performance of group-backed candidates seemed to have a demonstration effect on other political activists. But the uncertainty of the political structure of the future HKSAR, which was still waiting to be framed at the time, had made it difficult for political activists to chart their path of advancement in the power structure. The limited powers of the DBs and the UrbCo had not provided enough incentive for those who had already occupied the key position in the political structure, like the appointed non-official members in the ExCo and the LegCo, or for those who had already acquired prominent status in their own career, to participate. Whether to join the electoral competition or to wait for government appointment would be up to individual's choice, but indeed it was a hard choice.

Table 5.2   Performance of Political Groups in 1985 District Boards Elections

Group Name	Nominations	Elected	%
Hong Kong People's Association	8	8	100.0
Meeting Point	4	4	100.0
Hong Kong Affairs Society	3	3	100.0
Eastern Coalition	11	11	100.0
Group of 12	12	10	91.7
Hong Kong People's Council on Public Housing Policy	11	9	81.8
Professional Teachers' Union	30	24	80.0
Reform Club of Hong Kong	33	17	56.7
Hong Kong Civic Association	54	21	36.4

* The above figure does not reflect the fact that some candidates received support from more than one group.

Source: Leung Chun-man, "The Criteria of Appointing District Boards Members and the Training of Leaders Capable for Governing Hong Kong: An Interview with Mr Albert C.C. Lam," (in Chinese) *Hong Kong Economic Journal Monthly* 97 (1985):4-6.

The Mobilization Stage, 1985-1989

This stage of development differed from the previous one in several aspects. First of all, the political future of Hong Kong was fixed after Britain and China reached an agreement in late 1984. The Sino-British Joint Declaration signified not only the reversion of sovereignty from Britain to China, but also the eventual power devolution as implied in the Joint Declaration, i.e. the introduction of popular elections to the LegCo and possibly the Chief Executive. Second, the established elites began their mobilization drive to form political groups because the then existing political recruitment method had to change from exclusive appointment to elections. Third, the resistant attitude of the Chinese government towards party politics had started to be revised to a more accommodating one in late 1988. This helped to remove the major hurdle to forming political groups. Fourth, the Daya Bay anti-nuclear movements in 1986, the 1987 political review, and the drafting of the Basic Law from late 1985 onwards had, in one way or another, stimulated the alignment of political forces and exposed the whole society to the immense mobilization efforts of the concerned political forces.

Shortly after the signing of the Sino-British Joint Declaration in December 1984, four more political groups declared their formation in this period: the Progressive Hong Kong Society (PHKS, February 1985), the Association of Democracy and Justice (ADJ, April 1985), the Hong Kong Association for Democracy and People's Livelihood (HKADPL, October 1987), and the New Hong Kong Alliance (NHKA, May 1989). As examined in the following paragraphs, the PHKS and the NHKA were formed by prominent figures from the political and economic establishments whose political outlook was quite conservative, while the ADJ and the HKADPL were led by the active social activists who had championed social justice since the 1970s. Besides, the PHKS and the NHKA stood for the interests of the business sector and wanted to maintain the status quo. The ADJ and the HKADPL represented the grass-roots' interests and worked towards the coming of representative government.

After planning for six months in the dark and reportedly having London's and Beijing's understanding, Maria Tam, a heavy-weight political figure who had maintained good ties with local community leaders and was then concurrently ExCo, LegCo, UrbCo and DB member, and later also Basic Law drafter, had declared the formation of the Progressive Hong Kong Society (PHKS) in March 1985 with Philip Kwok of the Wing On Group as vice-chairman (Au Yung, 1985:14-6, 88). The PHKS was different from the above-mentioned groups because it aimed to build-up a cross-sector political group and attempted to integrate the loosely knit political forces of the establishment. Probably, this was the first time in Hong Kong history that the established elites had engaged overtly to form a political group. The formation of the PHKS also represented their awareness of the inevitable reform of the then rather closed political structure. It enlisted support from a variety of social sectors as was well reflected in its promoters' list. Among them were: Cheung Yan-lung, LegCo member and prominent rural leaders; Gerry Forsgate, vice-chairman of the UrbCo; Raymond Wu, president of the Medical Association; Kan Fook-yee, chairman of the Hong Kong Institute of Land Surveyors; Leung Chun-ying, a chartered estate surveyor; Vincent Lo, Kenneth Fung, Victor Fung, Veronica Wu and J.K. Lee, entrepreneurs and offspring of renowned families; Lam Chak-piu and Tong Kam-biu, UrbCo members and social activists; Chan Pun, Lee Fung-ying and Lee Kai-ming, leaders of the Federation of Hong Kong and Kowloon Labour Unions; Wong Wai-hung, chairman of the Federation of the Civil Service Unions; Edward Chen, director of Hong Kong University's Centre of Asian Studies; and others (*HKS*, 27 March 1985). Denis Bray, former Secretary for Home Affairs, reportedly joined the group (*SCMP*, 15 May 1985).

Although not regarding itself as a political party because of the sensitivity of the term in Hong Kong society and the resistant attitude of the Beijing government towards party development in Hong Kong in mid-1980s, the PHKS was *de facto* the most influential and powerful combination of individuals with an eye on the power vacuum left behind in the power devolution process. Echoing the PHKS's stated aims "To encourage and support its members to take part in the administration of public affairs in Hongkong", Tam had personally supported 30 candidates in the 1985 DB elections, of which 27 were elected (*SCMP*, 10 and 16 March 1985). It was also reported that the PHKS had over 80 members serving in major government advisory bodies, including 5 LegCo members, 8 municipal council members and 49 DB members in late 1988. In addition, 5 members had served in the Basic Law Consultative Committee and another 2 in the Basic Law Drafting Committee (*SCMP*, 3 December 1988; *HKS*, 28 January 1989). Attempts to enlist support from other political groups, like the MP, the HKAS and the HKCA, were also tried (*SCMP*, 30 March and 10 May 1985).

Some leaders of the rival democratic camp, such as Lo Lung-kwong, Ding Lik-kiu, and Lau Chin-shek, had given birth to the ADJ in mid-1985. This was the first step for the various pressure groups to maximize their resources and effectiveness for political participation. As Ding, a veteran democratic reformer who had led an ad hoc delegation to London to ask for the reform of the colonial political structure in 1984, made clear, "There will be fewer pressure groups in their conventional form. Future pressure group leaders are bound to work within the system itself instead of as outside critics of Government policies" and "It's time to go into politics and exert direct influence on Government policies". The ADJ, therefore, was an election-oriented association aimed "at promoting the spirit of democracy and social justice while upholding the prosperity and stability in Hongkong" (*SCMP*, 6 April 1985).

The democrats had further organized and merged to form a bigger coalition after the forming of the ADJ. Several pressure groups, such as the ADJ, the NHKS, the Hong Kong People's Council on Public Housing Policy, the Society for Social Research, the Septenrio Academy, and the Sham Shui Po Concerned Group on People's Livelihood, had met together to discuss possible merger with each other. After several months of discussion and preparation, the HKADPL was formally established in October 1986 with Ding Lik-kiu as chairman, Fung Kin-kee and Lee Wing-tat as deputy chairmen. The significance of its formation was the integration of the grass-roots activists into a more organized and politically-oriented group. It also laid the foundation for subsequent development of the democrats.

The HKADPL had about 100 members including an UrbCo member, two RegCo members and 9 DB members at the time of founding. Among others, the HKADPL aimed "to advocate a rational distribution of social resources and to improve the quality of life of the lower and middle social strata" (*SCMP*, 30 April 1986; Cheng, 1989:13). The group believed that "People's livelihood will not be improved without democratic and equal participation in political life" (*HKS*, 27 October 1986). Thus, they actively worked with other democrats in demanding the introduction of popular elections to the LegCo in 1988 and the adoption of the "190 Proposal" in the still-drafting Basic Law. Furthermore, the democratic groups of the HKAS, the MP, and the HKADPL had altogether supported 75 candidates, over 30% of the total (N=264), in the 1988 DB elections (Kwan, 1988:6-7). The first two democratic groups had only supported 7 candidates in 1985 DB elections (see Table 5.2).

In contrast, some younger business and social figures, like LegCo members Allen Lee, Stephen Cheong and Selina Chow, had adopted a cautious approach. They represented the "liberal" wing within the established elites whose judgement on political group formation differed from those of the PHKS. They were more inclined to form a political party and were the more "liberal" in their outlook among the established elites in early 1980s. Their idea of forming a political party was said to have developed in May 1983 when Lee had led a delegation of young professionals to Beijing. The leaders of the delegation formed the backbone of the planned party. Also involved in the plan were three LegCo members: Chan Ying-lun, Rita Fan and Martin Lee. Their plan did not materialize at this period. This was partly due to their lack of first hand information on the current political development and this coloured their judgement. The information flow was blocked because none of them were either ExCo members or Basic Law drafters in this period, except Martin Lee who actually had broken away from this clique at the very beginning of the Basic Law drafting process and joined hands with the democrats because of the clique's non-action orientation to party-building. As a result, they decided to adopt a wait-and-see attitude and stressed the importance of timing and political climate in forming a party. As a result, Cheong said that they wanted "to wait for the decision on the Basic Law Drafting Committee and Joint Liaison Group" because "We don't want to be groping in the dark" (*SCMP*, 31 March 1985).

Given that Xu Jiatun, the then Director of the Hong Kong Branch of the NCNA, had overtly aired his disapproval of constitutional reforms in the transitional period in late 1985, their plan to form a political party was therefore given up. When announcing the decision to shelve the plan temporarily until the 1987 political review, Allen Lee was quoted as saying: "There was Chinese resistance on any local party formation and going opposite to China is not very wise". And he further added that "It's still too early to form a party because we don't know the outcome of the 1987 review" and "It won't be too late to organise one then when direct elections are to be introduced" (*HKS*, 29 December 1985; *SCMP*, 30 December 1985).

Regarding the trend of forming political groups in early 1985, the Hong Kong government seemed to hold an encouraging attitude and welcomed the move. Edward Youde, the then Hong Kong Governor, had reportedly regarded the trend of party formation as a natural development and said "Don't get stuck with the labels (of party), look at the objectives". He further added that those groups formed at the time had the objective of assisting in maintaining the stability and prosperity of Hong Kong. Chung Sze-yuen, the then senior member of the ExCo, also recorded his acceptance of political parties and said: "When we talk about democracy, we cannot avoid that people have different views and therefore we cannot avoid that people will form parties" (*SCMP*, 11 April 1985).

But Beijing seemed not to favour the introduction of party politics in Hong Kong. Chinese officials voiced their opposition to party politics on several occasions. Following the warning of Xu Jiatun in late 1985, Lu Ping, the then Secretary-General of HKMAO, had reportedly told a group of LegCo members that Hong Kong could not and should not have its own political party (*HKS*, 1 February 1986). When touching on the issue of CCP activities in Hong Kong, Li Hou, the then deputy-director of the HKMAO, had said: "If other political parties have already been set up, then I can't say whether the Chinese Communist Party members would act openly or not" (*SCMP*, 3 June 1986).

The signal was clear, as expounded in the SCMP's editorial (4 June 1986) that "Hong Kong could be playing with fire if party politics were allowed to develop in the future Special Administrative Region". The editorial went on:

> This is the first time that China has set down a clear line on party politics. Hongkong must realise that politics could never develop here on traditional Western party line by excluding the Communist Party. . . . The course towards Westminster-style politics would mean an open invitation for politicking of a potentially destructive kind, in the sense that struggles for the seat of government with the certain (and only) winner being the Communist Party could extinguish the spirit of the Joint Declaration, which calls for Hongkong people ruling Hongkong. . . . Those who espouse the cause of party government should be admired for their direct and broad-minded approach to representative politics. But they would be wise to consider whether such politicking would serve exclusively Hongkong interests.

But Beijing's negative attitude towards party politics seemed to soften in late 1988. It seemed that China had came to see the inevitability of having organizational support once the popular elections were put in place. In response to whether the political party would have a bad influence on the future political structure, Li Hou said the forming of political organizations was inevitable and would be further developed as Hong Kong would have elections, especially popular elections. He also employed intentionally the term "political organization" instead of "political party" as he had objected to the term in June 1986 (*Ta Kung Pao*,

23 November 1988). By using the term "political organization", China seemed to convey the message that political organizations in Hong Kong would not be allowed to become the ruling party of the HKSAR, and thus, avoided the usage of the term "political party" which may have the meaning of ruling in Western democratic polities. In January 1989, Xu Jiatun had conveyed his view to political activists in Hong Kong that they were free to form political organizations. This move seemed to give tacit approval for the formation of political parties (*HKS*, 27 January 1989). Later, Xu had reportedly qualified his message by stating that political parties formed in Hong Kong would be prohibited from advocating the independence of Hong Kong or engaging in anti-communist activities (*HKS*, 16 February 1989). This might be interpreted as the no-go areas that the Chinese government would not tolerate. That means the development and presence of political parties in Hong Kong would not threaten the socialist system and communist rule in China. But the developments after the Tiananmen Incident in 1989 had invaded these no-go areas and had, thus, strained Sino-Hong Kong relations.

Being relieved from the pains of party-phobia, various political forces once again embarked on the road of party-building. At least four groups of political activists were on their way in late December 1988 and early 1989. Their major proposers were: Stephen Cheong Kam-chuen, Martin Lee, Lo Tak-shing, and Lau Chin-shek and Cheung Man-kwong. First of all, Cheong, "Group of 89" member, had revived Allen Lee's abortive party plan in December 1988. The core members were, more or less, the same as those of 1985, except Allen Lee and Martin Lee (*SCMP*, 3 December 1988). It was believed that the political status of Allen Lee, the then senior member of the LegCo, had prevented him from overtly participating in the plan. Allen Lee had been the key contender against Maria Tam within the political establishment and this prevented him from merging with the PHKS or coordinating to form a new group.

Second, because of contrasting attitudes towards popular elections and political reforms with Allen Lee's group since 1985, Martin Lee, the then LegCo member and Basic Law drafter, had come out with his own party plan announced in late December 1988 (*SCMP*, 31 December 1988). Martin Lee had been a vocal democracy reformer and a campaigner against undue Chinese interference in the Basic Law drafting process. He revealed that he would opt either to start a new party or merge with some or all of the following political groups to form a new one: the Joint Committee for Promotion of Democratic Government, the MP, the HKAS, and the HKADPL. At the same time, the "Big Three" democratic groups of the

MP, the HKAS and the HKADPL had also tried to hammer out a merger plan (*HKS*, 7 January 1989).

Third, Lo Tak-shing,[9] a vice-chairman of the BLCC and former ExCo and LegCo member, was said to have discussed with some of the "Group of 89" members, like Philip Kwok, Raymond Wu, and Kan Fook-yee, the possibility of forming a party in early March 1989. Maria Tam, chairwoman of the PHKS, was also reportedly involved.

Fourth, Lau Chin-shek of the HKCIC and Cheung Man-kwong of the HKPTU had engaged in forming a bigger "democratic league" in March 1989. Being frustrated by the slow progress of the "Big Three" merger plan and the reach of such party if it succeeded, the two proposed to develop "a political party with strong grass-roots support" with membership between 100,000 and half-a-million (*SCMP*, 21 March 1989).

Among the above political forces, only Lo's group had transformed its plan into action before the Tiananmen Incident in June 1989. The NHKA was formally established in May aiming "to work for the resolution or compromise of conflicting interests". The move had signified the first big step in formal party-building by the conservative clique amongst the established elites. But the leaders of the PHKS, like Maria Tam, did not join the NHKA. One of the reasons advanced by Tam for not joining was the incompatibility of the NHKA's aim at influencing government policies and her own role as ExCo member (*Oriental Daily News*, 9 March 1989:3). It was believed that Tam was still involved in it informally. The division of labour between Lo and Tam had been described as: " T.S. [Lo] has got the brains and Maria [Tam] is the worker ant--it's a perfect match" (*SCMP*, 4 March 1989:15). Nevertheless, the NHKA's general committee had 32 members, of whom 21 were from the "Group of 89" and 10 from the PHKS, and at least 6 belonged to both "Group of 89" and the PHKS. In order to clear away the impression of being led by a single leader, the NHKA decided to elect an honorary secretary instead of a chairman. Lo Tak-shing, was elected honorary secretary, LegCo member Peter Wong Hong-yuen as treasurer, Veronica Wu and Raymond Wu as press secretaries, and UrbCo member Pao Ping-wing as recruitment officer (*HKS* and *SCMP*, 2 May 1989).

The Consolidation Stage, 1989-Present

The Democrats The suppression of the democratic movement in June 1989 and the subsequent labelling of Hong Kong as a "subversive" base by the Chinese government had created a confidence crisis and intense concern about China's and Hong Kong's future. As mentioned in Chapter 3, the whole society of Hong Kong was shocked by the Tiananmen Incident and the democrats had become deeply engaged in supporting the democratic movement in Beijing. The Hong Kong Alliance in Support of the Patriotic Democratic Movement in China (HKASPDMC) was formed under the leadership of prominent democratic figures, Szeto Wah and Martin Lee, right after the military crackdown in Beijing. By organizing rallies and a donation campaign, and participating in smuggling the key leaders of the Chinese democratic movement out of mainland China, the democrats became the prime target of Chinese verbal attacks because the no-go areas of party development, as mentioned earlier in this chapter, set by the Beijing government had been invaded by the democrats. Reinforced by the breakdown of the Soviet Union and the liberalization of Eastern Europe in late 1989, the then Beijing leadership was desperately worried about its regime security, the possible peaceful evolution from within, and the "subversive" role of Hong Kong.

As a result, the party-building efforts cooled down because some political activists began to adopt a low-profile attitude at the time. As one democrat recorded there was difficulty in having incumbent Municipal Councils and DB members seek re-election in 1991 elections (*SCMP*, 3 September 1989). The party-building efforts also suffered from the exodus of the middle-class, like the professionals, intellectuals, social workers, and so on. An estimated 62,000 Hong Kong people emigrated to overseas in 1990. Nevertheless, the June 1989 events had stimulated the passive Hong Kong people to think afresh about their destiny which had long been controlled by others and about the closeness of their relationship with China.

The Tiananmen Incident, ironically, initially delayed the emergence of a budding territory-wide party system which had gone through nearly ten years of alignment, dealignment and realignment by the various political forces and groupings. But, once the situation had become stable in late 1989, the trend to form political groups was restored. On the democrat side, their prominent role played in supporting the democratic movement in China had further reinforced their image and popularity among the Hong Kong people. But, on the other hand, their relationship with the Chinese government had totally deteriorated as the democrats had condemned the way the Chinese government suppressed the democratic movement.

The official *People's Daily* carried a commentary entitled "No Sabotage of the One Country, Two Systems Policy Tolerable" on 21 July 1989, issuing a strongly worded warning to those democrats who played a significant role in supporting the democratic movement in China, accusing them of engaging in subversive activities, and condemning them for planning to form a political party in Hong Kong. Because of such developments, the idea of forming a united democratic party seemed to be blocked by the Chinese hostility towards it and the very survival of that party after 1997. The China factor coincided with the unresolved conflicts over ideological orientation and the nature and timing of the new party among key participants which had contributed to the slow progress of forming a new democratic party (*SCMP*, 6 August 1989; Wong, 1990; Lo, 1990:38-9). In addition, self-centred calculation also played a role. To quote Ding Lik-kiu's words, "Some of the liberals [democrats] say the time is not ripe for political parties. Others are reluctant to give up their hard won identities for the sake of a bigger group" (*HKS*, 15 May 1989). Because of such differences, the MP and the HKADPL later opted not to join the new democratic party--the United Democrats of Hong Kong (UDHK), and retained their separate group labels and identities. Nevertheless, some members of these two groups, like Yeung Sum, did join the new democratic group.

Although the pressure from China was felt, the democrats did manage to form a new political organization, though still not calling itself a political party, with their decision not to dissolve other democratic groups. The UDHK seemed to be taking shape in late 1989 and was formally established in April 1990 with about 210 founding members (*Contemporary*, 30 December 1989:29-30). The UDHK was chaired by Martin Lee with Yeung Sum of the MP and Albert Ho of the HKAS as vice-chairmen at the time of founding. Members mainly comprised professionals, lawyers, social workers, educationalists, and so on. Both the Hong Kong government and NCNA's officials were invited to attend the founding ceremony but they were not present. It was because China regarded some leaders of the UDHK as "subversive" and thus the Hong Kong government officials wanted to distance themselves from the conflict. Because of the overlapping leadership with the HKASPDMC, the UDHK stressed in its founding declaration that:

> The UDHK, being a local political organisation, will focus its attention on local affairs. It will not seek to participate or be involved in the politics of the Central People's government or of other regions in the People's Republic of China.

The intentional separation of the HKASPDMC and the UDHK did not bear fruit because the Chinese government treated these two groups as if there was no difference between them.

While the negotiation among "core" democratic groups and individuals was in progress, the Hong Kong Democratic Foundation (HKDF), first initiated by LegCo member Jimmy McGregor and subsequently chaired by LegCo member Leong Che-hung, declared its formation in October 1989 with support from leading foreign businessmen, like Hari Hariela, Ian Tomlin, Matthew Oram and Kewlram Sital (*SCMP*, 21 October 1989). Martin Lee was reportedly involved in the plan but later opted not to play an active role in the HKDF because he was deeply involved himself in a party bid with the "Big Three" and other leading democrats. The HKDF could be viewed as the conservative clique of the democratic forces. Their business interests seemed to prevent their merger with the grass-roots oriented democrats, and the adoption of confrontational attitude towards China. In its manifesto, the HKDF regarded itself as "an independent, multi-racial, multi-cultural political organisation . . . committed to developing a pluralistic democracy in Hong Kong" and it aimed "to shape government policy in order to make Hong Kong a more open, progressive society in which all people can share the fruits of its success".[10] With the proliferation of democratic parties after 1991, the HKDF chooses to play the role of a "political discussion group".

With the landslide victory of the joint ticket of the UDHK and the MP in the 1991 LegCo popular elections (for details, refer to Chapter 6), the democrats had a sizeable presence in the LegCo for the first time in Hong Kong political history. The effort of building a democratic alliance materialized in 1994 by the merger of the UDHK and the MP to form the Democratic Party (DP). The HKADPL was kept in the dark when the merger was under deliberation but was invited to join after the plan was finalized. Understandably, the core members of the HKADPL refused to join the new party and maintained a separate group identity. Other than the reasons mentioned above that separated them, one more reason that kept them apart was their split over the proper attitude towards the Beijing government in the late transitional period. While the DP insisted on adopting an uncompromising approach, the HKADPL adopted an accommodating attitude towards the Beijing government.

In the context of fighting for more popularly-elected seats in the LegCo, some democrats were frustrated by the mainstream democrats not asking for a full popularly-elected LegCo when the Patten's reform bill was debated in the LegCo in 1994. The frustrated democrats formed the

United Ants (UA) after the LegCo debate and later developed into a political group called Frontier in 1996. The Frontier may be regarded as a radical wing of the democrats as they are fighting for a quicker pace of democratization and are adopting an even more uncompromising attitude towards the Beijing government than the DP.

The Conservatives On the conservative side, a split emerged as the NHKA proposed to adopt the "Bicameral Model" in the future HKSAR's legislature in late August 1989 (*SCMP*, 28 August 1989). This move, as mentioned in Chapter 3, had caused a head-on confrontation with the supporters of the "4-4-2 Model", which was supported by such members of the "Group of 89", like Vincent Lo. Five pro-Beijing members of the NHKA, including Lo Tak-shing, had even tried to block the adoption of the "4-4-2 Model" by the "Group of 89" as a compromise with the democrats and the moderates. One of them reportedly concluded that the compromise "is aimed at using democracy to resist China" through the early introduction of universal suffrage (*SCMP*, 19 and 20 September 1989). Subsequently, some key members, such as Peter Wong Hong-yuen, Raymond Wu, Veronica Wu, and Philip Kwok, quit the NHKA in early 1990 (*SCMP*, 6 January 1990).

Because of this split, the conservative camp needed to develop another political group to prepare for the 1991 elections. The backbone of the planned group mainly comprised members from the PHKS and the "Group of 89", like Maria Tam, Hu Fa-kuang (former appointed LegCo member), Raymond Wu and Philip Kwok. Maria Tam was believed to be acting as a locomotive of the planned group. The group appeared to have difficulty in attracting prominent businessmen to join. Her rivals, Allen Lee, Stephen Cheong and Vincent Lo had, in one way or another, showed that they would not join the group (*Pai Shing*, 16 November 1990:34). The planned group further suffered from the charge of Tam's alleged conflict of interest and her reportedly censoring a reporter tracing her case in mid-1990.[11] The accusation not only damaged her public image but also hampered her coalition-building efforts for the planned group (Tang, 1993:283-4).

Tam had been regarded as "a political penny stock broker" who appeared to enjoy trust and acceptance from both the Beijing and the Hong Kong governments (Tang, 1993:269). She had engaged in bridging the "territorial conservatives" of the big businessmen and the "local conservatives" of community leaders and attempted to consolidate an influential conservative party so as to counter the surge of the democrats after the mid-1980s (Tang, 1993:280-1). Because of her important role in the party-building drive, the outbreak of the scandal had contributed to the low acceptance of the planned group by the mass public. Nevertheless, the planned group had gone through the crisis and formally declared the formation of the Liberal Democratic Federation (LDF) in November 1990 with Hu Fa-kuang as chairman, Maria Tam and Philip Kwok as vice-chairpersons. The LDF's members were recruited mainly from the business community, professionals and local community leaders.

The group led by Allen Lee and Stephen Cheong Kam-chuen did not manage to form a mass party before the 1991 LegCo elections. One of the reasons was the transformation of this group into a close government coalition after the downfall of Maria Tam in 1990. The government had, thus, relied on this group to guard against the expected surge of the democrats in the LegCo after 1991 popular elections. Under the leadership of Allen Lee, the Cooperative Resources Centre (CRC) was formed after the 1991 LegCo elections and comprised mainly the appointed members of the ExCo and the LegCo. In fact, the CRC became the pro-government force in the LegCo. Because of the arrival of the new Governor Christopher Patten and the subsequent "resignation" of the CRC's members from the ExCo in 1992, and the definite abolishment of the LegCo's appointed seats in 1995, the CRC was forced to develop a mass-oriented political party. As a result, the CRC was transformed into the Liberal Party (LP) in early 1993. Being a pro-business conservative party, it surprised the political circle by naming itself a "political party". Although Allen Lee participated in the 1995 LegCo popular election and won, his colleagues have still concentrated their efforts in the functional constituency elections. His advocacy of participation in popular elections was further frustrated by his defeat in the 1998 LegCo popular elections by a narrow margin. Nevertheless, the LP did manage to return ten LegCo members (none are from popular elections) in the 1998 LegCo election.

With the blessing of the Beijing government, the pro-business Hong Kong Progressive Alliance (HKPA) was formed in 1994. Its members mostly come from the professionals, small businessmen, and local political leaders. Like the LP, the HKPA has tried to develop its strength in popular elections but the results have been very discouraging.

The Leftists Like the democrats, the leftists have long been committed to protecting and promoting working class interests and thus they have enjoyed a certain level of working class support. As mentioned before, the role of the leftists is quite difficult to play because (1) the Beijing government is very concerned with the likely pressure generated by the combined efforts of the leftists and the democrats to safeguard the working class and grass-roots interests, and their possible domination in the electoral market. As a result, Beijing believes that this would give rise to welfare expansion and cause harm to the economic prosperity of Hong Kong; and (2) if the leftists adopt a high profile in political participation, this may cast doubt on Beijing's promise of "Hong Kong people governing Hong Kong" for Hong Kong people would take it as a sign of the indirect participation of Beijing in Hong Kong domestic affairs.

The above factors are believed to have had a negative effect on whether the leftists should form a full-fledged political party and participate actively in the electoral game of the day. The landslide victory of the democrats in the 1991 LegCo popular elections raised alarms amongst the leftists about their vulnerability in the virgin electoral market and the possible loss of political influence in society. The institutional rationality of the popular election has dictated the leftists to get organized because the popular election has been established as the only game in town in distributing political power. The leftists have also come to know that the best way to contain the upsurge of the democrats is to compete with them in the popular electoral market, under which the CE and all the LegCo members will be ultimately returned as stipulated in the Basic Law.

Drawing support from the FTU and other local leftists, the Democratic Alliance for Betterment of Hong Kong (DAB) was established in 1992. In the founding declaration, the DAB declared that:

> ... [I]t is our common wish and aspiration to welcome the return of Hong Kong to China and to continue to stay in Hong Kong to build a better home after 1997 to realize the vision of "One Country, Two Systems" and "Hong Kong People Governing Hong Kong".
>
> . . . . .
>
> The objective of our political participation is to create for Hong Kong the best possible democratic system which represents the will of the citizens, monitor the government's work, protect citizens' basic rights, guarantee equality for all before the law and independence of the judiciary, and maintain an election system that is free and fair. We maintain that democratic developments should be in line with the actual needs of the circumstances, be advantageous to maintaining social stability and economic prosperity; we are in favour of gradual and orderly development of a democratic government with the ultimate aim that the Chief Executive and all members of the Legislative Council will be elected by universal suffrage.

The forming of the DAB signified the acceptance by the local leftists of the importance of election for the political life in Hong Kong as well as the possible toleration of party development by the Beijing government. As will be discussed in Chapter 6, the DAB has established itself as a viable player in both the electoral market and the LegCo. Although the DAB did not pass with flying colours in the 1995 LegCo popular election, it did manage to have 6 LegCo members after the election. With the change of the majority system to a proportional representation system in the 1998 LegCo popular elections, the DAB took the windfall from the system change and managed to return 5 LegCo members in the popular election.

One interesting observation concerning the dynamic relationship between the DAB and the Hong Kong government before and after 1997 can be noted. The DAB acted as an opposition force in the colonial era, but has been playing a pro-government role since 1997. This transformation signified (1) the lack of a government supporting party in the LegCo after 1997, and (2) the intimate relationship between the DAB and the HKSAR government renders the former an ideal partner for the latter in the post-1997 governing of Hong Kong. This strategic move of the DAB to side with the HKSAR government may neutralize the DAB's support from the working class and the grass-roots in the long run.

The Budding Party Market in the 1990s

After more than a decade of development, various political forces had, in one way or another, consolidated and gradually undergone an institutionalisation process sparked off by the political reforms in the mid-1980s. Three rival camps of political forces had been emerged: the conservatives, the leftists and the democrats. As shown in previous section, the conservatives comprised mainly the established elites and its allies in the local community. They were of the opinion that the unreformed political system before the 1980s had served Hong Kong well and why bother to change it. By siding with the Chinese government from the mid-1980s, the conservatives tried hard to scale down the pace and scope of democratization and thus, contain the growth of the democrats. Their reasons to adopt a resistant attitude towards political reforms were the possible loss of their privileges and exclusive access to political power and influence, and uneasiness at the projected growth of the tax burden as a result of the welfare approach of the democrats. They often hold a cooperative attitude towards Beijing for business reasons, and thus are labelled as "pro-Beijing". Their approach to change largely relied on the building of a patron-client network, in which the patrons (the established elites) and the clients (the local community leaders) were threaded together by power brokers or go-betweens. This had an advantage when forming a political group within a short period of time, but the lack of direct communication between the patrons and the clients, and the limited reach of the clients' personal network proved to be an ineffective way to mobilize support and to develop the cohesiveness of the group. Furthermore, the group would suffer if the power brokers lost his/her credibility in the public eye.

However, the conservatives have tried to build-up their support in the popular election since the 1991 LegCo elections by participation. A typical example was the joining of Allen Lee, the then chairman of the LP, in the 1995 LegCo popular elections. But the conservatives seem not to have a clear consensus and strong commitment to join the popular election. It is therefore not surprising to see that they have retreated somewhat in frustration with the popular electoral market as was the case after the defeat of Allen Lee in the 1998 LegCo popular elections.

On the democratic side, they acted as an anti-establishment force and urged the government to carry out social reforms in the 1970s and the political reforms in the 1980s. They were inspired by the promise of "Hong Kong people governing Hong Kong" and the eventual devolution of power resulting from the Sino-British Joint Declaration and embarked on the road of political group-building. They were pro-China in the sense that some of the leading democrats, like Szeto Wah and Yeung Sum, were the first batch of social activists to advocate the return of Hong Kong to China when the 1997 issue first appeared in the early 1980s. But their differences over the pace and scope of democratic reforms emerged gradually from the mid-1980s. The Beijing leaders and the democrats had confronted each other in the Daya Bay anti-nuclear movement and the drafting of the Basic Law, and their relationship totally deteriorated after the Tiananmen Incident in 1989. Comparatively speaking, they were more organized than the conservatives, but their mobilization strength and organizational development were hampered by the lack of institutional support and favourable political conditions conducive to the growth of party politics. Although their demands for democratic reforms only received support from the small attentive middle-class professionals, their role of fighting for the grass-roots' interests had a wider acceptance in the mass public.

The conflict between the conservatives and the democrats in the late 1980s was mainly over the composition of the legislature, and the timing and pace of introducing popular elections. The release of two sets of Green and White Papers in 1984 and 1987-1988 had provided the occasions for various advocate groups to mobilize their respective supporters. Through wide media coverage and the mobilization efforts of concerned groups, the attentive public was no longer confined to a small group of people.

In the mid-1980s, the conflict between the conservatives and the British-Hong Kong government, on the one hand, and the democrats, on the other, had added a new dimension. China had intervened in the internal conflict of Hong Kong over the pace and direction of democratization. In the 1987 political review, the Hong Kong government had been accused by the democrats of instituting a political structure that would not be controlled by the public but instead by the already privileged well-to-do people through the introduction of functional constituency elections and the not-so-significant portion of popularly-elected seats in the legislature.

But this contradiction was transformed to one between the Chinese government and the democrats, as Beijing adopted a cautious but more restrictive attitude towards the political reforms. Beijing's stance was well reflected on the occasion of the 1987 political review and in the drafting process of the Basic Law. By adopting a conservative stance, Beijing seemed to put all the political forces under its reach and manoeuvre. By siding with the business tycoons and turning down the democrats' demands, the Chinese government engaged itself in a head-on confrontation with the democrats. The intervention of China had provided an opportunity for the conservatives to exploit its strategic economic role in the transitional period to counter the emergence of the democrats. The Tiananmen Incident blew away any remaining possibility of cooperation between the Chinese government and the democrats. The Sino-British conflicts over the 1994-95 electoral arrangements and the support by the democrats for Patten's reform had even further intensified the tension between the Beijing government and the democrats.

The leftists share views with the democrats on social reforms and on the protection of grass-roots interests, especially before the 1980s. But they depart on the issue of democratization and the degree of autonomy enjoyed by Hong Kong. The leftists argued that the social and economic stability would be the prime objective during the transitional period and in the first couple of years after 1997, and thus there was no hurry for democratization as the Basic Law has already laid down the path of political development after 1997. They also tend to put "one country" before the "two systems" in case there is disagreement between mainland China and Hong Kong. This kind of thinking comes very close to what the Beijing government has in mind. As a result, the leftists joined hands with the conservatives in preventing Hong Kong from the so-called "radical" democratization. The leftists advocated that the political reforms have to be followed and be in line with what has been stipulated in the Basic Law.

The orientation of various political forces in the budding party market in the 1990s can be summarized by using the two political cleavages identified and discussed in Chapters 3 and 4. First, the collective consumption (with redistribution effect) issue had long been a bone of contention in the territory. From the outset, the democrats and the leftist trade unionists had fought for a reasonable distribution of social resources and asked the government to adopt policies with redistribution effects. By contrast, the conservatives from the establishment, such as the bureaucrats, the business tycoons and the appointed non-official ExCo and LegCo members, have tended to uphold the capitalist mode of market distribution (individual consumption). Second, the centre-periphery issue has also divided the political community since the mid-1980s. The democrats asked for a faster pace of democratization and a higher degree of autonomy enjoyed after 1997, but the conservatives and the leftists wanted to have a slower pace of democratization and a degree of autonomy allowed by the Beijing government. The respective positioning of the various political groups can be roughly sketched in the following Figures 5.1 and 5.2.

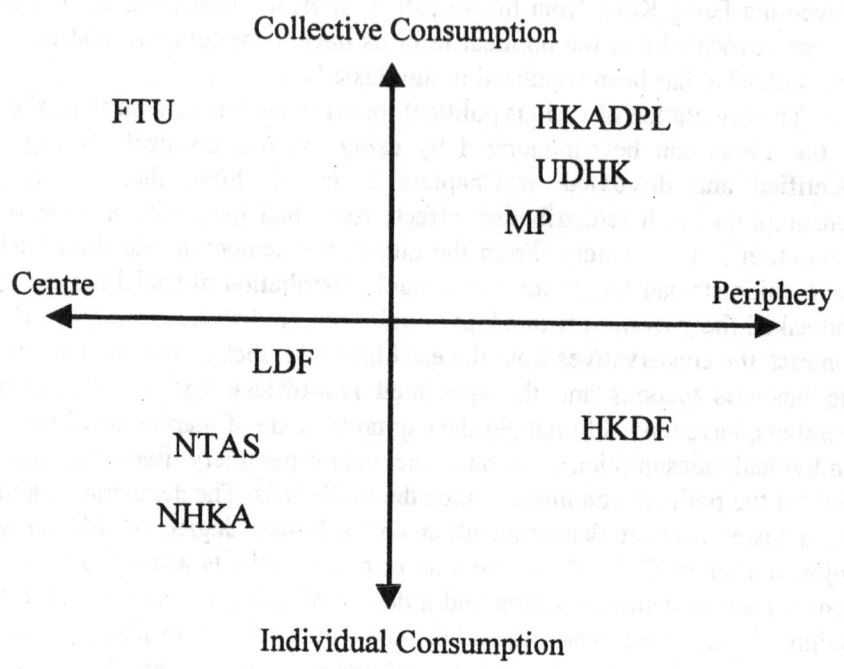

Figure 5.1   The Budding Party Market in 1991: A Sketch

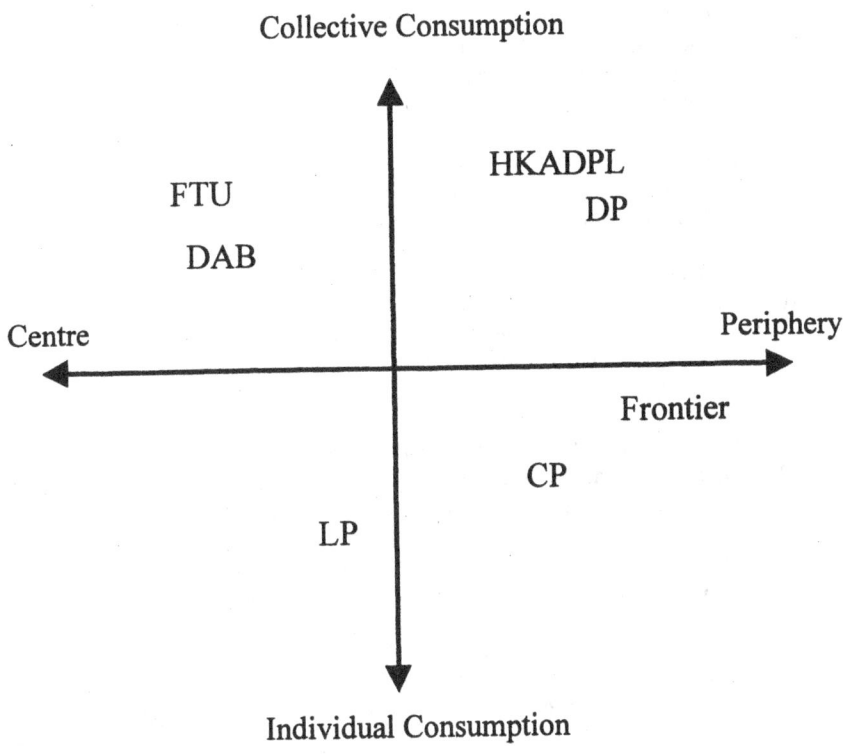

Figure 5.2   The Budding Party Market in 1998: A Sketch

Notes

1 The term "rightists" is used, throughout this book, to denote those people or organizations that are affiliated with the Kuomintang (KMT) or its related organizations, and also those who are the supporters of the KMT.
2 The 23 categories defined in the 1965 Working Report were:
   1. Persons on the Jury List;
   2. Persons who would be qualified for Jury Service but for being over 60, deaf, blind or similarly infirm;
   3. Teachers;
   4. Taxpayers;
   5. Members of the Defence Force and Auxiliary Services;

6. Pensionable Officers of the Hong Kong Government and Civil Service Pensioners;
7. Barristers-at-Law and Solicitors in actual practice and their Clerks;
8. Medical Practitioners, Dentists;
9. Editors, Reporters, Photographers, Commentators;
10. Chemists and Druggists;
11. Clergymen, Priests, Monks;
12. Professors, Lecturers, Full-Time Students, Graduates of the University of Hong Kong and the Chinese University of Hong Kong;
13. Pilots, Navigators;
14. Engineer;
15. Postmaster General;
16. Nurses;
17. Official and Unofficial Justices of the Peace;
18. Persons on the Current Rating List;
19. Architects;
20. Auditors;
21. Persons who are Members of some Professional Bodies;
22. Holders of School Certificates, Matriculation Certificates, General Certificate of Education "O" Level Certificates, and technical college certificates; and
23. Persons on the existing Electoral Register.

For details, see *The Report of the Working Party on the Urban Council Franchise and Electoral Registration Procedure* (Hong Kong: Government Printer, 1965), pp. 7-16.

3   In 1991, the HKCIC was under the leadership of Lau Chin-shek, a popularly-elected LegCo member since 1991, who had joined the HKCIC in 1972.
4   Szeto Wah had a younger brother working in the NCNA's Hong Kong Branch.
5   They are Anna Wu and Christine Loh. See *Eastern Express* 17 June 1994:1.
6   The term "political discussion groups" is used to denote those political groups whose activities are largely confined to the discussion of government policies and social issues, and thus their mode of participation is not action-oriented.
7   Yeung Sum is a LegCo member and Vice-Chairman of the Democratic Party (DP), which was formed by the merger of the UDHK and the MP in 1994.
8   *Wide Angle Monthly*, 160 (January 1986):74-5. The term "Three Principles of the People" was used by Sun Yat-sen, a respected Chinese revolutionary leader and Provisional President of the Republic of China in 1911, to describe his own political philosophy.
9   Lo Tak-shing is a grandson of Robert Hotung whose family has close ties with the establishment of Hong Kong. In 1985, he suddenly resigned from the posts of ExCo and LegCo member in protest at London's failure to accept its responsibility towards the Hong Kong people by giving them the full British passports. The resignation was the first of its kind in the one and a half centuries of British rule.
10 HKDF, Manifesto: *Hong Kong Democratic Foundation Towards a Democratic, Stable, Prosperous, Just and free Society.*
11 Maria Tam was accused of owning a certain amount of shares of a taxi company and the holding company of a bus company while chairing the Transport Advisory Committee.

6 The Embryonic Electoral Market in the 1990s

This chapter examines the popular elections held since 1991 and the subsequent emergence of the embryonic electoral market in Hong Kong. First of all, the landscape of the Hong Kong electoral market will be discussed. Second, the context of the first-ever 1991 LegCo popular elections and the interaction of the participants will be examined. Third, the last effort made by the British government in framing the electoral system for the 1994-95 election cycle and China's reaction to such an effort will be explored. The result of these elections will be examined in the context of the electoral market and party development. Fourth, a comparison of vote share of the leading political parties will be discussed in the context of the first HKSAR LegCo elections held in 1998.

Electoral and Party Markets in the Making

Elections in Hong Kong have a recorded history of more than a century. Starting from 1888, the Sanitary Board (founded in 1883 and renamed as the Urban Council (UrbCo) in 1936) had begun to have elected members, though the franchise was highly restrictive. Only those who had their names on the jury lists had the right to vote (Endacott, 1964: chapter 9). Not until the 1980s, almost a century later, would Hong Kong have the universal franchise in place. Moreover, given the colonial nature of the government, election and elected members have played only a marginal role in the Hong Kong policy-making process during that century.

As mentioned in previous chapters, the high institutional barrier of entry to the political game, the very low degree of government intervention in the Chinese society before the 1970s, the refugee mentality of the Hong Kong residents, and the yet-to-be-developed self-identity of "Hong Kong Person" have contributed, in one way or another, to the insignificance of political life in Hong Kong. This, in turn, made no room for the nutrition of election-oriented politicians. Through cooption or "administrative absorption", the socio-economic elites have been drafted in by the Hong Kong Government to become part-time politicians. Given that the coopted elites have no constituency in the society at large, their relations and links with the wider public could not be as strong as those enjoyed by politicians in a western polity. Because of such a structural constraint, the coopted elites have usually been insulated from the masses and have held a conservative political outlook. These characteristics proved to be a liability when the election mechanism began to be instituted gradually by the Hong Kong government as an alternative but promising method of political recruitment.

The situation started to change as the 1997 issue emerged in the early 1980s. In the past two decades, Hong Kong has undergone a series of "substantial" political reforms which have diverged from the previous "change within tradition" (Hook, 1983). Following the establishment of the District Boards in 1982 and the Regional Council (RegCo) in 1986, the introduction of universal franchise in 1982 and elected elements into the LegCo in 1985, the three-tier legislature has been developed into a promising vehicle to carry the weight of public opinion.

Expanding Pools of Participants and Politicians

With the lowering of the barrier of entry into the political game, the political and electoral markets have been rapidly developed. First of all, the electorate of Hong Kong has grown from 9,000 (0.4% of the then total population) in 1952 to over 2.79 million (42.99% of the total population) in 1998, as shown in Table 6.1.

Second, the actual number of voters varies in the pre-1982 period, from 1,914 in 1955 to 12,426 in 1979; but there is a progressive growth of voters in the post-1982 period, from 342 thousand in the 1982 DBs elections to 1.49 million in the 1998 LegCo popular elections.[1]

Third, the political posts opened for popular election grew from 2 in 1952 to 425 (346 for DBs, 32 for UrbCo, 27 for RegCo, and 20 for LegCo) in 1994 and 1995.

Fourth, the numbers of candidates being nominated grew from 9 in 1952 to 1030 (757 for DBs, 75 for UrbCo, 60 for RegCo and 138 for LegCo) in 1994 and 1995 (see Table 6.2). The appointment of Hong Kong Affairs Advisors (HKAAs) and District Affairs Advisors (DAAs) by the Chinese Government has also widened the pool of politicians. 858 persons

(188 as HKAAs and 670 as DAAs) have been appointed to the above posts.[2]

Table 6.1   The Electorate and Population of Hong Kong, Selected Years

Year	Electorate	Population	Electorate/ Population (%)
1952	9,000	2,250,000	0.40
1961	26,039	3,129,648	0.83
1971	37,788	3,936,630	0.96
1981	34,381	5,109,812	0.67
1982	899,559	*5,109,812	17.60
1986	1,441,540	5,495,488	26.23
1991	1,916,925	5,752,000	33.33
1995	2,572,124	6,156,100	41.78
1998	2,795,371	**6,502,100	42.99

Notes:
1. The electorates of 1952, 1961, 1971 and 1981 are the Urban Council's figures; 1982 is the District Boards' figure; 1986 is the Urban and Regional Councils' figure; 1991, 1995 and 1998 are the Legislative Council's figures.
2. The population figures of 1981, 1982 and 1986 include residents temporarily away from Hong Kong.
3. * 1981 Census' figure.
4. ** 1997 estimated mid-year population.

Sources:
1. Updated from Li (1995b:56);
2. Electorate's figures supplied by the Registration and Electoral Office, Constitutional Affairs Branch (Bureau);
3. For the population of Hong Kong (except 1952) before 1991, see *Hong Kong Annual Digest of Statistics*, 1994 ed., p. 11, Table 2.1; in and after 1991, see *Hong Kong Annual Digest of Statistics*, 1998 ed., p. 3, Table 1.1; for 1952 figure, see *Hong Kong Annual Report 1952*, p. 27.

178 *Hong Kong from Britain to China*

Table 6.2 The Number of Candidates in the Three-tier Legislature Elections by Years

Year	DB	UrbCo	RegCo	LegCo: EC	LegCo: FC	LegCo: PE
1982	403	-	-	-	-	-
1983	-	41	-	-	-	-
1985	501	-	-	39	25	-
1986	-	39	40	-	-	-
1988	493	-	-	26	20	-
1989	-	30	23	-	-	-
1991	467	37	24	-	40	54
1994	757	-	-	-	-	-
1995	-	75	60	18	70	50
1998	*	*	*	25	60	81
Sub-total	2621	222	147	108	215	185
Grand Total						3498

* No election has been held for these Boards and Councils since July 1997. The new election cycle for these Boards and Councils is expected to be held in late 1999 and 2000.

Abbreviations:
DB   District Board
UrbCo   Urban Council
RegCo   Regional Council
LegCo: EC   Legislative Council: Electoral College (1995 or before)/
            Election Committee (1998)
LegCo: FC   Legislative Council: Functional Constituency
LegCo: PE   Legislative Council: Popular Election

Source: Compiled from information provided by the Registration and Electoral Office.

The First-Ever 1991 LegCo Popular Elections

The first-ever popular elections to the LegCo signified a milestone in the political history of Hong Kong not only because of the establishment of an institutional linkage which provided a more direct representation for the mass public, but also because it was a transitional step leading to a fully-fledged legislature with an independent base and role that will remove it from the executive's direct influence and will enable it to wield decisive power within its own jurisdictions, i.e. the passage of the government's bills and the annual scrutiny of the government's budgets. These powers would be effective weapons to pressurize the government to make compromises if there were a clear majority of opinion within the legislature.

Needless to say, the LegCo popular elections in 1991 did not serve to change the government and to transfer the executive power from one party to another. That means no executive power was to be transferred to the winner of the LegCo popular elections. The executive-dominated political structure, which is formally not subject to any electoral pressure, would still be in place whatever the result of the elections. There was no hope of winning the LegCo elections and becoming the ruling party of Hong Kong. So the 1991 LegCo popular elections could not be regarded as having the same degree of significance and importance as those in former British colonies elsewhere when Britain decided to grant them independence through the institution of a Westminster-type of government.

But, in fact, the 1991 LegCo popular elections would strengthen the representativeness of the legislature and the input from the mass society. If viewed from a structural perspective, the introduction of popular elections to the LegCo would, in one way or another, challenge the legitimacy of the non-elected executive and may transform the relationship between the legislature and the executive in the long run. But the rather long-term nature of such a change, coupled with the negative Chinese attitude towards a stronger legislature, did contribute to the low key evaluation of the 1991 LegCo popular elections by the mass public. For the mass public, the 1991 LegCo popular elections only had a symbolic meaning of exercising civic rights rather than an electoral game devised to empower those among the attentive public to shape the political landscape of the transitional Hong Kong. "Votes without power", as the title of a book on 1991 LegCo popular elections suggested, seemed to represent their perception towards the said elections (Kwok, Leung and Scott, 1992).

Furthermore, the formal design and composition of the LegCo has prevented the emergence of a majority party in the legislature. There are four kinds of membership in the LegCo: 3 ex-officio members, 18 appointed members, 21 elected members from functional constituency elections, and 18 elected members from geographical popular elections. This composition had contributed to not only a fragmented legislature but also a lack of keen participants in the popular elections. Most of the prominent politicians, like Allen Lee and Maria Tam, saw no urgency about joining the 1991 popular elections. In answering the question why he decided not to stand in the 1991 LegCo popular elections, Allen Lee, then an ExCo and senior LegCo member, revealed in 1993 that the then Governor David Wilson had advised him not to join the said election, as he would reappoint him so as to maintain the continuity of the LegCo. Allen Lee later stated that his decision to accept Wilson's offer was a wrong one.[3]

This contributed to quite an unbalanced picture in which the potential candidates from the establishment and the conservatives relied on government re-appointment or functional constituency elections. On the other hand, the democrats concentrated their efforts on the geographical constituency popular elections. As a result, the electoral market had been further distorted as if the democrats had dominated the popular election market. This distorted picture further gained ground from the fact that the democrats (mainly from the UDHK, the MP and the HKADPL) had altogether nominated over 20 candidates for the 1991 LegCo popular elections (see Table 6.3).

Although the party market had been growing and evolving in the decade of the 1980s, the organizational strength and mobilization power of the political groups still remained elementary. Two indicators can be used to illustrate this point: membership and nomination rate. First, up to the moment of the 1991 LegCo elections, the election-created political groups were still small in scale in terms of membership (see Table 6.4). The membership of those formed before the Sino-British Joint Declaration in 1984 had ranged from 20 to 50 (except the MP), and those formed after that event usually had about or over 150 members (except the NHKA). It seemed that political forces had undergone realignment in the late 1980s and had merged into a comparatively larger coalition for fighting the 1991 electoral battles.

Second, as shown in Table 6.3, there were difficulties for the political groups in nominating enough candidates to stand in the 1991 LegCo popular elections. No single political group managed to have full participation in all 9 geographical constituencies. The UDHK was no exception. Although nominating a total of 14 candidates and contesting in full in 5 constituencies, the UDHK needed to form a coalition with the MP in three constituencies and had only one nominated candidate in the Kowloon West constituency. The LDF had nominated only 5 candidates in 4 constituencies, the HKADPL nominated 3 candidates in 2 constituencies, the MP nominated 3 candidates in 3 constituencies, the NHKA nominated 2 in 1 constituency, the HKDF nominated 1 candidate in 1 constituency. Three candidates in 3 constituencies had the apparent support of the leftists.

Table 6.3 Contest of Political Groups by Constituencies in the 1991 LegCo Popular Elections

	HKIE	HKIW	KE	KC	KW	NTE	NTS	NTW	NTN
FTU				1					
HKADPL					2				1
HKAS				(1)					
HKCA				(1)	(1)				
HKCF	1								
HKDF	1(1)								
KTMCA			1						
LDF		1	(1)		1			1	1(1)
MP			1					1	1
NHKA		2							
NWSC							1		
OR			1						
RCHK				(1)					
TUC			1						
UDHK	2	2	1	2	1	2	2	1	1

Abbreviations:
1. Groups' Name:

FTU	Federation of Trade Unions
HKADPL	Hong Kong Association for Democracy and People's Livelihood
HKAS	Hong Kong Affair Society
HKCA	Hong Kong Civic Association
HKCF	Hong Kong Citizen Forum
HKDF	Hong Kong Democratic Foundation
KTMCA	Kwun Tong Man Chung Association
LDF	Liberal Democratic Federation
MP	Meeting Point
NHKA	New Hong Kong Alliance
NWSC	Neighbourhood and Workers Service Centre
OR	October Review
PHKS	Progressive Hong Kong Society (dissolved in 1990)
RCHK	Reform Club of Hong Kong
TUC	Trades Union Council
UDHK	United Democrats of Hong Kong

2. Constituency:

HKIE	Hong Kong Island East
HKIW	Hong Kong Island West
KE	Kowloon East
KC	Kowloon Central
KW	Kowloon West
NTE	New Territories East
NTS	New Territories South
NTW	New Territories West
NTN	New Territories North

Notes:
1. The figure in the table means the exact number of candidates being nominated by that political group in the constituency;
2. The figure in brackets means those candidates who had been previously affiliated with or who still belonged to the group but did not ran under the group's banner.

Table 6.4 Membership of Selected Political Groups before 1991

Name	A	B	C
Hong Kong Observers	50	30	-
New Hong Kong Society	20	20	-
Meeting Point	190	190	127
Hong Kong Affairs Society	50	100	-
Hong Kong People's Association	30	20	-
Progressive Hong Kong Society	-	150	-
Hong Kong Association for Democracy and People's Livelihood	-	160	140
New Hong Kong Alliance	-	36	-
Hong Kong Democratic Foundation	-	340	-
United Democrats of Hong Kong	-	520	600
Liberal Democratic Federation	-	150	208

Sources:
1. For figures in column A, Yip Tze-chin, "The Political Wake-up of Hong Kong's New Generation of Intelligentsia," (in Chinese) *Hong Kong Economic Journal Monthly* 92 (1984): 40-3;
2. For figures in column B, Fong Wah, "Hong Kong Political Organizations: Easy to Form But Difficult to Grow," (in Chinese) *Ming Pao Monthly* 26 (April 1991):8-9;
3. For figures in column C, *Open Magazine* 75 (March 1993):50-1, (in Chinese).

The democrats had failed to arrive at a nomination list acceptable to all sides and a grand election coalition because of their different attitudes towards the Beijing government after the Tiananmen Incident, their ideological differences and personality conflicts. The HKADPL held a relatively soft attitude towards Beijing and a more welfare-oriented ideology, while the UDHK adopted a rather confrontational attitude and a more middle-class political orientation. The MP's attitude towards Beijing was closer to that of the HKADPL, while its political ideology was nearer to that of the UDHK. Even more, the HKADPL's candidates had engaged in a head-on competition in 2 constituencies with other democrats' candidates, in which one competed with a UDHK's candidate and the other competed with candidates from the UDHK-MP coalition. On the conservative side, any coalition effort was hampered by Maria Tam's scandal (discussed in Chapter 5) and the lack of urgency and incentive, created by the nature of the political system, to join the popular election game. They were further impeded by their "freshness" in wooing and pinning down grass-roots organization networks. Therefore, it seemed that a territory-wide conservative election coalition had failed to emerge in the 1991 LegCo popular elections. The leftists seemed to be constrained by the unfavourable political climate at the time and adopted a low-profile attitude in nominating candidates. Tsang Tak-shing, the chief-editor of the communist paper, *Ta Kung Pao*, claimed that:

> There was no organized fielding of candidates. For the eighteen seats contested in the direct elections, there were only three candidates from *established pro-Beijing [leftist] circles*, and they had all decided to run on their own initiatives [sic]. There was *no Chinese official attempt* to contact more would-be candidates with enticement [sic] to run. (Tsang, 1992:44; italics mine)

This above assertion was only half true. It was true that only three candidates were came from the "established pro-Beijing circles" and there was "no official Chinese attempt" to field more candidates, but the Beijing government had strategically supported, through the NCNA's Hong Kong Branch, those who competed against the UDHK's candidates, as will be demonstrated in the next section. Furthermore, the electoral campaigns of the leftists and their supported candidates were fought with vigorous support from the Chinese and the leftist establishments in terms of both funding and manpower (for details, see the following section). The leftist FTU mobilized one thousand "voluntary workers" to help promote voter registration in three possible running LegCo constituencies in June 1991. The FTU also planned to make a home visit to every voter in the Kowloon Central constituency, which political activists had long regarded as a "liberated area" because of the alleged popular support and influence the FTU enjoyed there (*Ming Pao*, 24 June 1991).

Political Mobilization in the 1991 LegCo Popular Elections

The Hong Kong government had put enormous efforts into the 1991 popular elections so as to ensure its success. The significance of success would not only help to prove the wisdom of introducing popular elections but also provide a chip for London to bargain with Beijing that more popularly-elected seats should be introduced before 1997. London's calculation had been embedded in the secret diplomatic exchange in February 1990 when China and Britain came to an understanding that there should be no less than 20 popularly-elected seats in the LegCo in 1995. The words "no less than" had hinted that London might raise the issue afterwards if it saw fit. The British Foreign Minister with special responsibility for Hong Kong stated in September 1990 that the Basic Law could be amended so as to accommodate the current developments in Hong Kong (*Bauhinia Magazine*, 2 (November 1990):11). Even as late as early September 1991, Prof. Wang Gungwu, then an ExCo member, urged Hong Kong people to demand more LegCo popularly-elected seats from the Chinese government if the turn-out rate reached as high as 60% in the LegCo popular elections (*HKS*, 14 September 1991). What mattered here was the linkage between the voting turnout in the 1991 LegCo popular elections and the possible increase of popularly-elected seats in 1995.

The slogan that the Hong Kong government employed in urging people to vote was: "vote: it's power in your hands!".[4] On the surface, this catchword was quite attractive and it implied that significant change could be possible if one did go to vote. But this claim did not match up with the then political reality as less than one-third (18 seats) of the total LegCo had been set aside for popular elections. Numerically speaking, a political force could manage to command a majority of the popularly-elected seats but still remain as a minority in the whole legislature. This short-term calculation and the negative Chinese attitude towards a stronger legislature had made the mass public feel that there existed a credibility gap.

On the Chinese side, the stance was very clear. No such link existed and the Basic Law could not be amended before it was put into practice in 1997. Two days before the designated polling day, an official statement from the State Council's HKMAO, put through by the semi-official China News Service, remarked:

> Over a period of time recently, [some people in] Hongkong have time and again given such view -- If the Legislative Council direct elections succeeded and there is a high turnout, [we should] demand China quicken the pace of democracy and give more directly elected seats in 1995. . . . It is absolutely

impossible and an unrealistic fantasy that the composition of the legislative assembly can be amended before 1997. (quoted in *SCMP*, 14 September 1991)

It warned that the LegCo constituted in 1995 would have to be dissolved in 1997 if the composition was not in accord with the stipulations of the Basic Law.

Beijing had, in one way or another, expressed openly its view that it would like to see the election of those who love China and Hong Kong, support Hong Kong's reunion with China and the Basic Law in the LegCo popular elections. Beijing had also made it clear that election of the democrats' candidates would do no good to the already strained Sino-Hong Kong relationship and reminded Hong Kong voters to be careful in choosing which candidates to vote for. In commenting on whether to vote for the pro-Beijing candidates, a signed article in the NCNA affiliated *Bauhinia Magazine,* which was widely cited by other media, stated that:

> In the present stage of Hong Kong, if the so-called "pro-China" means accepting the Chinese government, supporting "one country, two systems", the Basic Law and the unification of China, and advocating the strengthening of communication and cooperation between Hong Kong and mainland, then what is the problem? ... Taking into consideration the political reality [of reunion with China], voters should demand they love their country, accept or at least not to confront and even not to subvert the Chinese government when choosing political representatives to participate in the governing of Hong Kong. ... Some politicians in Hong Kong have regarded themselves orally as "not anti-China", and have only criticised some Chinese Communist Party's measures towards Hong Kong. But as a matter of fact, their behaviours are not so simple. ... they have lobbied western countries to apply economic sanctions towards China, ... they have setup political organizations that aimed at subverting Chinese government ... if people like this become Legislative Councillors, do they promote accord and cooperation between Hong Kong and mainland? Do they contribute to the smooth development of Hong Kong? ... Based upon the intimate and undividable relationships between Hong Kong and mainland, and the future of Hong Kong, it is worthy to consider from the angle of the above questions what kinds of people have to be chosen to institute the Hong Kong legislature. (*Bauhinia Magazine*, 12 (September 1991):13; original in Chinese, my own translation)

In order to minimize the democrats' chance of being elected, Beijing seemed to adopt an united-front strategy of supporting the local leftists and non-democrat candidates. An internal document drafted in September 1990 highlighted the following strategies:

1. to mobilize all possible forces, including those of the pro-Beijing, and apparently moderate but pro-Beijing groups, to participate in the 1991 LegCo elections;
2. to encourage and support business and professional organizations, like the LDF and the NTAS, to participate so as to minimize the democrats' chances of being elected or at least to prevent them from being elected uncontested;
3. owing to the fact that there are various factions within the democrats' camp and the lack of consensus towards China, we can adopt differential treatment towards the democrats' camp; in the hope of isolating and challenging the anti-communist figures, like Martin Lee and Szeto Wah, to the maximum degree, we could conditionally support the Meeting Point's and the HKADPL's candidates in those constituencies where the strength of the democrats has prevailed and we do not have suitable candidates to nominate;
4. given that they are not anti-communist, we could also conditionally support candidates from the British-Hong Kong establishment, whether they are pro-British or not. (Yip, 12 September 1991; original in Chinese, my own translation)

These strategies seemed to match the repeated urging of Chinese officials, i.e. Li Hou and Zhou Nan, during 1990 that businessmen should get organized and participate in the 1991 three-tier legislature elections (*Sing Tao Jih Pao*, 18 February 1990; *Bauhinia Magazine*, 2 (November 1990):11). Lu Ping had also publicly supported the left-wing FTU' participation in the 1991 elections (*Ming Pao*, 11 March 1991). In addition, the Beijing government had reportedly been involved in the electoral campaign by giving money to the left-wing LegCo candidates. The maximum amount the Beijing-supported candidates could receive was HK$100,000 and the "money would be channelled by Chinese companies in Hongkong through the Federation of Trade Unions". It was also reported that staff of China-run enterprises, i.e. the Bank of China and China Travel Service, had also been drafted in to campaign for the left-wing candidates (*Ming Pao*, 12 September 1991; *SCMP*, 15 September 1991).

Beijing's fear of the growth of the democrats was further fuelled as the UDHK, the flagship of the democrats' camp, urged the Governor to appoint ExCo members in proportion to the seat-share that the relevant political groups and individual candidates received in the LegCo popular elections (*Ming Pao*, 24 June 1991). Though article 55 of the Basic Law has stipulated that the HKSAR chief executive should appoint ExCo members from "among the principal officials of the executive authorities, members of the Legislative Council and public figures", Beijing showed its dislike of the democrats' move. This negative response could be seen as a move to prevent the UDHK, especially those who had a close relationship with the HKASPDM, presumably Szeto Wah and Martin Lee, from acquiring more influence or popularity in the transitional period.

The Surge of Democratic Forces in the 1991 LegCo Elections

The first-ever LegCo popular elections held on 15 September 1991 recorded the highest turnout, in terms of both rates and figures, in the electoral history of Hong Kong up to that moment, although it was quite low in comparison with those of Western democratic polities and newly independent states. Except those of the United States and Switzerland, the turnout rates for the industrialized countries ranged from 69.1% (Spain) to 89.2% (Australia where voting is compulsory) in the period 1985-89. The respective figures for the US and the Switzerland were 52.8% and 46.1% (Lane, McKay and Newton, 1991:123). Regarding the Asian developing countries in the early 1990s, the turnout rates, in general, were lower than those of the OECD countries. The respective turnout rates of Bangladesh, Malaysia, Republic of Korea, and Thailand were 52%, 70%, 71.9% and 59.27% (Inter-Parliamentary Union, 1991: Vol. 25, pp. 39 & 101; and 1992: Vol. 26, pp. 139 & 159). Nearly forty percent (39.15%, N=750,467) of the registered electorate in Hong Kong went to the polling stations and cast their votes. But in the calculation and interpretation of the turnout rate in Hong Kong it is necessary to take into consideration the following factors: the de-politicized context and its socialization effect, the obsolete electoral roll which had not been updated since the early 1980s, and the high rate of internal movement due to the rapid urbanization of the New Territories. Thus, according to a post-election study, the real turnout was estimated to lie in the range of 47.5% to 51.8% (Louie, et al., 1993:32-4).

Whatever the turnout rate may be, it was certainly the single political event in Hong Kong that attracted the greatest involvement of the local Hong Kong people up to date. In fact, the absolute numbers of voters had

The Embryonic Electoral Market in the 1990s 189

increased from about 390,000 in the UrbCo elections in May 1991 to 750,000, but the Hong Kong and Chinese officials, mass media and commentators still focused their discussion on the relatively "low" turnout rate. This agenda of discussion seemed to be set well before the election day by the British-Hong Kong Government's plan to request Beijing to increase the proportion of the LegCo popularly-elected seats if the 1991 LegCo elections proved to have a high turnout rate (see Chapter 3 for details).

Among the 18 elected LegCo members, 16 either came from the democrats or were pro-democrat independents. As shown in Table 6.5, the UDHK succeeded in returning 12 out of 14 LegCo candidates; the MP returned 2 out of 3; the HKADPL 1 out of 3; and one out of the pro-democrat independents. On the other hand, the rural conservatives managed to return only 1 LegCo member.[5] The leftists and the rightists had failed to grasp any seats. With regard to vote share by political inclination, the democrats and the pro-democrat independents had received 66% of the total actual vote, the conservatives and the pro-conservative independents 19.5%, and the leftists 7% (see Table 6.5).[6]

Table 6.5　Comparison of the 1991, 1995 and 1998 Popular Elections Results

Name	1991 CF(E)	1991 VR(%)	1995 CF(E)	1995 VR(%)	1998 NLNCF(E)	1998 VR(%)
Democrats						
UDHK	14 (12)	45.1	-*	-*	-	-
MP	3 (2)	7.2	-*	-*	-	-
DP	-	-	15 (12)	42.3	5/18 (9)	42.9
HKADPL	3 (1)	4.4	5 (2)	9.5	2/4 (0)	4.0
HKDF	1 (0)	1.4	-	-	-	-
NWSC	1 (0)	2.8	-	-	1/1 (1)	2.6
UA	-	-	2 (0)	2.0	-	-
Frontier	-	-	-	-	2/4 (3)	10.0
Citizens Party	-	-	-	-	2/2 (1)	2.8
Pro-Democratic Independents	3 (1)	5.0	2 (2)	7.3	1/1 (0)	0.8
Sub-Total	25 (16)	65.9	24 (16)	61.1	13/30 (14)	63.1

	CF(E)	VR(%)	CF(E)	VR(%)	NLNCF(E)	VR(%)
Conservatives						
LDF	5 (0)	5.1	1 (0)	1.3	-	-
Rural	3 (1)	5.3	2 (0)	3.0	1/1 (0)	0.5
NTA	-	-	-	-	1/5 (0)	1.8
NHKA	2 (0)	0.9	-	-	-	-
LP	-	-	1 (1)	1.7	4/12 (0)	3.4
HKPA	-	-	2 (0)	2.8	-	-
Pro-Conservative Independents	6 (0)	8.2	2 (0)	1.9	1/1 (0)	0.7
Sub-Total	16 (1)	19.5	8 (1)	10.7	7/19 (0)	6.4
Leftists						
FTU	1 (0)	3.3	-	-	-	-
HKCF	1 (0)	2.2	-	-	-	-
KTMCA	1 (0)	1.6	-	-	-	-
DAB	-	-	7 (2)	15.7	5/20 (5)	25.2
Pro-Beijing Independents	-	-	2 (0)	2.2	-	-
Sub-Total	3 (0)	7.1	9 (2)	17.9	5/20 (5)	25.2
Rightists						
TUC	1 (0)	0.2	-	-	-	-
123 DA	-	-	-	-	1/4 (0)	0.2
Sub-Total	1 (0)	0.2	-	-	1/4 (0)	0.2
Others	9 (1)	7.2	9 (1)	10.3	8/8 (1)	5.0
Grand Total	54 (18)	99.9	50 (20)	100.0	34/81 (20)	99.9

* Indicates party merged.

Abbreviations:
1. Political Parties (Groups):
   - 123DA — 123 Democratic Alliance
   - DAB — Democratic Alliance for Betterment of Hong Kong
   - HKPA — Hong Kong Progressive Alliance
   - NHKA — New Hong Kong Alliance
   - NTA — New Territories Alliance
   (others, please refer to Table 6.3)
2. Column Labels:
   - CF(E) — Candidates Fielded (Elected)
   - NLNCF(E) — Number of Lists / Number of Candidates Fielded (Elected)
   - VR(%) — Vote Received (%)

Source: Updated from Li and Newman (1997:223).

As predicted by many pre-election polls, the prominent leaders of the HKASPDM and the UDHK were all returned by a very large margin of voters' support. Martin Lee Chu-ming in the HKIE (for full constituency name, see Table 6.3) had obtained the territory-wide highest votes of 76,831, three-quarters (74.6%) of the voters in his constituency voting for him. The next three highest candidates in terms of vote share were: Szeto Wah in the KE (70%, 57,921 votes); Yeung Sum in the HKIW (65.4%, 45,108 votes); and Lau Chin-shek in the KC (62.2%, 68,489 votes) (see Table 6.6, Vote Share A).

Furthermore, the UDHK and its coalition partner MP won the top two highest votes in each of the following six constituencies: HKIE, HKIW, KE, KC, NTS, and NTN. Where their combined vote share of these winning candidates in the said constituencies ranged from 70.2% (KE) to 52.8% (NTN) of the total votes cast (see Table 6.6, Vote Share B). Nevertheless, the UDHK's candidates were defeated in the NTE constituency where they had only managed a combined 29.9% of the vote and lagged far behind the top three candidates in that constituency.

Table 6.6 Vote Share of the 1991 LegCo Popular Elections

Constituency/Name (Voters Number)	Vote Given	Vote Share (A)	Vote Share (B)
HONG KONG ISLAND EAST (103,028)			
LEE Chu-ming, Martin*	76831	74.6	40.2
MAN Sai-cheong*	43615	42.3	22.8
CHENG Kai-nam	29902	29.0	15.6
CHAN Ying-lun	19806	19.2	10.4
LEUNG Wai-tung, Diana	15230	14.8	8.0
CHOW Kit-bing, Jennifer	5805	5.6	3.0
HONG KONG ISLAND WEST (68,979)			
YEUNG Sum*	45108	65.4	34.8
HUANG Chen-ya*	31052	45.0	24.0
CHAN Yuk-cheung, David	29413	42.6	22.7
CHANG Yau-hung, Alexander	12145	17.6	9.4
WONG Man-chiu, Ronnie	6113	8.9	4.7
CHEUNG Wai-sun, Winnie	5821	8.4	4.5

KOWLOON EAST (82,405)

SZETO Wah*	57921	70.3	37.8
LI Wah-ming*	49643	60.2	32.4
HAU Shui-pui	21225	25.8	13.9
POON Chi-fai	16625	20.2	10.9
CHAN Cheong	3431	4.2	2.2
LI Ting-kit	3393	4.1	2.2
LI Koi-hop, Philip	865	1.0	0.6

KOWLOON CENTRAL (110,043)

LAU Chin-shek*	68489	62.2	34.2
LAM Kui-shing, Conrad*	56084	51.0	28.0
CHAN Yuen-han	44894	40.8	22.4
CHAN Chi-kwan, Peter	14145	12.9	7.1
YEUNG Lai-yin, Cecilia	8257	7.5	4.1
YOUNG, Dragon John	6273	5.7	3.1
CHEUNG Chung-ming, Justin	2158	2.0	1.1

KOWLOON WEST (69,483)

FUNG Kin-kee, Frederick*	36508	52.5	28.9
TO Kun-sun, James*	26352	37.9	20.9
LEE Yu-tai, Desmond	21471	30.9	17.0
SIT Ho-yin, Kingsley	18634	26.8	14.8
LAW Cheung-kwok	17145	24.7	13.6
NG Kin-sun	6098	8.8	4.8

NEW TERRITORIES EAST (96,637)

LAU Wai-hing, Emily*	46515	48.1	26.3
WONG Wang-fat, Andrew*	39806	41.2	22.5
KAN Chung-nin, Tony	37126	38.4	21.0
LAU Kong-wah	26659	27.6	15.1
WONG Hong-chung, Johnston	26156	27.1	14.8
CHOI Man-hing	348	0.4	0.2
LEUNG Ka-ching, Eric	306	0.3	0.2

NEW TERRITORIES SOUTH (91,780)

LEE Wing-tat*	52192	56.9	32.0
CHAN Wai-yip, Albert*	42164	45.9	25.9
LEUNG Yiu-chung	38568	42.0	23.7
YEUNG Fuk-kwong	30095	32.8	18.5

NEW TERRITORIES WEST (81,468)			
NG Ming-yum*	42319	51.9	29.4
TAI Chin-wah*	30871	37.9	21.5
WONG Wai-yin, Zachary	27243	33.4	18.9
TANG Siu-tong	23389	28.7	16.3
TSO Shiu-wai	20018	24.6	13.9
NEW TERRITORIES NORTH (46,644)			
FUNG Chi-wood*	23267	49.9	27.3
TIK Chi-yuen*	21702	46.5	25.5
CHEUNG Hon-chung	16221	34.8	19.1
WONG Chi-keung, Johnny	15350	32.9	18.0
CHOW Mei-tak, Ronald	7117	15.3	8.4
TONG Wai-man	1429	3.1	1.7

Notes:
1. Vote Share (A) = % of vote given over the number of voters presented and voted in that constituency;
2. Vote Share (B) = % of vote given over the total number of votes cast in that constituency;
3. Invalid votes are excluded in the electoral figures;
4. The symbol "*" denoted the returned candidates.

Source: Compiled and calculated from the data bank supplied by the Registration and Electoral Office, Constitutional Affairs Branch, Government Secretariat, Hong Kong Government.

The victory of the democrat candidates brought home a clear message that the voters wanted to have the possibility of an alternative voice in the LegCo. The result had contributed to the birth of a relatively solid, though still minority, opposition group in the government official- and business-dominated legislature.

The leftist candidates had contested in the following three constituencies: the HKIE, the KE, and the KC, and they all finished in third place. Chan Yuen-han (KC) had secured 44,894 votes (22.4% of the total valid vote in that constituency); Cheng Kai-nam, 29,902 votes (15.6%); and Hau Shui-pui, 21,225 (13.9%). The relative wide margin of votes between the democrat and the leftist candidates seemed to remove the "sure win" thesis that the leftists would have an overwhelming advantage in popular elections. The narrowest margin was that between Lam Kui-shing and Chan Yuen-han. Lam led Chan by nearly 12,000 votes, approximately 5.6% of the total actual vote in the KC constituency.

However, relatively speaking, the leftist candidates, in general, showed up better than the conservatives and the independents in terms of the number of votes a single candidate received.

The LDF had shown up badly with none of their candidates being elected. Despite being strongly supported by Maria Tam, then an ExCo and LegCo member, Alexander Chang Yau-hung had received less than 10% of the vote in the HKIW constituency. Cheung Hon-chung and Johnny Wong Chi-keung appeared to be closer challengers to the democrat candidates in the NTN constituency, but they still lagged behind by a margin of over 6% of the vote.

The rural conservatives seemed to have maintained certain support in the NTW constituency where Tai Chin-wah had obtained 21.5% of vote and finished in the second place. At the LegCo constituency level, the rural forces seemed to fail to strike back against the surge of the democrats in their influential New Territories' constituency (for an analysis at the District Boards level, see Li, 1993).

New But Fragile Rules of the Electoral Game

The arrival of Governor Christopher Patten in 1992 further intensified China's mistrust. Governor Patten's reform proposal had been criticized by both the Beijing Government and the conservative politicians in Hong Kong. It was because the effect of the reform would not only further lower the threshold of representation in the three-tier legislature, but also tip the political balance in favour of the democrats. This was especially the case in the regional and central tiers of the legislature. Although there was no proposal to increase the number of popularly-elected seats, the demarcation of the electorate for the new 9 functional constituencies and the composition of the election committee have been proposed in such a way to have the same effect as of the popular election, i.e. a very broad-based franchise.

Sino-British Negotiation on the Arrangement of the 1994-95 Elections

After a prolonged exchange of harsh words with each other, Beijing and London finally entered into negotiations on the arrangements for the 1994-95 elections in April 1993. London reiterated that Patten's reform package conformed to the letter and spirit of the Sino-British Joint Declaration, the Basic Law and the related agreements. But Beijing regarded the reform as a plot to prevent China from regaining the sovereignty of Hong Kong as well as to plant pro-British elements in the political establishment after 1997. The gap between the two was so wide that it could not be narrowed in the near future. After 17 rounds of negotiations, Beijing and London failed to resolve the issue (Hong Kong Government, 1994; Ministry of Foreign Affairs, PRC, 1994). The 1997 "through train" had been finally derailed. China resorted to setting-up its own "stove": the Preliminary Working Committee (PWC) of the Preparatory Committee for the Hong Kong Special Administrative Region.

In March 1994, Governor Patten proceeded to put his second part reform bill before the Legislative Council (Patten, 1998:55-80). Before the scheduled date for the second and third readings, political forces within and without the Legislative Council were mobilized to build up their own voting coalition. These included: the pro-Beijing groups, the conservatives (represented by the LP), the democrats (represented by the UDHK, the MP, and the HKADPL), and the non-aligned group (represented by the "Breakfast" group). Given that the reform bill would have tremendous effect on the political ecology of Hong Kong both before and after 1997, Beijing, London and Taipei were reportedly involved in influencing the voting choices of some Legislative Councillors.

There were altogether 16 amendments to the reform bill and one private member's bill, proposed by Emily Lau Wai-hing, for making all 60 LegCo seats become popularly-elected. After a lengthy and hot debate, Patten's reform bill was passed with minor amendments on 29 June 1994. The passage of Patten's reform bill fixed the format of the 1994-95 three-tier legislatures' elections. The major points of the reform included:

- lowering the voting age to 18;
- single-vote-single-seat system;
- abolition of all appointed seats in the District Boards and Municipal Councils;
- individual voting for the 21 old functional seats, instead of corporation voting;
- 9 new functional seats returned by the whole working population; and
- 10 election committee seats returned by the popularly-elected District Board members.

China's Plan for Take-over

Faced with the "non-cooperative" attitude of the British-Hong Kong Government, China adopted a self-help approach to prepare for the resumption of Hong Kong sovereignty. In August 1994, the National People's Congress Standing Committee resolved unanimously to dismantle the existing political structure on 1 July 1997 (*SCMP*, 1 September 1994, pp. 1 & 7). In October, the PWC political sub-group recommended establishing the Provisional LegCo so as to avoid a legislative vacuum just after the transfer of sovereignty in 1997 (*Hong Kong Economic Journal*, 7 October 1994, p. 7). The recommendation was later echoed by Lu Ping, the director of the Hong Kong and Macau Affairs Office (HKMAO), and was formally accepted by the PWC in December (*Wen Wei Pao*, 10 October 1994, p. A12 and 14 October 1994, p. A2; *Ming Pao*, 27 October 1994, p. A6; *Wen Wei Pao*, 11 December 1994, pp. 1, 2 & 5). Furthermore, the political sub-group reportedly preferred proportional representation for the election of the post-1997 Legislature (*Ming Pao*, 20 March 1995, p. A4).

China's reaction cast serious doubt on the continuity of the pre-1997 political structure. But, nevertheless, the Basic Law stipulates that elections would play a significant role in allocating political power. Articles 45 and 68 state squarely that:

> The Chief Executive of the Hong Kong Special Administrative Region shall be selected by election or through consultations held locally and be appointed by the Central People's Government....
>
> ....
>
> The Legislative Council of the Hong Kong Special Administrative Region shall be constituted by election....

Although China and the anti-popular election forces could play around with the word "election" or adopt their favour electoral system, elections could not be abolished totally after 1997. Therefore, it is not a question of have or have-not, but rather a question of degree.

The Last Election Cycle under British Rule in 1994-95

1994 DBs' Elections

Nearly 700,000 voters turned up in the September DB elections. Only 24, out of 140, appointed DB members and none of the DB chairmen who are concurrently appointed members joined the competition (*Hong Kong Economic Journal*, 16 August 1994, p. 6 and 28 August 1994, p. 2).

A record of 757 candidates entered into competition for 346 DBs' seats (including 50 uncontested seats) in September 1994. The major political parties (groups) fielded nearly half of the candidates. These included: the UDHK and the MP jointly nominated 133 candidates; the HKADPL nominated 40; the DAB, major rival of the democrats, nominated 83; the LP nominated 88; and the LDF nominated 27.[7]

But no single political party sought to field enough candidates so as to capture the majority of seats in all the 18 District Boards. We use the nomination rate to measure each of the major political party's intention of occupying the steering power in each of the DBs. We found 7 occasions when the parties fielded 50% or above candidates in one of the DBs. These included: the DAB in Wan Chai (50%), the LDF in Kowloon City (52.4%), the LP in Tai Po (73.7%), the HKADPL in Sham Shui Po (65%), and the DP in Central & Western, Wan Chai, and Kwai Tsing (78.6%, 70% and 51.9%, respectively).

Moreover, if we combined the nomination of the DAB and the LDF as well as those of the DP and the HKADPL, there were 5 more occasions that the combined nomination rate exceeded 50% of the total seats of that DB. These included: the DAB and the LDF in Central & Western and Eastern (50% and 52.9%, respectively), and the DP and the HKADPL in Wong Tai Sin, Tuen Mun, and Sai Kung (50%, 77% and 53.9%, respectively).

Given that the above nomination rates are mainly clustered around 50%, we can infer that the major political parties have generally demonstrated no eagerness to dominate in any of the DBs, whatever the reason would be. But there are some exceptions for the DP and the HKADPL. The nomination rate of the DP in Central & Western and Wan Chai, and those of the combined DP's and HKADPL's in Sham Shui Po, Tuen Mun, and Kwai Tsing are 70% or above.

The democrats won about 30% of the seats: the UDHK and the MP returned 75 seats and the HKADPL grabbed 29 seats. The DAB managed to have 37 seats. The Liberal Party suffered from an unexpected poll result: it secured only 18 seats. The LDF grabbed 12 seats. Over half of the seats (N = 175) were occupied by the minor parties and non-aligned candidates.

In terms of the balance of political forces in each of the DBs, only the democrats have a clear majority in the following DBs: Central & Western (DP: 57.1% of the total number of seats), Sham Shui Po (HKADPL: 55%;

DP: 15%), Tuen Mun (DP: 34.6%; HKADPL: 15.4%), and Kwai Tsing (DP: 33.3%; HKADPL: 22.2%).

Although the leftist and the conservative parties did not have a numerical majority in the DBs, their strength should not be underestimated. It is understood that many of the non-aligned DB members, in fact, hold a conservative political outlook or have a close relationship with the leftists and/or the conservatives. The election of the DB representatives to the UrbCo among DB members themselves would put some backing behind the above claim. The DAB and the LDF only have a combined seat share of 13.3% (2 out of 15 seats) in the Yau Tsim Mong DB, but Ip Kwok-chung (DAB member) managed to win the said election. The same also happened in the Wan Chai DB.

According to the above figures, political parties did not take full advantage of the abolition of appointed seats at the District Board level. Two reasons could account for this situation. First, the small size of the DB constituency has worked in favour of those candidates who have established their networks and personal ties in the locality for years. This is noticeably unfavourable to the democrats because most of them have had only a short time to make their names known to the public.

Second, the shortage of supply of potential candidates. The progressive growth of elected seats in the past decade has put pressure on the political groups to find enough candidates to run the elections under the group's or party's name. As shown in Table 4.5 (in Chapter 4), the elected DB members has grown from 132 in 1982-85 to 346 in 1994. This represented a growth of 262%. Given that the expansion has been on such a scale, the political parties (groups) clearly need some time to develop a sufficient pool of candidates.

The Election of DBs' Chairs and DBs' Representatives to the Municipal Councils As mentioned before, the abolition of appointed seats was bound to tip the power balance at the LegCo and Municipal Councils levels. But the effect was not so significant in the DB elections. The election of DBs' chairs and DBs' representatives to the Municipal Councils can provide hints to support this argument.

In 1994, the democrats (the DP and the HKADPL) managed to return three DBs' chairs, instead of one as in 1991. These included: Central and Western District, Sham Shui Po District, and Kwai Tsing District. Tuen Mun District appeared at first to be most likely chaired by the democrats, but the split of the democrats had cleared the way for the re-election of rural Heung Yee Kuk chair Lau Wong Fat as the chair. In addition, the rural leaders have been elected to the chairs of the following DBs: Tsuen Wan, Tuen Mun, Yuen Long, North, and Islands. The DAB and the LDF have each chaired one DB (Tai Po and Kowloon City, respectively). The remaining eight DBs are chaired by non-aligned DB members.

The election result of DBs' representatives to the Municipal Councils is similar to that of the election of DBs' chairs. The rural forces managed to secured 4 representatives (Yuen Long, North, Sai Kung, and Islands). The democrats grabbed 3 representatives (Central & Western, Sham Shui Po, and Kwai Tsing). The DAB returned 2 representatives (Wan Chai and Yau Tsim Mong). The LDF and the LP each secured one representative (Kowloon City and Shan Tin, respectively). The remaining 7 representatives were won by the non-aligned members or minor parties.

LegCo's Election Committee The DBs' election result also shaped the LegCo election committee election. Under the formula designed by Governor Patten and at the recommendation of the Boundary and Election Commission, the ten election committee seats would be returned by those elected DB members who were not qualified to register in Municipal Councils and Rural Functional Constituencies. Based upon the 1995 Final Register of Election Committee Constituency, 283 electors had be registered. This would mean that 26 DB members would qualify to elect one election committee member. As a result, the democrats (the DP and the HKADPL) captured 3 seats, the leftists (the DAB) 2 seats, each of the HKPA, the LDF and the 123DA one seat, and the remaining two seats went to the pro-Beijing non-aligned.

1995 Municipal Councils Elections

The Municipal Councils elections in March 1995 attracted 135 candidates, of which 87 (64%) have political affiliation.[8] 561,778 voters turned up in the elections and the turn-out rate was 25.8%. Compared with that of the 1991 polls (N=393,764; 23.1%), there was a growth of 168,014 voters in absolute terms. This represented a 42.7% of growth above that of 1991's.

No single political party could manage to field their candidates in up to half of the total seats of the Urban and Regional Councils. The DP fielded the largest number of candidates among the major political parties. They nominated 18 candidates each in both councils. The respective nomination rates are 43.9% (UrbCo) and 46.2% (RegCo). The DAB nominated 12 (29.3%) candidates in the UrbCo and 5 (12.8%) candidates in the RegCo. The HKADPL nominated altogether 9 candidates, 5 (12.2%)

in the UrbCo and 4 (10.3%) in the RegCo. The LDF and the LP fielded less than 10% of the total seats in each of the councils.

One interesting point to note here is that the combined nomination figure of the DP and the HKADPL exceeded the 50% threshold (56.1% in UrbCo; 56.4% in RegCo). They could have had a chance to capture the driving seats in both councils if they could manage to win the elections with flying colours or to build-up successfully a democratic coalition with the help of the pro-democrat non-aligned members.

The election result in the Urban Council brings the democrats such a chance. Including the DB representatives to the UrbCo, the DP grabbed 13 seats (31.7%) and the HKADPL won 6 seats (14.6%). Moreover, two pro-democrat non-aligned candidates managed to be returned. That meant the democrats altogether occupied 21 seats and might have held the driving seat in the UrbCo if they had successfully struck a deal. But the DP and the HKADPL failed to produce a mutually-acceptable package for the election of the Municipal Councils' chairs, and the UrbCo and RegCo functional constituencies of the LegCo. The DP only liked to discuss with the HKADPL the election of the Municipal Councils and related committee chairs, but the latter just wanted it to be linked with that of the Municipal Councils functional constituencies of the LegCo.

This conflict of calculation had not been resolved by the time the election came and thus resulted in a fatal blow to the democrats in the Urban Council. Given that a consensus on the council chair had been arrived at amongst the members, Ronald Leung Ding-bong, the incumbent chair, was returned uncontested. But the election of vice-chair signified the rift within the democrats. The DP's candidate, Lee Wah-ming, only secured 15 votes (without 6-vote support from the HKADPL) and was beat by the leftist DAB's candidate, Ip Kwok-chung, who managed to have 20 votes. Regarding to the election of 14 UrbCo committee chairs, the DP only returned 1 chair and 3 vice-chairs. The HKADPL's UrbCo members abstained in most of the elections mentioned above (*Ming Pao*, 4 April 1995, p. A4; *Hong Kong Economic Journal*, 4 April 1995, p. 7).

The split was not confined only to the democrats, but also to the rural camp in the election of RegCo chairs. The coalition of the rural, the conservatives and the leftists held the majority of seats in the Regional Council and could have had the capacity to prevent the democrats from electing to any position in the Council. The split within the rural camp was reflected by the fact that they nominated two candidates, both from the Heung Yee Kuk, to compete for the RegCo chair. With the help of the DP's councillors, Lam Wai-keung secured 21 votes and beat his rival rural

The Embryonic Electoral Market in the 1990s 201

candidate Liu Ching-leung, who only got 13 votes. In return, Lam's faction supported the DP candidate, Chow Yick-hay, to run for the vice-chair. Although the DP had only 12 seats in the Council, Chow managed to get 18 votes (without the HKADPL's support) and beat his rival DAB member Ngan Kam-chuen (*Ming Pao*, 4 April 1995, p. A4; *Hong Kong Economic Journal*, 4 April 1995, p. 7). Predictably, the election result of the RegCo committee chairs was similar to that of the UrbCo's.

The exchange of support between Lam's faction and the DP once again demonstrated the dynamics of politics: there is no forever friend nor foe, but only interests. This has also given proof of the situational nature of politics. The democrats, especially the DP, have, in some critical occasions, challenged the privileges the rural indigenous residents enjoy. Moreover, the DP has been the prime target of "containment" by the coalition of the rural forces, the conservatives, and the leftists. For the general public, it is very hard for them to comprehend the fact that the Lam's faction could trade with the DP in the election of the RegCo chairs. For the close watchers of politics, this is only realpolitik.

1995 Legislative Council Elections

The September 1995 LegCo elections were held under the most unusual of circumstances of any Hong Kong election to date. The three major blocs of candidates, the democrats, the leftists and pro-Beijing candidates, and the conservatives squared off for four-year terms knowing that the mainland government had already announced that anyone elected in September 1995 would be turned out on 1 July 1997. This rejection of the elected LegCo, by the Chinese authorities, held even though it was the first Hong Kong legislature in which all its members were elected.

Fifty candidates competed for the twenty popularly-elected seats with the democrats, leftists, conservatives, and the non-aligned fielding twenty-four, nine, eight and nine candidates, respectively. Compared to the 1991 election, the leftists and pro-Beijing party nominated three times as many candidates in 1995 (nine vs. three) and the conservatives nominated half as many (eight vs. sixteen). The democrats fielded roughly the same number of candidates (twenty-four vs. twenty-five).

The 1995 LegCo popular elections produced results similar to those of 1991. The democrats won sixteen seats (80 percent of the twenty popularly-elected seats). The remaining four seats were divided up between the leftists (two seats), the conservatives (one seat), and the non-aligned (one seat). The respective vote share for the democrats, the conservatives, and the leftists was 61.1 percent, 10.7 percent, and 17.9 percent. Non-aligned candidates received 10.3 percent of votes. The democrats and the conservatives both experienced a decline in electoral support (in terms of vote share); the drop for the conservatives (from 19.5 percent to 10.7 percent) was larger than that experienced by the democrats (from 65.9 percent to 61.1 percent). On the other hand, the leftists and non-aligned candidates received more votes than they did in 1991. The leftists gained ten more percentage points (from 7.1 percent to 17.9 percent), while the non-aligned gained three more (from 7.2 percent to 10.3 percent).

The democrats drew support primarily from the geographic constituencies and the nine newly created, broad-based, functional constituencies. The Liberal Party managed to win one geographical constituency seat that they contested and captured a total of ten legislative council seats. The DAB and its supporters in the FTU captured only one geographic seat and a total of six additional seats. Table 6.5 contrasts the results from the 1991 and 1995 LegCo popular elections.

The election result was somewhat unexpected. First, while many analysts attributed the 1991 landslide LegCo victory of the democrats to post-Tiananmen Square concerns on the part of the electorate, some believed that once emotions settled, the degree of support for the democrats would decline (Leung, 1993). Rather, the democrats remained the single dominant political force in Hong Kong -- commanding the support of more than 60 percent of the voters in 1995 -- despite Chinese government statements warning Hong Kong electors of the danger of supporting the local democratic movement. The democrats successfully exploited both their uncompromising attitude towards Beijing and their grass-roots populist platform. Hence, the democrats successfully straddled the two most important cleavages in the Hong Kong electorate (Li, 1996).

In the functional constituency elections, nine of the twenty-one old functional seats were uncontested. In the twelve contested old functional seats, 42,885 votes were cast compared with 393,521 votes cast in the nine new functional constituencies. The average turnout in the old constituencies was 78.67 percent while the average turnout in the nine new constituencies was 38.37 percent. The turnout in the nine new constituencies was generally viewed favourably given how broad some of the constituencies were.

The more surprising result was that the leftists failed to return three party leaders in the geographical constituency elections -- shocking election watchers both in and out of Hong Kong. More importantly, the growth in the leftist vote (from 7.1% in 1991 to 17.9% in 1995) may not have been as significant as it appears since the leftists fielded more than twice the number of geographical constituency candidates in 1991 than in 1995 (three vs. seven). For decades, the leftists had organized grass-root interests and had successfully knitted a well organized community network. Therefore, the leftists were defeated not by their failure to provide community services or their record, but rather because they were unable to convince the voters of their ability to protect local rights and interests against the claims of the Chinese government either before or after 1997.

The conservatives' pro-establishment values and ideology also failed to attract widespread voter support. In addition, their lack of enthusiasm for participating in the popular elections was reinforced by the continued existence of the functional constituencies which have been a more reliable way for the conservatives to win elections. For instance, the LP, one of the more influential conservatives groups fielded only one candidate in popular elections but managed to elect a total of ten members to the LegCo. It will prove difficult for this party, or the conservatives generally, to claim broad legitimacy until they are also prepared to field candidates in more popular elections.

Provisional LegCo in 1997 and the First HKSAR LegCo Elections in 1998

The Provisional LegCo in 1997

In response to Governor Patten's electoral reforms, the mainland Chinese authorities announced that the elected sitting legislature would not serve beyond 1 July 1997. This decision effectively ended the notion that the elected legislature would serve as a "through train" of continuity serving from 1995 to 1999. Because of the derail of the "through train", the origin stipulations in the Basic Law of forming the first HKSAR LegCo do not match with the developments in the late transitional period. As a result, China resorted to the extra-ordinary measure that a Provisional LegCo, comprised of sixty members, would be selected by the same committee (Selection Committee) charged with (s)electing the first chief executive of the HKSAR. The task of selection fell to a committee of 400 members which was selected in turn by the Preparatory Committee -- a committee of

150 members, a majority of whom were from Hong Kong, established under the Basic Law to facilitate the transfer of sovereignty.

The Selection Committee, convened on 19 December 1996 in Shenzhen, China and (s)elected the sixty members of the Provisional LegCo to serve from before the transition until the election of the first elected legislature. Of the sixty elected members, ten of the successful candidates had earlier been defeated in the popular elections held in 1995. These included Tam Yiu-chung, vice chairman of the DAB and the largest vote getter in the Provisional LegCo election. Also elected was Tsang Yok-sing, chairman of the DAB who had announced during the 1995 election that if he was defeated in the popular election, he would not serve in the appointed legislature.

While no DP members of the legislature sought positions on the Provisional LegCo, thirty-four members of the 1995 legislature sought election to the Provisional LegCo and thirty-three were elected. Only Samuel Wong Ping-wai, the representative from the engineering functional constituency failed to get re-elected. One former member of the DP, Chan Choi-hei, a member of the District Board, defected from the DP to seek election to the Provisional LegCo. He was successful.

The final results indicated that no democrats were elected to the Provisional LegCo while the LP retained 10 seats in the legislature and the DAB increased its representation from 6 to 10 seats. If one had to summarize the criteria sought by the electors, it was legislative and political experience with many of the candidates having current and former experience in either LegCo or ExCo, and service in an advisory capacity to the Beijing government.

The First HKSAR LegCo Popular Elections

Despite the bad weather in the election day, a total of 1.49 million electors cast their votes in the first HKSAR LegCo popular elections in May 1998. A turnout rate of 53.29% was recorded, the highest in the electoral history of Hong Kong. The reasons for such a high turnout may be many. It may be due to the change of attitude towards elections as election itself becomes the symbol of practising "Hong Kong people governing Hong Kong" after 1997; it may be a political expression of social frustration generated by the financial crisis of the time as well as by the controversial government policies, such as the plan to build an average of 85 thousands apartments per year; it may be due to the hope of the voters to show their dissatisfaction with the Provisional LegCo; or it may simply just out of civic duty. Whatever the reasons, the HKSAR is definitely governing a more active and rights-aware population than that under the British rule.

By the time of 1998 LegCo election, Hong Kong had adopted three different kinds of electoral system in only seven years (Lo and Yu, 1996). The reform of any electoral system is a very political exercise and it is no exception here in Hong Kong. Starting from the 1991 LegCo elections, Hong Kong experienced three kinds of electoral system. In 1991 LegCo popular elections, the double-seat double-vote system was adopted. That means each elector has two votes to cast for in a double-seat constituency. Because of the claimed presence of the coat-tailed effect, the disadvantaged under the then electoral system demanded reform. As a result, the single-seat single-vote was adopted in the 1995 LegCo popular elections. After the said election, the democrats had still received more than 60% of the votes cast, but occupied 80% of the seats. The issue of inproportionality became a hot debated topic after the election. For those who defended the majority system, they argued that the popularly-elected LegCo members only constituted one-third of the 60-member LegCo. They regarded the adoption of the majority system as a compensation for the lack of popular participation in the functional constituency elections. On the contrary, those who demand the adoption of proportional representation system counter that the principle of equality should be adopted as far as possible and justice should be done in the popular elections first. For the politicians, their concern over adopting which kind of electoral system may be a matter of realpolitik more than a matter of principle.

If we put the issue of electoral system in the context of the political development in the transitional Hong Kong and Beijing's Hong Kong policy, it would be easy to guess what kind of electoral system would be in place in the 1998 LegCo popular elections. After hot debates and discussions, the proportional representation system was adopted with five medium-sized constituencies (each has three to five LegCo members) in the 1998 LegCo popular elections.

There were altogether 34 lists with a total of 81 candidates. Of which, the democrats nominated 13 lists with 30 candidates in all the five constituencies. As the flagship of the democrats, the DP had one list in each constituency with a total of 18 candidates. The leftists, as represented by the DAB, had a full participation in all five constituencies with a total of 20 candidates. The conservatives fielded altogether 7 lists with a total of 19 candidates. Of which, 4 lists with 12 candidates were nominated by the LP.

In terms of the result, the democrats still commanded more than 60% of the voter support and grabbed 70% of the 20 popularly-elected seats. Although there was no significant change in the vote and seat share of the democrats at a whole, the zero return (2 in 1995) of the HKADPL did put through a message that the "moderate" wing of the democrats have lost their electoral support as there was a drop of more than 5% of the total votes cast for the HKADPL (from 9.5% in 1995 to 4% in 1998). With the support of one-fourth of the total voters, the leftists yielded a historic result of returning 5 seats, one in each constituency. The leftists have received 7% more than what it did in 1995. The increase of the leftists' vote support seems to be at the expense of the conservatives and the non-aligned. The conservatives experienced a rapid downfall in electoral support, from 19.5% in 1991 to 10.7% in 1995, and then further came down to 6.4% in 1998. Although the LP experienced modest growth in vote support, none of their candidates was elected, not even chairman Allen Lee. The non-aligned candidates also lost their support by more than 5% compared with 1995 (for details, see Table 6.5 above).

After nearly two decades of development and mobilization, the electoral market of Hong Kong has taken shape. As noted above, the democrats have acquired more than 60% of the voter support and the leftists came second with about 25% voter support. The combined electoral market share of the democrats and the leftists is close to 90%. The conservatives and the non-aligned candidates have played a diminishing role in the popular elections. Although it is still early to say that the party and electoral markets of Hong Kong are in a stable condition, there is already a trend of development leading to the segmentation of party development, whereby the democrats and the leftists concentrate their efforts in the popular election market, and the conservatives rely nearly solely on the functional election market to maintain their influence in the policy-making process. To a larger extent, this kind of segmentation is due to the institutional incentive offered by the existing political structure. The uncertainty of when to return the CE and all the LegCo members by mean of popular elections has, in one way or other, given a rather high incentive for the less competitive political forces in the popular election to maintain their stronghold in functional elections. The competition between the popularly and functionally elected LegCo members will become keen as time goes by, but the more serious question is whether that kind of institutional arrangement is capable of managing social conflicts, especially at a time of economic downturn.

Notes

1. The election figures in this book are supplied by the Registration and Electoral Office, Constitutional Affairs Branch, except where stated otherwise
2. Collected and calculated from the newspapers of Hong Kong
3. Interview with Allen Lee, 1 July 1993, Hong Kong.
4. This phrase was found in the government's election advertisements in the major printed media.
5. Tai Chin-wah resigned from the post before the formal swearing-in ceremony. He was then under investigation by the police concerning his alleged fraudulent qualifications to practise as a solicitor.
6. The electoral qualifications for the 1991 LegCo popular elections were: any person who is a registered elector and who has been ordinarily resident in Hong Kong for the 10 years immediately preceding the nomination date is eligible to be nominated as a candidate; and any Hong Kong permanent resident who is 21 years old or over, or any person who is ordinarily resident in Hong Kong for 7 years immediately preceding the date of his/her application is eligible to register as an elector. See the *Electoral Provisions Ordinance* (Cap. 367), sections 8, 9, and 18.
7. Compiled and calculated from the newspapers of Hong Kong
8. The data on political affiliation is based on the information package for municipal councils elections provided by the Government Information Services on 5 March 1995.

7 Institutional Design and Conflict Management

Amid the surge in the number of new democracies around the world since the 1980s, studies of democratic transition have been flooding the fields of comparative politics and third world development (Mainwaring and Scully, 1995; Stepan and Skach, 1993; Powell, 1989; Shugart and Carey, 1992; Huntington, 1991; Sartori, 1994; Mainwaring, 1993; Riggs, 1988). Among this literature, one will note that institutional arrangements and design have been emphasized by several scholars as playing a significant role in building up the new political order and therefore would contribute to successful democratic transition. Putting it in more specific terms, what kinds of regime type (presidential, parliamentary or hybrid system) would be more conducive to the stability of a newly established polity? What kinds of electoral and party systems would work more harmoniously with the chosen regime type? What kinds of representation system could help to reflect the relative strength of social forces and contribute to consensus-building? How low should the institutional threshold be so as to accommodate as many social forces, which want to have political representation, as possible? Or how high should it be so as not to discriminate against some minor forces? What kinds of voting system would be best for bringing voters' preferences into the decision-making process?

Although Hong Kong did not follow the usual path of decolonization and become an independent state, the transition from a British colony to a Special Administration Region of the PRC does involve some kind of institutional reform and restructuring. The need for institutional reforms stems from (1) the change of political status after 1997: from a colony to an integrated part of a sovereign state, and (2) China's promise to let "Hong Kong people governing Hong Kong" under the parameter of "one country, two system". The dual transition of sovereignty and regime has a profound impact upon the colonial political structure and order, and this in turn gives rise to a new political market, in which partisan alignment, de-alignment and realignment have taken place.

Faced with this tremendous transformation, the designing of a new institution that has the capability to cope with the turbulence of realignment of political forces is significant and critical to the political stability of Hong Kong and the legitimacy of the emerging political order. This chapter, therefore, aims to explore the dynamic relationships between as well as the institutional designs of the executive and the legislature in the post-1997 Hong Kong and to examine the institutional arrangements in terms of their capacity for conflict resolution and management.

Constitutional Engineering

It is easy to detect the "drastic" institutional changes that have been laid down in the Sino-British Joint Declaration and the Basic Law. The changes are "drastic" in the sense that elections were to replace the appointment system in returning the chief executive (governor) and all members of the legislature in twelve years' time (1985-97).

"Drastic" or not is in the eye of beholder. Those people who advocate democratic government would argue that the reforms of the Victorian colonial political structure have been delayed for a long period of time. In addition, they argue, Hong Kong possesses the necessary socio-economic conditions that would facilitate the development of democratic government. But, for those people who have reservations about the pace of the political reforms, they would argue that the reforms would jeopardize the stability and prosperity of Hong Kong if carried out in such a short period of time and at such a "drastic" pace.

No matter how the proponents and opponents argue their case, the reality is that the foundation of the colonial political order has been eroded and should, therefore, give rise to a new political order. The various political forces within and without Hong Kong would try to shape the emerging political order to their favour. As a result, the direction and pace of the change would be a sensitive and an explosive issue. Therefore, the access to the constitution-making process is a vital step in shaping the emerging constitutional order.

The "subjective" dimension of the constitution-making process is the aspiration and values that the participants want to materialize as well as the consensus or compromise with which they have to come to terms. Therefore, one scholar notes that:

> Constitutions are man-made designs. These designs reflect the constitution-makers' values, their expectations of the consequences of various arrangements, their often laboriously negotiated compromises. (Powell, 1982:66)

If most of the significant forces are included in the constitution-making process, the resulting constitutional framework would be a lasting one. If not, it will face possible challenges from the excluded forces. At this juncture, the objective dimension of constitution-making comes into play.

The meaning of "objective dimension" is that: whether the new constitutional framework can successfully provide an open and fairer political arena in which various political forces can represent their constituencies to compete for power and to resolve inter-constituency's differences and conflicts. Therefore, the capability of conflict resolution is one of the most important indicators to see whether the emerging constitutional framework is legitimized or not. As R. Kent Weaver (1992:9) suggests,

> Successful conflict management in a democratic society does not mean that there is no conflict, but rather that conflict is resolved in a way that all parties accept as legitimate, even if the outcome is not particularly to their liking.

The failure of conflict management is said to be reflected in the following three ways: the suppression of political competition (*de jure* and *de facto*), political instability resulting from violent and disruptive conflict, and regime instability (Gunther and Mughan, 1993:273-4).

The matching between the "subjective" and the "objective" dimensions of the constitution-making process is indispensable for a political community. Needless to say, we are not hoping for a total matching for there is no such thing in reality. Instead, what we can look for is that the shorter the distance between the "subjective" and the "objective", the more the chance that the emerging constitutional framework can survive.

Accompanying the erosion of the British colonial political order is the need to re-frame the political institutions under which a new political order will be emerged. China, as the future sovereign state of Hong Kong after 1997, held the trump card in shaping the constitutional framework of the HKSAR. Although the British government had a role to play in that process, one may doubt about how decisive its say was.

It is widely believed that China plans to have as little political reform as possible. That means the "executive-led" government serves as the basic model in designing the post-1997 political institutions. But, for better or for worse, the replacement of the appointment system by election in returning the executive head and all members of the legislature has worked to undermine the very foundation of the "executive-led" government and would likely transform the legislature from a submissive to an assertive one. From the China's point of view, the potential conflicts between the chief executive and the legislature could be contained by tailoring an institutional framework under which a fragmented legislature would emerge. By doing so, the "executive-led" government would function as before.

Access to the constitution-making process is vital in the sense that the participants would have the prerogatives to mould the new rules of the political game and thus their rights and interests would be protected. For those sectors who are lucky enough to have their representatives in the process, their views and interests are more easily being articulated; for those sectors who find no representative in the process, their rights have to rely on the mercy of the participants. Control over entry into the constitution-making process is therefore highly political and manipulative.

The Framing of the Post-1997 Constitutional Parameters

In the Sino-British Joint Declaration period, the formal players were highly restricted to the Chinese and the British government. The Chinese side had reiterated that they opposed the ideas of "three-legged stool" for the then negotiations were held between sovereign states and there was no room for the government and people of Hong Kong to play. Moreover, China claimed to represent the views and interests of Hong Kong people in the negotiations. Although the British government tried in the initial period to include representatives from the Hong Kong government (the then Governor, Edward Youde), it met with strong opposition from China. The Governor and officials from the Hong Kong government joined the negotiation as members of the British delegation. Although the British government claimed to consult the ExCo members after each round of negotiation, the way the ExCo members had been recruited limited their representation in relation to the whole society. In a formal sense, only the Chinese and the British governments were involved in the negotiations over the sovereignty of Hong Kong and the detailed arrangements contained in the subsequent Sino-British Joint Declaration (signed in

December 1984). The exclusion of the Hong Kong people from the negotiations stimulated a sense of powerlessness which developed in response to the fact that they could not control their fate.

For the British part, the honourable withdrawal from Hong Kong was the possible second best option after China rejected the validity of the three "unequal" treaties and the idea of exchanging sovereignty with continued British administration after 1997. What the British negotiators could aim for was to bring the Chinese government to agree a set of principles based upon which the pre-1997 order could be maintained and safeguarded.

As far as the institutions of the executive and the legislature are concerned, the two governments came to terms laid down in Sino-British Joint Declaration's Section I of Annex I:

> The chief executive of the Hong Kong Administrative Region shall be selected by election or through consultation held locally and appointed by the Central People's Government. . . . The Legislature of the Hong Kong Special Administrative Region shall be constituted by elections. The executive authorities shall abide by the law and shall be accountable to the legislature.

Although the word "elections" is not clearly defined and may be subject to different interpretation, the nature of the relationship between the Governor (the Chief Executive) and the legislature has undergone drastic transformation. In twelve years' time, Hong Kong would be transformed from an appointed Governor and legislature to an elected chief executive and legislature. More important is the "spill-over" effect on the operation of the whole political system and the way of governance. It seems that the effect of the introduction of elections into the political system has been under-estimated. Retrospective speaking, although Hook has regarded the changes (the introduction of popular elections at the district level) in the early 1980s as "change within tradition" (Hook, 1983), the subsequent introduction of popular elections to the LegCo and the related structural changes seems highly logical and possible because of the British need to prepare for the "unusual" decolonization process.

In terms of constitution-making, the relevant clauses in the Sino-British Joint Declaration had effect on the drafting of the Basic Law. China had to transform the promises in the Sino-British Joint Declaration into an enforceable constitutional law. Needless to say, China held the upper hand in interpreting and transforming the promises into binding constitutional laws. Shifting from international negotiations to domestic constitution-making, China took the driving seat in steering the direction of constitutional change under the parameters of the Sino-British Joint Declaration.

From Political Principles to Institutional Arrangements

From the beginning, China was the single most powerful force in controlling access to the drafting of the Basic Law and its views on the design of the future political framework therefore became the dominant one. By allocating differential seat ratio to different sectors, China could monitor which social or political forces would have more say in the drafting process. In fact, the Basic Law Drafting Committee (BLDC) was formed in 1985 with altogether 59 members. Of which, 23 were from Hong Kong and these Hong Kong members have been overwhelmingly drawn from the business and industrial sectors. Although the Basic Law Consultation Committee (BLCC) had a wider representation and was formed to solicit opinions, its influence was limited by its advisory role. Opinions were encouraged to be expressed, but the real decision was made by the drafters, not the ones who were being consulted or expressing opinions.

The politics of appointment would set the parameters of the constitutional discussion and more important is the contribution of the majority members of the drafting committee to the final shape and content of the constitution. In theory, the drafting committee's members had to consider all views and proposals put forward before them. But, at the end of the day, their own views or interests prevailed and the final decision was made by numerical count.

Through the appointment system, China could keep the initiative in its own hands. This is not to suggest that China could do anything it liked, but it possessed the necessary resources to mobilize support for what it wants and to buildup opposition to what it does not want.

The final product of the constitutional framework, as stipulated in the Basic Law, has reflected both the "cautious" attitude of the Chinese government and the "conservative" approach of the business community towards democratization. As Kuan Hsin-chi notes, the final product of the Basic Law is "a pact between the Chinese government and the business and industrial elites in Hong Kong" (Kuan, 1991:785). But the more important thing is whether the emerging constitutional framework has the capacity to manage conflicts. Before going into discussion on this aspect, the role of and relationships between the executive and the legislature, as stipulated in the Basic Law, should be introduced.

The Chief Executive (CE) of the HKSAR is no more returned by appointment, but through consultation, nomination or election held locally. The responsibility of electing the CE is vested in the Selection Committee (Election Committee in and after the second term) of 400 people (800 in and after the second term). The S/Election committee is composed of four pre-defined functional sectors of industrial, commercial and financial; professional; labour, social services and religious groups; and political figures (Hong Kong deputies to the NPC, Hong Kong representatives to the National Committee of the Chinese People's Political Consultative Conference (CPPCC), and LegCo members, etc.). Each group has a quota of 100 (200 in the second term).

The CE is assisted by an appointed ExCo in policy-making. The members of the ExCo shall be appointed by the CE and shall be drawn from "the principal officials of the executive authorities, members of the Legislative Council and public figures" (Article 55).

If there is a need to change the s/election method of the CE, the earliest date of proposing amendment is 2007 and shall be subject to the following procedures:

- endorsement of a 2/3 majority of the LegCo;
- the consent of the CE; and
- be reported to the Standing Committee of the NPC for approval. (Annex 1 of the Basic Law)

The legislature is composed of members returned by different election methods in the first three terms. The methods and proportion of members returned by each method are summarized in Table 7.1.

Although the CE and the LegCo members both have the right to initial bills, the latter can not move any bills that have an effect on "public expenditure or political system or government operation". Furthermore, the LegCo members have to seek the CE's written approval before they can move any bills that relate to government policies (Article 74).

Table 7.1 The Composition of the Post-1997 Legislature

Year	Functional Constituency	Geographical Constituency	Election Committee	Total
1997	30 (50.0%)	20 (33.3%)	10 (16.6%)	60 (100%)
1999	30 (50.0%)	24 (40.0%)	6 (10.0%)	60 (100%)
2003	30 (50.0%)	30 (50.0%)	0 (00.0%)	60 (100%)

* Because of the establishment of the Provisional LegCo in 1997, the HKSAR LegCo elections listed above will be deferred by one year.

The influence and power of the LegCo are further kept under control by instituting a separate vote count mechanism under which all motions, bills and amendments to government bills introduced by LegCo members should have the majority support from "each of the two groups of members present". These two groups are: members returned by functional constituencies and members returned by geographical constituencies and by Election Committee.

The institution of the separate vote count mechanism has the merit of moderating a radical change of policy direction by imposing a higher threshold of approval and is, thus, conducive to an integrated executive leadership and a higher degree of policy continuity. This will have the effect of maintaining the status quo. But the limitation is its effect of limiting the chance of the minority, but popular, view from becoming the LegCo majority view. Any political forces who want to block the bills or motions initiated by individual LegCo members could do so by having only 16 votes. In fact, this threshold is low enough to defeat all initiatives taken by individual LegCo members and would therefore contribute to a weak legislature.

Like the CE, the composition of the legislature and the voting procedure of passing bills and motions could be amended subject to procedures similar to those of the CE, except for the requirement of seeking approval from the Standing Committee of the NPC (Annex 2).

Apart from the above institutional arrangements aimed at containing the emergence of a full-fledged legislature, the "executive-led" governing model is further maintained by the fact that the CE can dissolve the legislature if the former refuses to accept bills passed by the legislature twice or the legislature withholds its approval of the government budget or other important bills (Articles 49 and 50).

Although the CE has to resign when the new constituted legislature has passed the same bill or has withheld approval again, the legislature will find it very difficult to have a two-thirds majority on a particular issue or bill. Why is this so? It is due to the methods of returning LegCo members and the resultant fragmented legislature, and to the decision-making procedures the legislature have to follow.

The segmented methods of returning LegCo members by functional constituency (FC), popular election (PE) and election committee (EC) have the effect of limiting the chance of having a legislature with a clear majority voice, especially an opposition one. First of all, the functional constituency commands half of the LegCo seats up to 2007 and that proportion will probably maintained for a while even after 2007. One of the reasons advanced to justify the adoption of functional elections is to provide those functional groups which have contributed a lot to the "success" of Hong Kong with a certain level of representation in the legislature. But the diffuse nature of the functional groups has rendered difficult any coalition-building effort because of a more direct constituency linkage and more easily identifiable sectoral interests. In addition, their close relationship with the establishment both subjects them to tremendous executive pressure and makes them prime lobbying targets of government.

Secondly, the members returned through election committee have a pro-status quo tendency by default. It is because the constituency demarcation has followed, more or less, those of the functional constituency. Lastly, although the members returned by geographic constituency have a better chance of building a voting bloc within the legislature, they so often fall into ideological clashes or have different views and judgements over social welfare and political reforms.

From Institutional Arrangements to Rule-making Procedures

According to the Decision[1] adopted by the NPC on 4 April 1990, the Preparatory Committee:

> shall be composed of mainland members and of Hong Kong members who shall constitute not less than 50 per cent of its members. Its chairman and members shall be appointed by the Standing Committee of the National People's Congress. (Article 2)

From the membership list of the Preparatory Committee, one can note that most of the appointees come from the business, commercial and financial sectors. The under-privileged are greatly underrepresented in the committee.

In August 1996, the Preparatory Committee (established in January 1996) passed the policy document on the Formation Method of the Selection Committee which was charged with electing the first chief executive of the HKSAR and the Provisional LegCo.[2] The latter job is not mentioned in the Basic Law, but was added to the Selection Committee's responsibilities by the Preparatory Committee which was empowered by a resolution of the Standing Committee of the NPC in August 1994. This last-minute adjustment was due to the failure of the Sino-British negotiations over the 1994-95 electoral arrangements in 1994 which signified the overturn of the "through train".

As stated in Articles 2 and 5 of the Formation Method, the 400-member Selection Committee shall be returned by four pre-defined groups and each group has a quota of 100. Those who want to apply for a candidacy are free to choose which group s/he wants to apply to (except the group for political figures). The application has to be made through a registered association or organization. The full list of applications is first screened by the Preparatory Committee members and each of them shall then recommend 100 candidates for each group (except the group for political figures). Considering all the members' recommendation, the Presidium of the Preparatory Committee shall recommend at least 120 candidates for each group and forward the short-listed candidates to the Preparatory Committee members to vote for. No reason will be given to those applicants who do not have the recommendation of the Presidium. Each member is then allowed to vote for up to 100 candidates in each group and the top 100 candidates having the highest votes in each group will be declared elected.

The group for political figures was subject to another procedure. All the Hong Kong representatives to the NPC who are permanent residents of Hong Kong (26 in number) automatically became members of the Selection Committee. The Hong Kong representatives to the CPPCC had to elect among themselves to fill-up 40 seats. The rest of the seats (34) were open to nomination from any registered associations and from the Preparatory Committee members. The election rule was the same as those of the first three groups.

The Preparatory Committee also passed the methods of returning the CE and the Provisional LegCo in October 1996.[3] It stipulated that those who were interested in running in the CE election had to apply to the Presidium of the Preparatory Committee and the latter would examine the applicants' eligibility. For those who were confirmed as being eligible, they had to seek at least 50 Selection Committee members' nominations so as to qualify as a candidate of the CE. The double ballot would be adopted if the leading candidate failed to receive the majority support of the Selection Committee members.

As for the Provisional LegCo, each potential candidate was required to have the nomination of 10 Selection Committee members, and each Selection Committee member, in turn, could not nominate more than 5 candidates. Similar to the nomination procedure of the CE, the eligibility of the potential candidates had to be confirmed by the Presidium of the Preparatory Committee. Simple majority was adopted as the decision rule and each Selection Committee member was allowed to vote for up to 60 candidates.

As described in previous sections and summarized in Table 7.2, access to both the constitution-making process and the political positions charged with rule-making power for the institutions of the HKSAR was highly moderated by China. Through appointment, Beijing could easily shape the membership of the Preparatory Committee. Although the Selection Committee was open for nomination, the Presidium of the Preparatory Committee was empowered to screen the candidates' list. It is therefore widely believed that only those who could pass the "trust" test could successfully be selected as members of the Preparatory and Selection Committees, and the members of the latter were subsequently empowered to select the CE and the Provisional LegCo. It is quite clear that the Chinese government was in a strong position in defining the role and the relative strength of the participants in the constitution- and rule-making processes.

As a result, the colonial governing philosophy does find a new form in the HKSAR, with an elected but out-of-reach CE and a fragmented legislature. These institutional arrangements are made possible through the high institutional threshold of accessing the CE, the departmentalized methods of returning LegCo members, and the installation of multi-veto points in the decision-making procedures of the legislature. Two major, but related, effects resulted: the insulation of political figures who are responsible for policy-making from the citizens' control and their insensitivity to social demands and conflicts.

Table 7.2 Access to the Constitution-making and Decision-making Processes by the General Public

	Methods of Recruitment	Public Access
Sino-British Joint Declaration	Delegation	Highly Restricted
Basic Law Drafting Committee	Appointment	Restricted
Preliminary Committee of the Preparatory Committee	Appointment	Restricted
Preparatory Committee	Appointment	Restricted
Selection Committee	Nomination & Appointment	Restricted
Chief Executive	Consultation/ Nomination / Election	Restricted
Provisional LegCo	Nomination & Election	Less Restricted
LegCo (Functional Constituencies)	Nomination & Election	Less Restricted
LegCo (Election Committee)	Nomination & Election	Less Restricted
LegCo (Geographic Constituencies)	Nomination & Popular Election	Least Restricted

Election Dynamics and Cleavage System

As noted earlier, the major conflicts, in terms of the pace of democratization, during the constitution-making process in the late 1980s were the role of the legislature and its relations with the executive, the proportion of popularly-elected seats in the legislature, the decision-making procedures in the legislature and so on. China and the conservative elites wanted to maintain the political status quo as far as possible, while the democrats preferred a democratic reform to the colonial governing structure.

At the electorate level, the voters seem to align along the cleavage lines of centre-periphery and individual-collective consumption. The continued salience of these two cleavages would contribute to the dominance of the democrats in popular elections, in terms of vote share, not seat share. It is suggested that the raw support is better calculated on the basis of vote share than seat share because the latter is more sensitive to the kind of election system that will be adopted. As the twin cleavages have been discussed in previous chapters, the relevant concepts are only briefly restated here.

The centre-periphery cleavage is defined as: the clash of the "centre" dominant Chinese Government with the "periphery" constituted unit(s) of Hong Kong over the pace of democratization and the degree of autonomy enjoyed by the latter after 1997 (Li, 1995a:327). It also reflects the long-term historic distrust between the Communist Chinese government and the people of Hong Kong in general. Given that the restoration of Hong Kong sovereignty to Chinese government is inevitable, some kinds of institutional protection have been sought by the emerging middle class which will protect their exiting way of life. These included: an open and democratic government, a high degree of autonomy after 1997, and the rule of law. On the other hand, the Chinese government does promise what the middle class wants to have, but there is a credibility gap between what it agrees in principle and what it really does in the constitution-making process and the resultant executive-dominance governing model.

Those people, groups or parties who share or articulate these values and viewpoints, or fight to see them in place, could be classified as "pro-periphery". Those who do not share these values and see no reason to antagonize the Chinese government over the pace of democratization and the related institutional reforms could be termed as "pro-centre".

The application of the consumption cleavage concept in explaining voters' choice was first developed by Patrick Dunleavy in the late 1970s.

His line of reasoning is that: accompanying the state expansion is the state intervention into the consumption process; sectoral cleavages (collective vs. individualized consumption) emerge and crosscut the existing class cleavages. Any change in policy direction will be rejected by the affected sector(s) and any move to privatize the collective consumption goods will cause shifts in electoral support. In the context of Hong Kong, the consumption cleavage denotes the contraction of the Hong Kong state through the adoption of a privatization policy. The expansion of the social services programmes in the 1970s was made possible by the government's high-land price policy. That policy allowed the government to continue the traditional low tax policy while at the same time to expand her programmes in housing, education, health care, and so on. The state distanced herself from these resource-sucking programmes because of the sudden drop of land revenue as a result of the political uncertainty in the late 1970s and early 1980s. In order to keep tax low enough so as to compete with other developing countries, a government budget cut is a logical result. Under such circumstances, the privatization of some government services is deemed desirable, especially the provision of public housing and cheap health care services. Although the government uses the pretext of "cost recovery" and "user pay", the effect of moving the financial burden back to the user is the same as that of the privatization policy.

For those people who have a collective mode of consumption, they may reject the privatization policy and, therefore, logically support those groups or parties with the same orientation in the popular elections. They may be termed as "pro-collective consumption". For those people who have an individual mode of consumption, they may accept the privatization policy and, therefore, vote for those groups or parties which share the same attitude with them in the popular elections. They may be regarded as "pro-individual consumption".

The above mentioned twin cleavages of centre-periphery and consumption are believed to have been salient in the 1995 LegCo popular elections (Li, 1996:245-73). As sketched in Figure 7.1, the democrats seem to draw their majority support from those voters who held a pro-periphery attitude and have a collective mode of consumption. Given that the existing three major political forces (democrats, leftists and conservatives) did not compete in all constituencies, whether the democrats can maintain their electoral support in future LegCo popular elections is called into doubt.

However, the continued salience of the twin cleavages of centre-periphery and individual-collective consumption is highly possible. It is because once the cleavages gain prominence, they are quite durable. It is sure that cleavage transformation is possible, but it would be happened in a rather slow and gradual manner. Other things being equal, the partisan alignment along the twin cleavage lines is highly possible. As a result, the democrats may likely gain the majority support in terms of vote share in the popular elections in the near future.

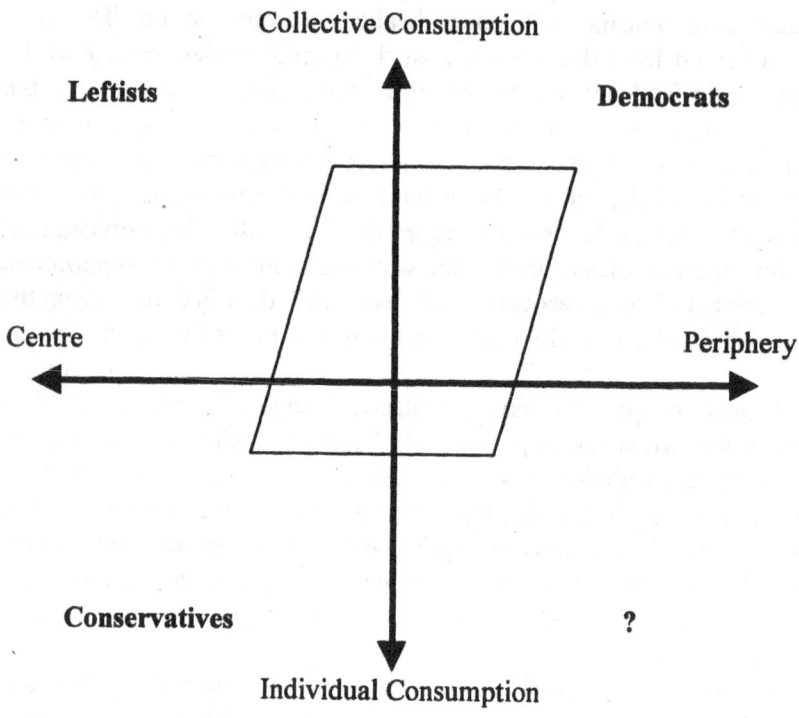

Figure 7.1   A Sketch of the Electoral Market of Hong Kong in 1998

The HKSAR Constitutional Order and Conflict Management

In the context of Hong Kong, even though the democrats or any other political forces receive the majority support in the popular polls, they are highly unlikely to become the majority force in the whole legislature, not to speak of in the election of the CE. The reason is simple. More than half of the LegCo seats are not returned by popular elections (half in 2003). Even when there a majority party emerges in popular elections, this party is most likely to be a minority party in the whole legislature. Moreover, the institutional arrangements between the executive and the legislature are not structured in such a way as to strengthen citizen control or public accountability of those who are involved in decision-making. The blocking of the popular will, if any, by institutional barriers has, in one way or the other, provided the basis of further reinforcing the existing cleavages system and the related partisan alignment. The under-privileged will sooner or later transform the policy conflicts into rule conflicts.

For illustrative purposes, Figure 7.2 is constructed to chart the political orientations of LegCo members returned by functional constituencies, election committee, and geographic constituencies. Scenarios (I) and (IV) reflect those LegCo members that share a common view or have arrived at a consensus on a particular issue. If this is the case, it would pose a tremendous pressure on the executive to act and the popular views are more likely to have effect on subsequent executive decision or policy-making. Scenarios (II) and (III) indicate that there are conflicting views among LegCo members and the LegCo which would become divisive on that particular issue. If this is the case, the executive could have more room in manoeuvring the decision-making.

Given the segmented methods of returning LegCo members and the different basis of interests representation and articulation inherited, a fragmented legislature is highly possible. Therefore, scenarios (II) and (III) are likely to happen more often than scenarios (I) and (IV).

If we further consider the number of seats in each category, a majority, in favour of the business and professional interests, apparently emerges. One of the effects is that the gap between the majority view of the LegCo and the popular views may become wider and, therefore, the conflicts between them may be escalated.

If the cleavage system is added to the above discussion, the conflicts between the majority LegCo view and the popular views become even clearer. As shown in Figure 7.3, the LegCo majority view (established interests) is likely to adopt a pro-centre and pro-individual consumption attitude (scenarios I and III), while the non-established (supposedly representing the popular views) a pro-periphery and pro-collective consumption orientation (scenarios II and IV).

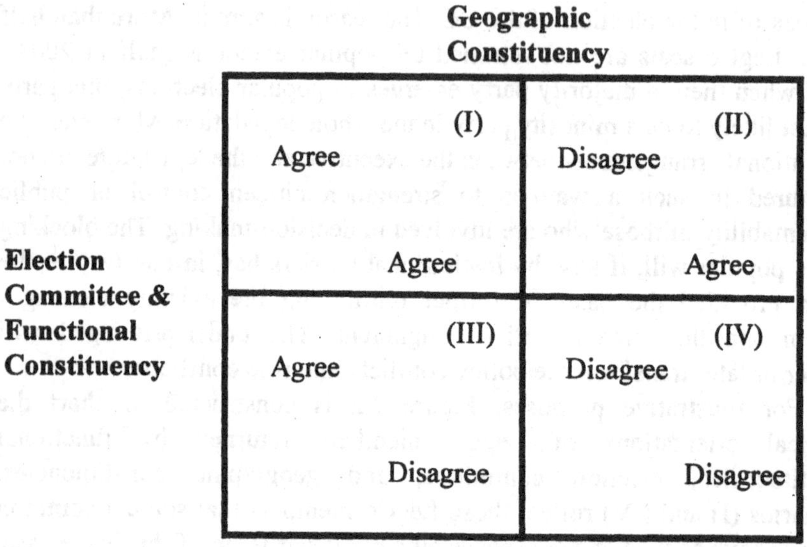

	Geographic Constituency	
	Agree (I)	Disagree (II)
Election Committee & Functional Constituency Agree	Agree	Agree
	(III)	(IV)
	Agree	Disagree
Disagree	Disagree	Disagree

Figure 7.2   The Dynamics within the LegCo

The separate origin and survival of the executive and the legislature will raise the issue of which institution is representing the popular views. In a typical presidential system, both the executive and the legislature are returned by popular elections or by electoral college comprised of popularly-elected members. So, there is not much problem. On the other hand, in a typical parliamentary system, the legislature is supposedly representing the popular views and the executive relies on the confidence of the legislature. The issue of representing popular views is therefore not an issue at all. But in the case of Hong Kong, the issue of representing the popular views is quite complicated. Based upon the institutional arrangements stipulated in the Basic Law, neither the executive nor the legislature could, on procedural grounds, claim that it is representing the popular views. Strictly speaking, only those elected in popular elections could qualify themselves to speak for the popular views.

Legislature

	Established	Non-established
Centre-periphery Cleavage	(I) Centre (conservative & leftists)	(II) Periphery (democrats)
Consumption	(III) Individual (conservatives)	(IV) Collective (democrats & leftists)

Figure 7.3 The Twin Cleavages and the LegCo

If this is the case, the popularly-elected representatives would more or less tend to challenge those representatives returned by other forms of election. Supported by the voters, these popularly-elected representatives will demand an increase in the proportion of popularly-elected seats. This, in turn, would entail opposition from those LegCo members who are returned by functional constituencies and election committee. The conflicts would not be so easily resolved because of the zero-sum nature of the change of the seat proportions.

The way the CE is being elected has prevented him/her from moving too close to the popular views. The rather small constituency and the close, interdependent relations within the constituency have to be responsible for that. The room for manoeuvre is not as large as that of the popularly-elected CE. The dominance of the established interests in the decision-making process and the suppression of the popular views in the LegCo would further force the voters to vote for the groups or parties that represented the grass-roots.

The conflicts mentioned above seem to be clustered around the rule and policy levels and the conflicting parties are judged to have been encapsulated, as defined in Chapter 1. If these judgements are correct, the pressing task at this moment is to re-design the institutional arrangements of the executive and the legislature in such a way as to contain the conflicts effectively and to ward-off the possible development towards non-encapsulation.

Alternative Arrangements

The fragmentation of the LegCo, the dominance of established interests in the LegCo, the distortion of popular views in the decision-making process, the insulation of the CE from popular election and the resultant weakening of public accountability of the CE may all work to antagonize and polarize the existing conflicts (as reflected in popular elections) which have, in turn, de-legitimated the newly-installed conflict resolution mechanism.

Which direction does the adjustment proceed if needed? The followings are some of the suggestions:

Policy Co-option

This method requires the CE and the executive to grant access for those related or interested parties to the policy-making process by policy area. The CE or the executive is obliged not only to consult those who are being identified in a particular policy network, but also to try to draw the common denominator among them. Because of its informal nature, its successful operation depends highly on the "will and skill" of the CE and the executive.

Institutional Co-option

In order to compensate for the high institutional threshold of entry of the CE and the resultant gap between the established and the non-established in the decision-making process, it would be better to appoint some popularly-elected LegCo members to the ExCo.[4] The expected effects are: (1) to strengthen the grass-roots' views or interests in the policy deliberation process and (2) to facilitate the emergence of elite consensus and integration.

Although LegCo members have been identified as one of the potential sources of appointing ExCo members (Article 55 of the Basic Law), reservations about appointing those LegCo members who have political affiliation has been expressed. Judging from the past three LegCo popular elections, nearly all the winners have party affiliation. It will, therefore, defeat the original idea of co-option if those LegCo members who are popularly elected and have party affiliation are excluded from the ExCo.

The appointment of those popularly-elected LegCo members to the ExCo may put pressure on the CE and the ExCo members to make compromises, but the resultant deals are very likely be the median option in the spectrum of policy choices.

Abolishment of Separate Vote Count Mechanism

The high institutional threshold imposed by the separate vote count mechanism to adopt LegCo individual bills or motions is designed in such a way as to counter the surge of the non-established interests in the LegCo decision-making process. But this mechanism also works to the disadvantage of the established interests. It is because only 16 votes can effectively block any individual bills or motions from passage. The abolishment or lowering of the threshold may ease the tension within the LegCo and more important, this may help reflect the societal preferences in a more proportional way.

Readjusting the Proportion of FC and GC Seats

As stated in the Basic Law, the LegCo members will be eventually returned by "universal suffrage" (Article 68). If this is going to happen, the earlier the time to make that adjustment, the less the conflicts will be. The timely and gradual manner of introducing the adjustment would help prevent the polarization of political forces within the LegCo. It is because: (1) the non-established may expect a growing role in the LegCo, so their frustration may, thus, be lessened; and (2) the adjustment will bring pressure on the established interests to join the popular elections and, therefore, their policy stance will be dictated by the logic of the electoral market.

Returning the CE through Popular Election

How to make the CE accountable to the public is a perennial question. However, as stated in the Basic Law, the "ultimate aim is the selection of the Chief Executive by universal suffrage upon nomination by a broadly representative nominating committee in accordance with democratic procedures" (Article 45). The designers' logic is clear. By balancing the non-established interests, "a broadly representative nominating committee" is used to screen the potential candidates and subject them to popular election. If implemented, this will bring the CE under periodic popular electoral pressure and thus, keep the CE in touch institutionally with the wider spectrum of interests. Although the method of organizing the "broadly representative nominating committee" does not workout at this moment, it is preferable not to set a high threshold of entry. Otherwise, the purpose of popular election will be defeated. Moreover, the earlier the time to return the CE through popular election, the better the chance to keep the conflicts at the policy level.

Given that no political institutions could remain intact in an age of rapid and dynamic changes, institutional reforms are always needed and desirable so as to enhance their capacity to cope with the emerging social conflicts or to fine-tune the existing mechanism for growing effectiveness.

Notes

1   "The Decision of the National People's Congress on the Method for the Formation of the First Government and the First Legislative Council of the Hong Kong Special Administrative Region" can be found in *The Basic Law of the Hong Kong Special Administrative Region of the People's Republic of China* (Hong Kong: The Consultative Committee for the Basic Law, 1990), pp. 65-7.
2   The full text of the formation method of the first HKSAR Selection Committee can be found in *Wen Wei Po*, 11 August 1996, p. A4.
3   For the relevant documents, see *Wen Wei Po*, 6 October 1996, pp. A1 & A6.
4   In Tung Chee-hwa's (the first CE of the HKSAR government) first ExCo from 1997 only one popularly-elected LegCo member is included.

8 Conclusion

The political configurations at the time that universal suffrage is introduced have a considerable effect on the development and salience of particular electoral cleavages. Once the electoral cleavages have emerged, the electoral market will be structured by the mobilization efforts of the concerned political groups or parties along these cleavage lines. In the context of Hong Kong, the removal of the institutional barrier of entry by the new political structure stipulated in the Sino-British Joint Declaration in 1984 paved the way for the entry of the new middle-class professionals into the political arena and this reflected the gradual breakdown of the monopolistic power structure, which the established elites had dominated since the founding of the Crown Colony of Hong Kong. The "1997 issue", therefore, not only signified the reversion of Hong Kong's sovereignty to China, but also the transformation of Hong Kong's political order as a result of the Chinese promise of "Hong Kong people governing Hong Kong". At this juncture of transformation, the privatization of collective consumption programmes and the expanding salaries tax net resulting from the drastic decline of land revenues as a result of political uncertainty in the early 1980s and the designated use of the land fund from 1985 alienated the low-income group and the middle-class professionals.

The LegCo popular elections were, thus, the result of the interaction among various historic and structural factors, such as the widespread distrust of the communist Chinese government by the Hong Kong people, the rise of new middle-class professionals, the tough Chinese policy towards Hong Kong's democratization, the privatization of government services resulted from the fiscal crisis of the British-Hong Kong government, and the Tiananmen Incident of 1989. All these events had, in one way or another, structured the political and electoral universe of Hong Kong, from which the enfranchised Hong Kong electors had being nurtured since 1945, and contributed to the salience of the centre-periphery and the individual-collective consumption electoral cleavages in the LegCo popular elections.

The Centre-Periphery Cleavage

The centre-periphery cleavage denoted, here, the clash of the "centre" dominant Chinese government with the "periphery" constituted unit(s) of Hong Kong over the pace of democratization and the degree of autonomy enjoyed by the latter after 1997. Electorally speaking, Hong Kong's political groups and voters could be divided into the pro-centre and the pro-periphery groupings, in which the former stands for a slower pace of democratization and accepts the degree of autonomy as allowed by China, while the latter supports a quicker pace of democratization and fights for the maximum degree of autonomy.

The centre-periphery cleavage also reflected the mistrust between the Chinese government, and the British-Hong Kong government and the Hong Kong people. On the one hand, the Chinese government appeared to have the perception that Britain did not wholeheartedly wish to see the reversion of Hong Kong's sovereignty to China and would adopt any measure to prolong the informal British presence in Hong Kong. This conspiratorial perception by Beijing coloured its judgements on the developments in Hong Kong and paved the way for the adoption of a cautious and conservative policy. For example, the political reforms initiated by the British-Hong Kong government from the mid-1980s have been viewed as a plan to take advantage of the distrustful feelings among the Hong Kong people by planting "pro-British" politicians into the political structure through elections after 1997, and the Hong Kong government's decision to build a new airport after the Tiananmen Incident of 1989 has been interpreted as a move to transfer Hong Kong's fiscal reserves back to Britain. Because of such an attitude, China tended to assert its authority by claiming, in the name of a smooth transition of power and convergence, to have a "veto" power in the transitional period. The Chinese suspicion and distrust further intensified after the Tiananmen Incident of 1989 when the Hong Kong people came out collectively to protest against the way the Beijing leaders had handled the democratic movement.

On the other hand, the Hong Kong Chinese have held negative feelings towards the communist Chinese government because most of them are either refugees or the children of refugees, who either had experienced or have been told of the misgoverning of the communist Chinese government. The historic distrust of the communist Chinese government had been moderated by the rise of China on the international stage in the early 1970s. China's entry into the United Nations and the

Sino-American rapprochement had softened the negative attitude of the Hong Kong people, especially the local-born young intellectuals and university students, towards the Chinese government. The emergence of the 1997 issue in the late 1970s, however, had, more or less, challenged their national identification and their related emotional feelings. The possible loss of freedom and existing living style resulting from the reversion of Hong Kong sovereignty to China had placed the Hong Kong Chinese in a very embarrassing position. Their national romance gave way to practical considerations of their way of life. Although China promised to keep Hong Kong unchanged for 50 years and to let Hong Kong people govern Hong Kong after 1997, the trust of the Hong Kong people was not high enough to make their own hearts really at ease. Their suspicion and distrust might have been alleviated if China had made the best use of the symbol of nationalism and handled skilfully its contradictions with Hong Kong society by acting with self-restraint as a referee, rather than as an arbiter, in the local political conflicts between the conservatives and the democrats.

The bone of contention between the Chinese government and the conservatives, on the one hand, and the democrats, on the other, lies in the pace of democratization and the degree of autonomy allowed after 1997. As the colonial political structure was given notice with the signing of the Sino-British Joint Declaration in 1984, political reforms were inevitable, but the pace and scope of political reforms in the transitional period was subject to differing interpretation. The mistrust between Britain and China had come into play at this critical juncture in the smooth transfer of power. The reforms aimed at having a full-fledged legislature and a more accountable executive system met with a suspicious reception from the Chinese. In order to control these developments, the Chinese government asserted that any "major" changes in the transitional period would better converge with the Basic Law then being drafted. The Sinologists within the British Foreign Office stressed the importance of cooperation with the Chinese government so as to secure a viable plan, which could extend beyond 1997, for the maximum actualization of the pledges contained in the Joint Declaration. For them, any unilateral move without China's blessing would prove to be short-lived and thus the confrontational approach would do no good for the continued stability and prosperity of Hong Kong.

The continued prevalence of this cooperative approach was challenged by the subsequent developments after the Tiananmen Incident in 1989. The upsurge of emotional feeling within Hong Kong at the time brought pressure on the British-Hong Kong government to do something to stabilize both the social order and the inner psychological uncertainty of most Hong Kong people. The pressure to do more was once again viewed by the Chinese government as a plot to prevent the smooth transfer of power. Even worse, China seemed to believe that the joint effort of Britain and other Western countries in sanctioning China and in supporting the pro-democratic Chinese activists was an offensive move to challenge the communist regime in Beijing. Thus, the mistrust and misunderstanding between Britain and China had reached the point of no return.

As for the local democrat activists, they had high hopes of reforming the colonial political system and smoothing the way for subsequent "Hong Kong people governing Hong Kong" in the early 1980s. This stance had been taken up by various political groups formed during or after the Sino-British negotiations, such as the MP and the NHKS. The demands for democratic government from such groups and political activists had become the prime source of conflict with the Hong Kong government and the conservatives in the mid-1980s, when the power devolution resulting from the Sino-British Joint Declaration had taken place. Later on, however, the contradiction shifted to one between the Chinese government and the democrats as a result of the Chinese intervention in Hong Kong domestic politics. This was well demonstrated in the 1987 political review which, under China's pressure, deferred the introduction of popular elections from 1988 to 1991, and the drafting of the Basic Law which adopted a conservative political model for after 1997. The conservative approach to political reforms and the alliance with the conservatives had put the Chinese government at odds with the democrats. The growing Chinese intervention in local Hong Kong politics had also brought up the question of how high the "high degree" of autonomy for Hong Kong promised by the Chinese leaders and stipulated in the Joint Declaration would be after 1997. Later in 1989, the Tiananmen Incident had not only politicized the Hong Kong society but also had driven the Hong Kong people to support the democrats' demands for a quicker pace of democratization so as to minimize the intervention from Beijing after 1997.

The salience of the centre-periphery electoral cleavage in terms of democratization and autonomy in the 1991 LegCo popular elections is reflected in both the salience of the issue during the electoral campaign process and the defeat of the leftist and the conservative candidates by a significant margin of votes by the leading democrats (Li, 1995a). The leftists had knitted together their local working class network for decades and believed themselves to have considerable support in the low-income groups. But the ecological data at the district level reveals that they actually showed up worse than the democrats in the working class districts (Li, 1995a: chapter 7). The pro-centre candidates, who strongly stressed a cooperative attitude towards China, obtained even less support than the leftists. By contrast, the democrats' leaders who played both an active role in Chinese and local democratic movements enjoyed the highest electoral support.

The centre-periphery cleavage seems to undergo transformation after 1997. The relative non-intervention of the central Beijing government into the domestic affairs of Hong Kong has the effect of sidelining the direct conflicts between the Beijing government and Hong Kong society. Nevertheless, the HKSAR becomes the focus of the conflicts. For those who do not have trust in Beijing's promise of "one country, two systems" and "Hong Kong people governing Hong Kong", their distrust has now shifted towards the HKSAR government as they believe that the HKSAR government does not enjoy a real autonomy in governing Hong Kong and lives under the shadow of the central Beijing government. For them, the handling of the right of abode issue by the HKSAR government and the subsequent request from the HKSAR government to the Standing Committee of the NPC to interpret the relevant clauses in the Basic Law have, among others, given support to their worry. The Court of Final Appeals ruled in January 1999 that children who born in mainland China and whose parent (either father or mother) is Hong Kong resident should become a permanent resident of the HKSAR. But the HKSAR government challenged the ruling by arguing that the issue is touching upon the relationship between the central and the HKSAR governments and thus requested the Standing Committee of the NPC through the State Council to interpret the relevant clauses of the Basic Law. The opponents to the request regarded the issue as a domestic one and thus falling within the jurisdiction of the HKSAR. Moreover, the issue has raised the question of how and under what circumstances should the relative priority of "one country" and "two systems" be placed. The hard fact is that this kind of issue will come up very often in the future, which is regarded as normal as "one country, two systems" is a new concept and under experimentation. The problem is whether there is a sound and credible mechanism or procedure in place to manage that kind of conflict.

The Individual-Collective Consumption Cleavage

The growing intervention of the Hong Kong government in the individual consumption process in the 1970s, resulting from the pressure of further capitalist economic development had two different consequences. First of all, most Hong Kong people improved their living standards as a result of massive government provisions of public housing, medical services and education. There was no doubt that most Hong Kong people benefited from it, especially those direct recipients, and appreciated the government's benevolent effort. Second, the affected population under the government's urban redevelopment scheme, slum clearance and land resumption drive complained of their poor or unfair treatment and poor compensation from the government. Although their grievances did not accumulate to the point of explosion, their negative feelings towards the government were reinforced and, thus, the government's efficiency in governing suffered.

On top of these were the growing costs of living resulting partly from the high land price policy of the Hong Kong government and the related chain effects of price rises on other daily necessities. In order to keep the tax low enough to attract foreign investment, the Hong Kong government had to rely on land revenues to support its massive expenditure on infrastructural construction and collective consumption programmes. The disproportionate reliance on land revenues exposed the vulnerability of the government's fiscal capability. The real challenge had come when the 1997 issues surfaced in the late 1970s. The confidence crisis resulting from the uncertainty over the political future of Hong Kong in the early 1980s plagued the land and property markets. Because of the sudden decline in land revenues, the government was forced into either contracting out its activities by cutting back government expenditure and adopting a privatization policy, or into finding new tax sources to replace the declining land revenues.

The results of the government contraction and the decline of land revenues were the shifting of the financial burden to the low-income group and the middle class. The effect of privatization would be tremendous because of the extensive scope of government provisions in public housing, medical services and education. Furthermore, the privatization drive has not only lessened the government financial commitment to the collective consumption programmes, but has also taken the form of "cost-recovery" in charging government services and facilities. As a result, more and more government departments or public bodies have or will adopt the market-oriented mode of operation, such as the Post Office, Water Supplies Department and so on.

Even worse, the low-income group further suffered by the transfer of the manufacturing industries to nearby Chinese special economic zones, the import of foreign labour, and the high inflation rates in the mid- or late 1980s. The middle class also suffered from the expanding salaries tax net resulting from government pressure to replace the loss of land revenues through the minor, inflation-proof adjustment in tax allowance. Although the over-taxing of the middle class has already been eased after the mid-1990s as the tax allowances have been adjusted significantly, the impact of state contraction, in the form of privatization, has deeply penetrated into all walks of life.

Understandably, the low-income group and the middle class would be prone to political and electoral mobilization, and thus, come to extend the reach of the political activists. Therefore, a territory-wide political market gradually emerged, in which the collective consumption issues became one of the principal concerns of the electors.

The Emergence of a "Distorted" Electoral Market

Added to the electoral cleavages mentioned above is the institutional factor that help to maintain the existing cleavage structure. The design of the existing political institutions is not capable of addressing the issues of democratization, autonomy and privatization. The problem lies not only in the substantial content of the concerned issues themselves, but in the authority and legitimacy of those people who exercise the policy-making power. Not subject to popular pressure, the CE and some functionally elected LegCo members find it hard to command the respect of the public, not to talk about whether they have the mandate to govern Hong Kong. The current institutional set-up also leads to the emergence of a distorted electoral market, which in turn intensifies the existing social conflicts.

After a decade of development, an electoral market is in the making. Faced with this new advancement, the conservatives have not adjusted well so far. Enjoying a political "free lunch" for more than a century, they have tended to resist the introduction of universal franchise and related institutional reforms. They have tried very hard to delay the pace of reforms and have made little preparation to take up the challenge of popular election. Nevertheless, the formation of the LP in 1993 signified a departure from this tendency. They aim high but without a solid mass support. But more important is the lack of "will and skill" to compete in the emerging electoral market.

The nominal participation of the conservatives in popular elections will only make things worse. It is most likely that they will rely on functional elections to maintain their influence in the LegCo or in the policy-making process. Therefore, the continuity of the functional elections becomes a life-and-death struggle for them. Any reform to decrease the proportion of functional seats would inevitably meet with their strong opposition.

With the insufficient voters' support for and the resulting minimum involvement of the conservatives in the popular election, the electoral market would be inevitably divided up by the leftists and the democrats. This has already been shown in the past few LegCo election results.

The leftists and the democrats have long been involved in the social and labour movements and have already established themselves as the "vanguard" of the grass-roots. Moreover, the leftists have the asset of having close ties with the Chinese Government. The plea of nationalism could be an effective tool to enlist support from those Hong Kong people who have a strong national sentiment. Nevertheless, this asset will also become a liability when there is a conflict of interest between China and Hong Kong, as quite often has been the case both before and after 1997.

The minimum participation of the conservatives, the overwhelming support for both the democrats and the leftists, and the resulting "distorted" electoral market reflect the inappropriate design of the existing political institutions. First of all, the non-elected governor before 1997 or the non-popularly-elected CE after 1997 and the "executive-led" government would inevitably produce an "opposition" legislature, in which the voters would expect their representatives to play a watch-dog role. Because of their close ties with the political establishment, the conservatives could not be trusted to take up such role. On the contrary, the democrats and the leftists would be the logic alternatives to vote for.

Second, the prolonged existence and the significant proportion of functional elections have been given the conservatives a convenient means to counter the expected surge of the democrats and the leftists in the LegCo. They, therefore, feel under no hurry to prepare for the popular elections or to adjust their policy orientation. This could direct the electoral traffic into two extremes: the conservatives would only focus on functional elections while the democrats and the leftists consolidate themselves largely through popular elections.

The conflicts between functionally elected and popularly-elected LegCo members, as well as between the non-popularly-elected executive and the elected legislature could be expected to intensify, which, in turn, would contribute to the tense political atmosphere both before and after 1997, and would also make it even harder for the concerned parties to compromise in the political review in or after 2004.

The sudden influx of these participants, politicians and political parties on to the political stage resulted from the top-down democratic reform which has had a significant impact on the political ecology of Hong Kong: from closed and responsible to more open and representative government. This has been reflected in the growing public role in the policy-making process and the repeated challenge to the "executive-led" government structure by the elected legislature. These developments have contributed to the re-discovery of politics in the "depoliticized" society of Hong Kong.

Dimensions of Electoral Support

Previous studies of the 1991 LegCo popular elections largely focused on the effect of the Tiananmen Incident on the alignment of political forces and on the voters' choice. This book develops these studies further by adding the domestic dimension of the social conflicts which have been developed within Hong Kong since the 1970s. Based upon these twin cleavages of centre-periphery and individual-collective consumption, a classification scheme has been constructed to frame the positioning of various political forces, which would contribute to the understanding of the electoral and political dynamics in the post-1997 Hong Kong. In short, it is possible to construct the following figure, based upon the centre-peripheral (in terms of democratization and autonomy) and the individual-collective consumption (in terms of privatization) cleavages, to demonstrate the possible electoral support for various political forces, presuming that the voters are expressing their own free will.

As shown in Figure 8.1, there are four possible situations:
1. the voters are positive towards democratization and autonomy, and hold a negative attitude towards privatization;
2. the voters are negative towards democratization and autonomy, and hold a negative attitude towards privatization;
3. the voters are negative towards democratization and autonomy, and hold a positive attitude towards privatization; and

4. the voters are positive towards democratization and autonomy, and hold a positive attitude towards privatization.

If situation (1) emerges, the democrats are likely to receive more electoral support; if situation (2) arises, the leftists are likely to have more electoral support; if situation (3) emerges, the conservatives are likely to get more electoral support; if situation (4) arises, there is no political force (group) clearly identify itself with this position at this moment.

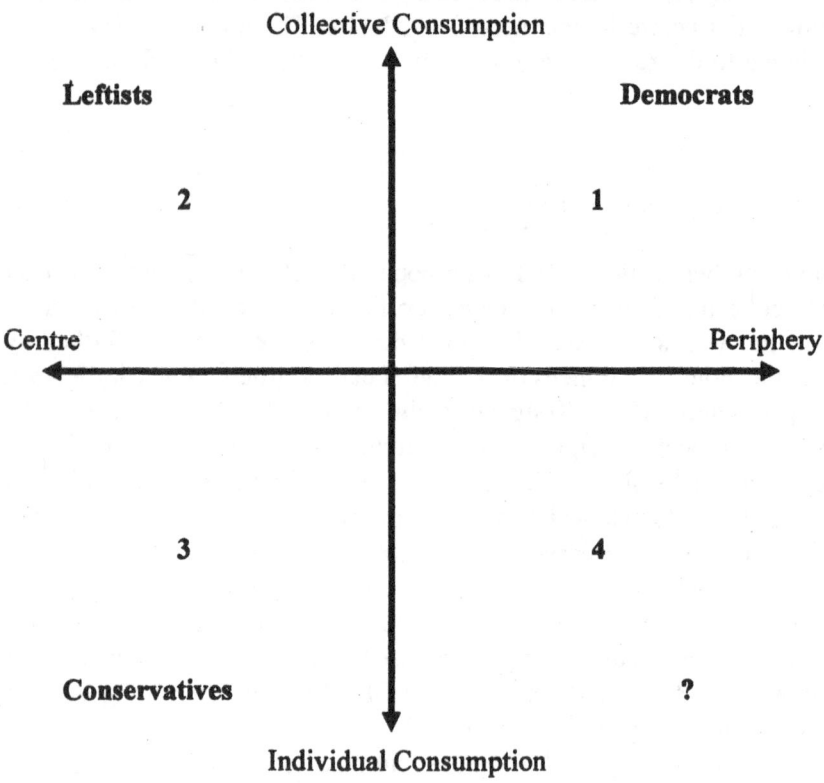

Figure 8.1   Possible Dimensions of Electoral Support

Conclusion 239

With the absence of the conservatives, the competition in the popular electoral market will be limited to the democrats and the leftists. Because of their common orientation towards privatization and collective consumption, the real competition between the democrats and the leftists will be on the issue of democratization and autonomy. So, the victory of the democrats in the past LegCo popular elections may be interpreted as if the majority of voters tended to be concerned more about the issues of democratization and autonomy than the issue of privatization when they decided on their vote choices. Situation (4) seems not to be viable because those voters who oppose the privatization drive would logically have to support more democratization as only more popularly-elected seats could effectively bring enough pressure to halt the privatization move. The conservatives are fighting an uphill battle because their negative attitude towards democratization and positive attitude towards privatization do not match with the interests and demands of the grass-roots. Moreover, the conservatives have yet to develop credibility and support in the popular electoral market. Therefore, situation (3) is not likely to emerge in the near future.

The Possible Developments Ahead

The discussions in this book have served to explore the development of a cleavage system in Hong Kong and its impact on the alignment of political forces and on the voters' choice in the LegCo popular elections, as well as the readiness of the political institutions to address the conflicts. Given that Hong Kong is a special administrative region of the PRC, the attitude of the Beijing government is critical to any further liberalization or democratization of Hong Kong's political system. Nevertheless, Hong Kong's emerging electoral cleavage structure, which is embedded in a particular pattern of social cleavages and conflicts, has been taking shape since the 1970s and will, in my view, probably remain in the near future. Other things being equal, the twin cleavages would have the same effect on voters' choice. How far the Beijing government will allow Hong Kong to have a full democracy and how high the autonomy which Hong Kong enjoys will be have yet to be confirmed, but the pressure generated by the cleavage structure and released during the electoral process sets the agenda for public discussion and policy debate after 1997, just as if it did before that date.

Looking into the future 10 or 20 years' political order of Hong Kong, it is very likely that the role played by the Hong Kong people in domestic politics will become more important than before. Two reasons can be adduced: (1) the promise of "one country, two systems", "Hong Kong people governing Hong Kong" and "high degree of autonomy"; and (2) popular elections have been instituted to elect certain numbers of political posts with the ultimate goal of returning the CE and all the LegCo members by popular elections as stipulated in the Basic Law. Therefore, six developments may emerge: (1) further mobilization and politicization of Hong Kong society along the twin cleavages of centre-periphery and individual-collective consumption will become inevitable; (2) the democrats will continue to receive electoral support and will remain as a significant player in the LegCo; (3) tensions and conflicts between the Executive and the Legislature will come to the forefront because of the built-in contradiction of the HKSAR's representation system; (4) the insulation of the Executive from the mass electoral pressure will give rise to a legitimacy crisis for the HKSAR government; (5) pressure to reform the "executive-led" government will surface and will lead to have some kind of reform, such as a kind of political appointment of the policy secretaries; and (6) the Beijing government will tolerate demands for political reform so long as these demands do not prevent it from exercising sovereign power over Hong Kong and so long as there is no significant spill-over effect into China.

Things happening outside Hong Kong will also have effect on the liberalization or democratization of Hong Kong. First of all, the absorption of the Chinese economy into the international capitalist system has made China more prone to the influence of the outside world. Given that the success of economic reforms in China is so important for the survival of the Communist regime and the contribution of Hong Kong to that effect is significant, the Chinese leaders would be more cautious and self-restrained in handling the governing of and political demands from Hong Kong. Second, the openness of Chinese leaders. The Chinese leaders seems likely to be a more open-minded and pragmatic leaders, who will try to balance conflicting demands in the economic liberalization process and will also subscribe to the capitalist logic of thinking. Therefore, a more relaxed atmosphere will emerge within China as well as between China and Hong Kong. Although China and the conservatives will be tempted to restrain the pace of democratization and the depth of political reforms, there is only a slim possibility of overturning what Hong Kong has already gained in the political system, such as popular elections, accountability, representation and so on. Optimistic though it may be, it still depends on the "will and skill" of the political leaders of China and Hong Kong to make compromises that would allow a positive sum political game to operate which can benefit both sides as well as their peoples.

Bibliography

Government Publications

Abercrombie, Patrick. [1948]. *Hong Kong: Preliminary Planning Report.*
Assessment Office. 1984. *Arrangements for Testing the Acceptability in Hong Kong of the Draft Agreement on the Future of the Territory. Report of the Assessment Office. Report of the Independent Monitoring Team.* Hong Kong: Government Printer.
Blackie, W.J. 1955. *Report on Agriculture in Hong Kong with Policy Recommendation.* Hong Kong: Government Printer.
Braga, J.M. 1965. *A Hong Kong Bibliography.* Hong Kong: Government Press.
Census and Statistics Department. 1969. *Hong Kong Statistics 1947-1967.* Hong Kong: Government Printer.
Census and Statistics Department. 1975. *Hong Kong Social & Economic Trend 1964-1974.* Hong Kong: Government Printer.
Census and Statistics Department. 1981. *Hong Kong Annual Digest of Statistics.* 1981 Edition. Hong Kong: Government Printer.
Census and Statistics Department. 1987. *Hong Kong 1986 By-Census, Main Report Vol. 1.* Hong Kong: Government Printer.
Census and Statistics Department. 1988. *Hong Kong 1986 By-Census: Graphic Guide.* Hong Kong: Government Printer.
Census and Statistics Department. 1992a. *Hong Kong 1991 Population Census: Basic Table for District Board Districts.* Hong Kong: Government Printer.
Census and Statistics Department. 1992b. *Hong Kong Annual Digest of Statistics.* 1992 Edition. Hong Kong: Government Printer.
Census and Statistics Department. 1993. *Hong Kong Annual Digest of Statistics.* 1993 Edition. Hong Kong: Government Printer.
Census and Statistics Department. 1997a. *1996 Population By-Census: Summary Results.* Hong Kong: Government Printer.
Census and Statistics Department. 1997b. *1996 Population By-Census: Graphic Guide.* Hong Kong: Government Printer.

Census and Statistics Department. 1999. *Estimates of Gross Domestic Product 1961 to 1998*. Hong Kong: Printing Department.
Colonial Secretariat. 1971. *White Paper: The Urban Council*. Hong Kong: Government Printer.
Commerce and Industry Department. 1958. *Report of the Hong Kong Commercial Mission to Caribbean Countries, Nov.-Dec. 1958*. Hong Kong.
Commerce and Industry Department. 1960. *Report of the Hong Kong Commercial Mission to West Africa, Jan.-Feb. 1960*. Hong Kong.
Commissioner for Resettlement. 1973. *Annual Departmental Report 1972-73*. Hong Kong: Government Printer.
Council of Social Service. 1958. *Working Together: A Survey of the Work of Voluntary and Government Social Organizations in Hong Kong*. Hong Kong: Government Printer.
Environment Branch. 1979. *Keeping Hong Kong Moving: The White Paper on Internal Transport Policy*. Hong Kong: Government Printer.
Finance Branch. 1989. *Public Sector Reform*. Hong Kong: Government Printer.
Fisher, N.G. 1951. *A Report on Government Expenditure on Education in Hong Kong 1950*. Hong Kong: Government Printer.
Freeman, R.A. 1964. *Report on an Export Credits Insurance Scheme for Hong Kong*. Hong Kong: Government Printer.
Gill, K.L. 1966. *'Recreation for Young People': A Survey*. Hong Kong: Government Printer.
Hamilton, G.C. 1969. *Government Departments in Hong Kong: 1841-1969*. Hong Kong: Government Printer.
Hong Kong Annual Report. Yearly.
Hong Kong Government. 1949. *Report of the Hong Kong Salaries Commission*. Singapore: Government Printer.
Hong Kong Government. 1952. *High Education in Hong Kong*. Hong Kong: Government Printer.
Hong Kong Government. 1953a. *Report on Technical Education and Vocational Training*. Hong Kong.
Hong Kong Government. 1953b. *Rent Control*. Hong Kong: Government Printer.
Hong Kong Government. 1954. *Papers on Development of Kai Tak Airport*. Hong Kong: Government Printer.
Hong Kong Government. 1956a. *Report of the Inter-Departmental Working Party on the Proposed Cross-Harbour Tunnel*. Hong Kong: Government Printer.

Hong Kong Government. 1956b. *Report of the Working Committee on Tourism.* Hong Kong: Government Printer.

Hong Kong Government. 1956c. *Report on the Riots in Kowloon and Tsuen Wan, October 10th to 12th, 1956.* Hong Kong: Government Printer.

Hong Kong Government. 1958a. *Report of the Advisory Committee on the Proposed Federation of Industries.* Hong Kong: Government Printer.

Hong Kong Government. 1958b. *Final Report of the Special Committee on Housing 1956-1958.* Hong Kong.

Hong Kong Government. 1959. *The Problem of Narcotic Drugs in Hong Kong.* Hong Kong: Government Printer.

Hong Kong Government. 1961a. *Report of the Hong Kong Trade Mission to Australia.* Hong Kong: Government Printer.

Hong Kong Government. [1961]b. *Reports of the Standing Committee and the Advisory Committee on Corruption, 1960-61.* Hong Kong: Government Printer.

Hong Kong Government. 1963a. *Statement on Government's Policy on the Re-organization of the Structure of Primary and Secondary Education.* Hong Kong: Government Printer.

Hong Kong Government. 1963b. *Report of the Fulton Commission 1963.* Hong Kong: Government Printer.

Hong Kong Government. 1963c. *Report of Working Party on Export Credit Insurance.* Hong Kong: Government Printer.

Hong Kong Government. 1963d. *Report of Working Party on the* Hong Kong Government. 1963e. *Report of the Hong Kong Trade Mission to the Middle East, 27th Dec. 1962--22nd Jan. 1963.* Hong Kong: Government Printer.

Hong Kong Government. 1963f. *Report of the Working Paper on Government Policies and Practices with Regard to Squatters, Resettlement and Government Low Cost Housing.* Hong Kong: Government Printer.

Hong Kong Government. [1963]g. *Development of Medical Services in Hong Kong.* Hong Kong: Government Printer.

Hong Kong Government. 1963h. *Shek Pik Water Scheme.* Hong Kong: Government Printer.

Hong Kong Government. 1964a. *Aims and Policy for Social Welfare in Hong Kong.* Hong Kong: Government Printer.

Hong Kong Government. 1964b. *Report of the Finance of Home Ownership Committee.* Hong Kong: Government Printer.

Hong Kong Government. 1964c. *Final Report of the Seamen's Recruitment Committee.* Hong Kong: Government Printer.

Hong Kong Government. 1964d. *Review of Policies for Squatter Control, Resettlement and Government Low-Cost Housing.* Hong Kong: Government Printer.

Hong Kong Government. 1964e. *Report of the Working Committee on Productivity.* Hong Kong: Government Printer.

Hong Kong Government. 1964f. *Report of the Hong Kong Government Trade Mission to the Common Market Countries, October 1963.* Hong Kong: Government Printer.

Hong Kong Government. 1965a. *Report of the Working Committee on Export Promotion Organization.* Hong Kong: Government Printer.

Hong Kong Government. 1965b. *The Report of the Advisory Committee on Gambling Policy.* Hong Kong: Government Printer.

Hong Kong Government. 1965c. *Education Policy.* Hong Kong: Government Printer.

Hong Kong Government. 1965d. *Report of the Governor in Council of the Working Party set up to Advise on the Adequacy of the Law in Relation to Crimes of Violence Committed by Young Persons.* Hong Kong: Government Printer.

Hong Kong Government. 1965e. *Development of Medical Services in Hong Kong.* Hong Kong: Government Printer.

Hong Kong Government. 1965f. *Report of the Hong Kong Trade Mission to the East Africa.* Hong Kong: Government Printer.

Hong Kong Government. 1965g. *The Report of the Working Party on the Urban Council Franchise and Electoral Registration Procedure.* Hong Kong: Government Printer.

Hong Kong Government. 1966a. *Report of Advisory Committee on Clinics.* Hong Kong: Government Printer.

Hong Kong Government. [1966]b. *Hong Kong Trade Mission to Cyprus.* Hong Kong: Government Printer.

Hong Kong Government. 1966c. *Report of the Ad Hoc Committee on the Future Scope and Operation of the Urban Council.* Hong Kong: Government Printer.

Hong Kong Government. 1967a. *Kowloon Disturbances 1966: Report of Commission of Inquiry.* Hong Kong: Government Printer.

Hong Kong Government. 1967b. *A Report by the Inter-Departmental Working Party to Consider Aspects of Social Security.* Hong Kong: Government Printer.

Hong Kong Government. 1967c. *Report of the Working Party on Local Administration.* Hong Kong: Government Press.
Hong Kong Government. 1968. *Report on the Operation of the Rice Control Scheme in 1967.* Hong Kong: Government Printer.
Hong Kong Government. 1971. *Chinese Language Committee Report: The First to the Fourth Report.* Hong Kong: Government Printer.
Hong Kong Government. 1973a. *Social Welfare in Hong Kong: The Way Ahead.* Hong Kong: Government Printer.
Hong Kong Government. 1973b. *The Five Year Plan for Social Welfare Development in Hong Kong, 1973- 78.* Hong Kong: Government Printer.
Hong Kong Government. 1973c. *The Machinery of Government: A New Framework for Expanding Services.* Hong Kong: Government Printer.
Hong Kong Government. 1974a. *The Further Development of Medical and Health Services in Hong Kong.* Hong Kong: Government Printer.
Hong Kong Government. 1974b. *Transport in Hong Kong: A Paper for Public Information and Discussion.* Hong Kong: Government Printer.
Hong Kong Government. 1974c. *Secondary Education in Hong Kong over the Next Decade.* Hong Kong: Government Printer.
Hong Kong Government. 1977a. *Integrating the Disabled into the Community: A United Effort.* Hong Kong: Government Printer.
Hong Kong Government. 1977b. *A Programme of Social Security Development in Hong Kong.* Hong Kong: Government Printer.
Hong Kong Government. 1977c. *Services for the Elderly.* Hong Kong: Government Printer.
Hong Kong Government. 1977d. *Development of Personal Social Work among Young People in Hong Kong.* Hong Kong: Government Printer.
Hong Kong Government. 1978. *The Development of Senior Secondary and Tertiary Education.* Hong Kong: Government Printer.
Hong Kong Government. 1979a. *Advisory Committee on Diversification Report.* Hong Kong: Government Printer.
Hong Kong Government. 1979b. *Social Welfare into the 1980's.* Hong Kong: Government Printer.
Hong Kong Government. 1980. *Green Paper: A Pattern of District Administration in Hong Kong.* Hong Kong: Government Printer.
Hong Kong Government. 1981a. *White Paper: District Administration in Hong Kong.* Hong Kong: Government Printer.
Hong Kong Government. 1981b. *Primary Education and Pre-Primary Services: White Paper.* Hong Kong: Government Printer.

Hong Kong Government. 1984a. *Green Paper: The Further Development of Representative Government in Hong Kong*. Hong Kong: Government Printer.

Hong Kong Government. 1984b. *White Paper: The Further Development of Representative Government in Hong Kong*. Hong Kong: Government Printer.

Hong Kong Government. 1984c. *A Review of Public Housing Allocation Policies*. Hong Kong: Government Printer.

Hong Kong Government. 1985. *Green Paper on Housing Subsidy to Tenants of Public Housing*. Hong Kong: Government Printer.

Hong Kong Government 1986a. *Report of the Committee on Housing Subsidy to Tenants of Public Housing*. Hong Kong: Government Printer.

Hong Kong Government. 1986b. *Report of the Working Party to Review Public Housing Rental Policy*. Hong Kong: Government Printer.

Hong Kong Government. 1986c. *Consultative Document: Redress of Grievances*. Hong Kong: Government Printer.

Hong Kong Government. 1987. *Green Paper: The 1987 Review of Developments in Representative Government*. Hong Kong: Government Printer.

Hong Kong Government. 1988. *White Paper: The Development of Representative Government: The Way Forward*. Hong Kong: Government Printer.

Hong Kong Government. 1994. *Representative Government in Hong Kong*. Hong Kong: Government Printing Department.

Housing Branch. 1997. *Homes for Hong Kong People: The Way Forward. Long Term Housing Strategy Review Consultative Document*. Hong Kong: Government Printer.

Ministry of Foreign Affairs, PRC, 1994. *Facts About a Few Important Aspects of Sino-British Talks on 1994/95 Electoral Arrangements in Hong Kong*. Hong Kong: Joint Publishing.

Office of Members of the Executive and Legislative Councils (OMELCO). 1989. *Comments on the Basic Law (Draft)*. Hong Kong: OMELCO.

OMELCO Standing Panel on Constitutional Development. 1988. *Report on Draft Basic Law*. Hong Kong: Government Printer.

Secretariat for Chinese Affairs. 1969. *The City District Officer Scheme*. Hong Kong: Government Printer.

Survey Office. 1987. *Public Response to Green Paper: The 1987 Review of Developments in Representative Government Report of the Survey Office: Part 1--Report*. Hong Kong: Government Printer.

Tomkins, H.J. 1962. *Report on the Hong Kong Banking System and Recommendations for the Replacement of the Banking Ordinance 1948*. Hong Kong: Government Printer.
Urban Council. 1957. *Hawkers: A Report with Policy Recommendations*. Hong Kong: Government Printer.
Urban Council. 1969. *Report of the Reform of Local Government*. Hong Kong: Government Printer.
Williams, Gertrude. 1966. *Report on the Feasibility of a Survey into Social Welfare Provision and Allied Topics in Hong Kong*. Hong Kong: Government Printer.
Younghusband, Eileen L. 1960. *Training for Social Work in Hong Kong: A Report Prepared for the Government of Hong Kong*. Hong Kong: Government Printer.

Books and Articles

Alavi, Hamza. 1972. "The State in Post-Colonial Societies: Pakistan and Bangladesh." *New Left Review* 74:59-82.
Alavi, Hamza. 1990. "Authoritarianism and Legitimation of State power in Pakistan." In Subrata Kumar Mitra, ed. *The Post-Colonial State: Dialectics of Politics and Culture*, pp. 19-71. New York: Harvester Wheatsheaf.
Alavi, Hamza and Teodor Shanin, eds. 1982. *Introduction to the Sociology of "Developing Societies"*. Hampshire: Macmillan.
Alford, Robert. 1963. *Party and Society*. Chicago: Rand McNally.
Apter, David E. 1971. *Choice and the Politics of Allocation: A Developmental Theory*. New Haven and London: Yale University Press.
Au Yung, Bun. 1985. "The Emergence and Breakthrough of Miss Maria Tam." *Hong Kong Economic Journal Monthly* 100:14-6, 88. (in Chinese)
Austin, D.G. 1980. "The Transfer of Power: Why and How." In W. H. Morris-Jones and Georges Fischer, eds. *Decolonisation and After: The British and French Experience*, pp. 3- 34. London: Frank Cass.
Bacher, B., O. Lorz, & L. Schuknecht. 1992. "Chinese Investment -- 'Hostages' for Hong Kong?" *Journal of Institutional and Theoretical Economics* 148:645-54.
Baker, Hugh D.R. 1983. "Life in the Cities: the Emergence of Hong Kong Man." *China Quarterly* 95:469-79.

Bartolini, Stefano and Peter Mair. 1990. *Identity, Competition, and Electoral Availability: The Stabilisation of European Electorates 1885-1985.* Cambridge: Cambridge University Press.

Berglund, Sten and Soren Risbjerg Thomsen, eds. 1990. *Modern Political Ecological Analysis.* Abo: Abo Akademis Forlag.

Bermeo, Nancy. 1987. "Redemocratization and Transition Elections: A Comparison of Spain and Portugal." *Comparative Politics* 19:213-31.

Bernacchi, B. A. [1989]. *Reform Club 40-Year History: A Brief History.* Mimeo.

Bernacchi, B. A., et al. 1979. *The Hong Kong Urban Council: The Case of the Elected Members.*

Berndtson, Erkki. 1985. "The Party System and the Future of the State in Advanced Capitalist Countries." *International Political Science Review* 6:65-80.

von Beyme, Klaus. 1985. "The Role of the State and the Growth of Government." *International Political Science Review* 6:11-34.

Bogdanor, Vernon. 1990. "Founding Elections and Regime Change." *Electoral Studies* 9:288-94.

Brown, Courtney. 1982. "The Nazi Vote: A National Ecological Study." *American Political Science Review* 76:285-302.

Budge, Ian. 1982. "Electoral Volatility: Issue Effects and Basic Change in 23 Post-War Democracies." *Electoral Studies* 1:147-68.

Budge, Ian and Dennis Farlie. 1983a. *Explaining and Predicting Elections: Issue Effects and Party Strategies in Twenty-Three Democracies.* London: George Allen & Unwin.

Budge, Ian and Dennis Farlie. 1983b. "Party Competition: Selective Emphasis or Direct Confrontation? An Alternative View with Data." In Hans Daalder and Peter Mair, eds. *Western European Party Systems: Continuity and Change*, pp. 267-305. Beverly Hills: Sage.

Budge, Ian; David Robertson and Derek Hearl, eds. 1987. *Ideology, Strategy and Party Change: Spatial Analysis of Post-War Election Programmes in 19 Democracies.* Cambridge: Cambridge University Press.

Burns, John P. 1987. "Immigration From China and the Future of Hong Kong." *Asian Survey* 27:661-82.

Burns, John P. 1988. "Succession Planning and Localization." In Ian Scott and John P. Burns, eds. *The Hong Kong Civil Service and Its Future.* Hong Kong: Oxford University Press.

Burton, John W. 1993. "Conflict Resolution as a Political Philosophy." In *Conflict Resolution Theory and Practice: Integration and Application*, pp. 55-64. Edited by Dennis J. D. Sandole and Hugo van der Merwe. Manchester and New York: Manchester University Press.

Butler, David and Donald Strokes. 1974. *Political Change in Britain: the Evolution of Electoral Choice*. 2nd ed. London: Macmillan.

Cameron, David R. 1978. "The Expansion of the Public Economy: A Comparative Analysis." *American Political Science Review* 72:1243-61.

Campbell, Duncan. 1980. "A Secret Plan for Dictatorship." *New Statesman* 2598:8-9, 12.

Castells, Manuel. 1978. *City, Class and Power*. Hampshire: Macmillan.

Castells, Manuel; L. Goh and R. Y-W. Kwok. 1990. *The Shek Kip Mei Syndrome: Economic Development and Public Housing in Hong Kong and Singapore*. London: Pion.

Central Intelligence Agency. [1993]. *The World Factbook 1993-94*. Washington: Brassey's.

Chan, Kai-cheung. 1993. "History." In Choi Po-king and Ho Lok-sang, eds. *The Other Hong Kong Report 1993*, pp. 455-83. Hong Kong: Chinese University Press.

Chan Lau, Kit-ching. 1973. "The Hong Kong Question During the Pacific War." *Journal of Imperial and Commonwealth History* 2:56-77.

Chan Lau, Kit-ching. 1990. *China, Britain and Hong Kong 1895-1945*. Hong Kong: Chinese University Press.

Chan, Ming K. 1991. "Democracy Derailed: Realpolitik in the Making of the Hong Kong Basic Law, 1985-90." In Ming K. Chan and David J. Clark, eds. *The Hong Kong Basic Law: Blueprint for "Stability and Prosperity" under Chinese Sovereignty?*, pp. 3-35. New York: M.E. Sharpe.

Chan, Ming K. and David J. Clark, eds. 1991. *The Hong Kong Basic Law: Blueprint for "Stability and Prosperity" under Chinese Sovereignty?* New York: M.E. Sharpe.

Chan, Thomas M.H. 1988. "The Political Organization of the Hong Kong Special Administrative Region." *Journal of Chinese Law* 2:115-22.

Chan, Wai Kwan. 1991. *The Making of Hong Kong Society: Three Studies of Class Formation in Early Hong Kong*. Oxford: Clarendon.

Chao, Chien-min. 1987. "'One Country, Two Systems': A Theoretical Analysis." *Asian Affairs* 14:107-24.

Cheek-Milby, Kathleen. 1989a. "The Changing Political Role of the Hong Kong Civil Servant." *Pacific Affairs* 62:219-34.

Cheek-Milby, Kathleen. 1989b. "The Civil Servant as Politician: The Role of the Official Member of the Legislative Council." In Kathleen Cheek-Milby and M. Mushkat, ed., *Hong Kong: The Challenge of Transformation*, pp. 256-91. Hong Kong: Centre of Asian Studies, University of Hong Kong.
Cheng, Joseph Y.S. 1982a. "The Future of Hong Kong: A Hong Kong Belonger's View." *International Affairs* 58:476-88.
Cheng, Joseph Y.S, ed. 1982b. *Hong Kong in the 1980s*. Hong Kong: Summerson.
Cheng, Joseph Y.S, ed. 1984. *Hong Kong In Search of a Future*. Hong Kong: Oxford University Press.
Cheng, Joseph Y.S, ed. 1986a. *Hong Kong in Transition*. Hong Kong: Oxford University Press.
Cheng, Joseph Y.S. 1986b. "The 1985 District Board Elections in Hong Kong." In Joseph Y.S. Cheng, ed. *Hong Kong in Transition*, pp. 67-87. Hong Kong: Oxford University Press.
Cheng, Joseph Y.S. 1987. "Hong Kong: the Pressure to Converge." *International Affairs* 63:271-83.
Cheng, Joseph Y.S. 1989a. "The Democracy Movement in Hong Kong." *International Affairs* 65:443- 62.
Cheng, Joseph Y.S. 1989b. "The Post-1997 Government in Hong Kong: Toward a Stronger Legislature." *Asian Survey* 24:731-48.
Cheng, Joseph Y.S. 1989c. "Political Modernization in Hong Kong." *Journal of Commonwealth and Comparative Politics* 27:294-320.
Cheng, Joseph Y.S, ed. 1989d. *The Road to Political Participation: Collected Essays of the Hong Kong Association of Democracy and People's Livelihood*. Hong Kong: Wide Angle. (in Chinese)
Cheng, Joseph Y.S. 1989e. "The 1988 District Board Elections: A Study of Political Participation in the Transitional Period." In Kathleen Cheek-Milby and Miron Mushkat, ed. *Hong Kong: The Challenge of Transformation*, pp. 116-49. Hong Kong: Centre of Asian Studies, University of Hong Kong.
Cheng, T.C. 1969. "Chinese Unofficial Members of the Legislative and Executive Councils in Hong Kong Up to 1941." *Journal of the Hong Kong Branch of the Royal Asiatic Society* 9:7-30.
Cheong-leen, Hilton. 1962. *Hong Kong Tomorrow: A Collection of Speeches and Articles*. Hong Kong.

Cheung, Anthony B.L. 1991. "Public Sector Reform in Hong Kong: Trends and Limitations." Paper presented at the conference *Public Sector Reform in Hong Kong: Progress-To-Date and Future Directions*, Hong Kong, 26 March 1991.

Cheung, Anthony B.L. 1995. "Financial, Managerial and Political Dimensions of Public Sector Reform." In Jane C.Y. Lee and Anthony B.L. Cheung, eds. *Public Sector Reform in Hong Kong: Key Concepts, Progress-To-Date and Future Directions*, pp. 39-68. Hong Kong: The Chinese University Press.

Cheung, Anthony B.L and Louie Kin-sheun. 1991. *Social Conflicts in Hong Kong, 1975-1986: Trends and Implications*. Hong Kong: Hong Kong Institute of Asia-Pacific Studies, The Chinese University of Hong Kong.

Cheung, Kit-fung; Yeung Kin-hing; Lo Wing-hung; and Chan Lu-tze. 1991. *No Change for Fifty Years? The Tug of War among China, Britain and Hong Kong over the Basic Law*. Hong Kong: Long-chiu. (in Chinese)

Cheung, Tak-shing. 1985. "An Overall Review on the District Boards Elections." *Wide Angle Monthly* 151:20-2. (in Chinese)

Chiu, Hungdah; Y.C. Jao; and Yuan-li Wu, eds. 1987. *The Future of Hong Kong: Toward 1997 and Beyond*. New York: Quorum.

Clubb, Herome M.; W.H. Flanigan; and N.H. Zingale. 1990. *Partisan Realignment: Voters, Parties, and Government in American History*. Westview Encore ed. Boulder: Westview.

Committee of Hongkong-Kowloon Chinese Compatriots of All Circles for the Struggle Against Persecution by the British Authorities in Hong Kong. 1967. *The May Upheaval in Hong Kong*. Hong Kong: Committee of Hongkong-Kowloon Chinese Compatriots of All Circles for the Struggle Against Persecution by the British Authorities in Hong Kong.

Conway, M. Margaret. 1989. "The Political Context of Political Behavior." *Journal of Politics* 51:3-10.

Cooper, John. 1970. *Colony in Conflict: The Hong Kong Disturbances May 1967--January 1968*. Hong Kong: Swindon.

Cottrell, Robert. 1993. *The End of Hong Kong: The Secret Diplomacy of Imperial Retreat*. London: John Murray.

Cradock, Percy. 1994a. *Experiences of China*. London: John Murray.

Cradock, Percy. 1994b. "China, Britain and Hong Kong: Policy in a Cul-de-sac." *World Today* 50:92-6.

Crewe, Ivor and D. Denver, eds. 1985. *Electoral Change in Western Democracies*. Beckenham: Croom Helm.

Crook, Richard C. 1987. "Legitimacy, Authority and the Transfer of Power in Ghana." *Political Studies* 35:552-72.
Cuthbert, Alexander R. 1991. "A Fistful of Dollars: Legitimation, Production and Debate in Hong Kong." *International Journal of Urban and Regional Research* 15:234-49.
Dahl, Robert A. 1967. *Pluralist Democracy in the United States: Conflict and Consent.* Chicago: Rand McNally.
Dalton, Russell J.; Scott C. Flanagan; and Paul Allen Beck, eds. 1984. *Electoral Change in Advanced Industrial Democracies: Realignment or Dealignment?* Princeton, N.J.: Princeton University Press.
Darwin, John. 1988. *Britain and Decolonisation: The Retreat from Empire in the Post-War World.* Hampshire: Macmillan.
Davies, S.N.G. 1977. "One Brand of Politics Rekindled." *Hong Kong Law Journal* 7:44-80.
Davis, S.G. 1949. *Hong Kong In Its Geographical Setting.* London: Collins.
Deutsch, Karl W. 1986. "State Functions and the Future of the State." *International Political Science Review* 7:209-22.
Devine, Joel A. 1985. "State and State Expenditure: Determinants of Social Investment and Social Consumption Spending in the Postwar United States." *American Sociology Review* 50:150-65.
Dicks, Anthony. 1983. "Treaty, Grant, Usage or Sufferance? Some Legal Aspects of the Status of Hong Kong." *China Quarterly* 95:427-55.
Dittmer, Lowell. 1986. "Hong Kong and China's Modernization." *Orbis* 30:525-42.
Domes, Jurgen. 1990. "Elections in the People's Republic of China." In Robert K. Furtak, ed. *Elections in Socialist States*, pp. 143-60. New York: Harvester Wheatsheaf.
Domes, Jurgen and Yu-Ming Shaw, eds. 1988. *Hong Kong: A Chinese and International Concern.* Boulder: Westview.
Doron, Gideon and Moshe Maor. 1991. "Barriers to Entry into a Political System." *Journal of Theoretical Politics* 3:175-88.
Downs, Anthony. 1957. *An Economic Theory of Democracy.* New York: Harper.
Drower, George. 1992. *Britain's Dependent Territories: A Fistful of Islands.* Aldershot: Dartmouth.
Duke, Vic and Stephen Edgell. 1984. "Public Expenditure Cuts in Britain and Consumption Sectoral Cleavages." *International Journal of Urban and Regional Research* 8:177-201.

Duncanson, Dennis. 1988. "The Anglo-Chinese Negotiations." In Jurgen Domes and Yu-Ming Shaw, eds. *Hong Kong: A Chinese and International Concern*, pp. 26-41. Boulder: Westview.

Dunleavy, Patrick. 1979. "The Urban Basis of Political Alignment: Social Class, Domestic Property Ownership, and State Intervention in Consumption Processes." *British Journal of Political Science* 9:409-43.

Dunleavy, Patrick. 1980a. "The Political Implications of Sectoral Cleavages and the Growth of State Employment: Part 1, The Analysis of Production Cleavages." *Political Studies* 28:364-83.

Dunleavy, Patrick. 1980b. "The Political Implications of Sectoral Cleavages and the Growth of State Employment: Part 2, Cleavage Structures and Political Alignment." *Political Studies* 28:527- 549.

Dunn, Lydia. 1985. "Hong Kong after the Sino-British Declaration." *International Affairs* 61:197-204.

Duvall, Raymond D. and John R. Freeman. 1981. "The State and Dependent Capitalism." *International Studies Quarterly* 25:99-118.

Duverger, Maurice. 1984. "Which is the Best Electoral System?" In Arend Lijphart and Bernard Grofman, eds. *Choosing An Electoral System: Issues and Alternatives*, pp. 31-9. New York: Praeger.

Eichenberg, Richard C. 1983. "Problems in Using Public Employment Data." In Charles Lewis Taylor, ed. *Why Government Grow*, pp. 136-53. Beverly Hills: Sage.

Endacott, G.B. 1962. *A Biographical Sketch-Book of Early Hong Kong*. Singapore: Eastern Universities Press.

Endacott, G.B. 1964. *Government and People in Hong Kong 1841-1962: A Constitutional History*. Hong Kong: Hong Kong University Press.

England, Joe and John Rear. 1975. *Chinese Labour Under British Rule: A Critical Study of Labour and Law in Hong Kong*. Hong Kong: Oxford University Press.

Etzioni, Amitai. 1964. "On Self-encapsulating Conflicts." *Journal of Conflict Resolution* 8:242-55.

Evans, Peter B. 1985. "Transnational Linkages and the Economic Role of the State: An Analysis of Developing and industrialized Nations in the Post-World War II Period." In Peter B. Evans, Dietrich Rueschemeyer, and Theda Skocpol, eds. *Bringing the State Back In*, pp. 192-226. Cambridge: Cambridge University Press.

Evans, Peter B.; Dietrich Rueschemeyer and Theda Skocpol, eds. 1985. *Bringing the State Back In*. Cambridge: Cambridge University Press.

Fifoot, Paul. 1991. "China's Basic Law for Hong Kong." *International Relations* 10:301-27.

Flora, Peter and Jens Alber. 1981. "Modernization, Democratization, and the Development of Welfare States in Western Europe." In Peter Flora and Arnold J. Heidenheimer, eds. *The Development of Welfare States in Europe and America*, pp. 37-80. New Brunswick & London: Transaction Books.

Flora, Peter and Arnold J. Heidenheimer, eds. 1981. *The Development of Welfare States in Europe and America*. New Brunswick & London: Transaction Books.

Foley, Duncan K. 1978. "State Expenditure from a Marxist Perspective." *Journal of Public Economics* 9:221-38.

Fong, Peter F.W. 1986. "Citizen Participation and Administrative Decentralisation in Hong Kong." *Habitat International* 10:207-17.

Fong, Wah. 1991. "Hong Kong Political Organizations: Easy to Form but Difficult to Grow." *Ming Pao Monthly* 26 (April):8-9. (in Chinese)

Fung, Yee-wang. 1973. "Some Contributory Factors to Student Movements in Hong Kong." *Asia Quarterly* 4:287-311.

Fung, Yuk-lin. 1990. *Embarking on the Road to 1997: Interviews with the Political Elites*. Hong Kong: Comos Books Ltd. (in Chinese)

Furtak, Robert K, ed. 1990a. *Elections in Socialist States*. New York: Harvester Wheatsheaf.

Furtak, Robert K. 1990b. "The Fundamentals, Characteristics and Trends of Elections in Socialist States." In Robert K. Furtak, ed. *Elections in Socialist States*, pp. 4-19. New York: Harvester Wheatsheaf.

Ghai, Yash. 1991. "The Past and the Future of Hong Kong's Constitution." *China Quarterly* 128:794-813.

Ginsberg, Benjamin. 1976. "Elections and Public Policy." *American Political Science Review* 70:41-9.

Goodstadt, L.F. 1969. "Urban Housing in Hong Kong, 1945-63." In I.C. Jarvie and J. Agassi, ed., *Hong Kong: A Society in Transition*. London: Routledge and Kegan Paul.

Gould, Frank. 1983. "The Growth of Public Expenditures: Theory and Evidence from Six Advanced Democracies." In Charles Lewis Taylor, ed. *Why Government Grow*, pp. 217-39. Beverly Hills: Sage.

Gould, Frank and Barbara Roweth. 1978. "Politics and Public Spending." *Political Quarterly* 49:222-7.

Grinberg, Lev Luis. 1993. "The Crisis of Statehood: A Weak State and Strong Political Institutions in Israel." *Journal of Theoretical Politics* 5:89-107.

Gunther, Richard and Anthony Mughan. 1993. "Political Institutions and Cleavage Management." In *Do Institutions Matter? Government Capabilities in the United States and Abroad*, pp. 272-301. Edited by R. Kent Weaver and Bert A. Rockman. Washington, D.C.: Brookings Institution.

H.K. Lamb. [1985]. *A Date with Fate*. Hong Kong: Lincoln Green.

Haddon-Cave, Philip. 1984. "The Making of Some Aspects of Public Policy in Hong Kong." In David Lethbridge, ed. *The Business Environment in Hong Kong*, 2nd ed., pp. xiii-xx. Hong Kong: Oxford University Press.

Hall, John A. 1986. "State and Economic Development: Reflections on Adam Smith." In John A. Hall, ed. *States in History*, pp. 154-76. Oxford: Basil Blackwell.

Hall, John A., ed. 1986. *States in History*. Oxford: Basil Blackwell.

Hambro, Edvard. 1955. *The Problem of Chinese Refugees in Hong Kong*. Leyden: A.W. Sijthoff.

Hanneman, Robert and J. Rogers Hollingsworth. 1992. "Refocusing the debate on the Role of the State in Capitalist Societies." In Rolf Torstendahl, ed. *State Theory and State History*, pp. 38-61. London: Sage.

Harris, Peter. 1975. "Representative Politics in a British Dependency: Some Reflections on Problems of Representation in Hong Kong." *Parliamentary Affairs* 28:180-98.

Harris, Peter. 1978. *Hong Kong: A Study in Bureaucratic Politics*. Hong Kong: Heinemann Asia.

Harris, Peter. 1986. "Hong Kong Confronts 1997: An Assessment of the Sino-British Agreement." *Pacific Affairs* 59:45-68.

Harris, Peter. 1988. *Hong Kong: A Study in Bureaucracy and Politics*. Hong Kong: Macmillan.

Harrop, Martin and William L. Miller. 1987. *Elections and Voters*. Hampshire: Macmillan.

Heaton, William. 1970. "Maoist Revolutionary Strategy and Modern Colonialism: The Cultural Revolution in Hong Kong" *Asian Survey* 10:840-57.

Hermel, Robert and John D. Robertson. 1985. "Formation and Success of New Parties: A Cross-National Analysis." *International Political Science Review* 6:501-23.

Hermet, Guy. 1978. "State-Controlled Elections: A Framework." In Guy Hermet, Richard Rose and Alain Rouquie, eds. *Elections Without Choice*, pp. 1-18. London: Macmillan.

Ho, Shuet Ying. 1986. "Public Housing." In Joseph Y.S. Cheng, ed. *Hong Kong in Transition*, pp. 331-53. Hong Kong: Oxford university Press.
Ho, H.C.Y. 1979. *The Fiscal System of Hong Kong*. London: Croom Helm.
Hoadley, J. Stephen. 1970. "Hong Kong is the Lifeboat: Notes on Political Culture and Socialization." *Journal of Oriental Studies* 8:206-18.
Hoadley, J. Stephen. 1973. "Political Participation of Hong Kong Chinese: Patterns and Trends." *Asian Survey* 13:604-16.
Holcombe, Randall G. 1991. "Barriers to Entry and Political Competition." *Journal of Theoretical Politics* 3:231-40.
Hong Kong Civic Association. 1974. *Hong Kong Civic Association: 20th Anniversary, 1954- 1974*. Hong Kong: Hong Kong Civic Association.
Hong Kong Civic Association. 1979. *Hong Kong Civic Association: 25th Anniversary, 1954-1979*. Hong Kong: Hong Kong Civic Association.
Hong Kong Federation of Students, ed. 1983. *A Review of the Student Movements in Hong Kong*. Hong Kong: Wide Angle. (in Chinese)
Hong Kong Observers. 1981. *Pressure Point*. Hong Kong: Summerson Eastern.
Hong Kong Observers. 1983. *Pressure Points: A Social Critique*. 2nd ed. Hong Kong: Summerson.
Hong Kong People's Council on Public Housing Policy (HKPCPHP). 1988. *HKPCPHP: 10th Anniversary Souvenir Publication, 1978-88*. Hong Kong: HKPCPHP. (in Chinese)
Hook, Brian. 1983. "The Government of Hong Kong: Change Within Tradition." *China Quarterly* 95:491-511.
Hopkins, Keith, ed. 1971. *Hong Kong: The industrial Colony*. Hong Kong: Oxford University Press.
Hsia, Ronald and Laurence Chau. 1978. *Industrialisation, Employment and Income Distribution: A Case Study of Hong Kong*. London: Croom Helm.
Hughes, Richard. 1976. *Borrowed Place, Borrowed Time: Hong Kong and Its Many Faces*. 2nd rev. ed. London: Andre Deutsch.
Huntington, Samuel P. 1968. *Political Order in Changing Societies*. New Haven, Conn.: Yale University Press.
Huntington, Samuel P. 1974. "Postindustrial Politics: How Benign Will It Be?" *Comparative Politics* 6:163-91.
Huntington, Samuel P. 1991. *The Third Wave: Democratization in the Late Twentieth Century*. Norman & London: University of Oklahoma Press.
Huntington, Samuel P. and Joan M. Nelson. 1976. *No Easy Choice: Political Participation in Developing Countries*. Cambridge, Mass. & London: Harvard University Press.

Hurley, R.C. 1925. *Picturesque Hong Kong and Dependencies*. Hong Kong: Commercial Press.
Inglehart, Ronald. 1977. *The Silent Revolution: Changing Values and Political Styles Among Western Publics*. Princeton N.J.: Princeton University Press.
Inglehart, Ronald. 1984. "The Changing Structure of Political Cleavages in Western Societies." In Russell J. Dalton, Scott C. Flanagan and Paul Allen Beck, eds. *Electoral Change in Advanced Industrial Democracies*, pp. 25-69. Princeton N.J.: Princeton University Press.
Inter-Parliamentary Union. 1991. *Chronicle of Parliamentary Elections and Developments*, Vol. 25. Geneva: Inter-Parliamentary Union.
Inter-Parliamentary Union. 1992. *Chronicle of Parliamentary Elections and Developments*, Vol. 26. Geneva: Inter-Parliamentary Union.
Jao, Y.C.; Leung Chi-keung; Peter Wesley-smith; and Wong Siu-lun, eds. 1985. *Hong Kong and 1997: Strategies for the Future*. Hong Kong: Centre of Asian Studies, University of Hong Kong.
Jarvie, I.C. 1969. "A Postscript on Riots and the Future of Hong Kong." In I.C. Jarvie and Joseph Agassi, eds. *Hong Kong: A Society in Transition*, pp. 361-9. London: Routledge & Kegan Paul.
Jarvie, I.C. and Joseph Agassi, eds. 1969. *Hong Kong: A Society in Transition*. London: Routledge and Kegan Paul.
Jeffries, Charles. 1960. *Transfer of Power: Problems of the Passage to Self-Government*. London: Pall Mall Press.
Johnson, Graham E. 1986. "1997 and After: Will Hong Kong Survive? A Personal View." *Pacific Affairs* 59:237-54.
Johnston, R.J. 1990. "Lipset and Rokkan Revisited: Electoral Cleavages, Electoral Geography, and Electoral Strategy in Great Britain." In R.J. Johnston, F.M. Shelley, and P.J. Taylor, eds. *Developments in Electoral Geography*, pp. 121-42. London: Routledge.
Kam Yiu-yu. 1992. "The Memoirs of Kam Yiu-yu: The History of the Ebb and Flow of the Chinese-side Newspapers in Hong Kong." *Contemporary Monthly* 19 (1992):81-8. (in Chinese)
Katz, Richard S. 1980. *A Theory of Parties and Electoral Systems*. Baltimore: Johns Hopkins University Press.
Keung, John. 1985. "Government Intervention and Housing Policy in Hong Kong: A structural Analysis" *Third World Planning Review* 7:23-44.
Key, V.O., Jr. 1955. "A Theory of Critical Elections." *Journal of Politics* 17:3-18.

Key, V.O., Jr. 1959. "Secular Realignment and the Party System." *Journal of Politics* 21:198- 210.
King, Anthony. 1973. "Ideas, Institutions and the Policies of Governments: A Comparative Analysis, Parts I and II, III." *British Journal of Political Science* 3:291-313, 409-23.
King, Ambrose Yeo-chi. 1975. "Administrative Absorption of Politics in Hong Kong: Emphasis on the Grass Roots Level." *Asian Survey* 15:422-39.
King, Ambrose Yeo-chi and Rance P.L. Lee, eds. 1981. *Social Life and development in Hong Kong*. Hong Kong: Chinese University Press.
Kirkbride, Paul S.; Sara F.Y. Tang; and Robert I. Westwood. 1991. "Chinese Conflict Preferences and Negotiating Behaviour: Cultural and Psychological influences." *Organization Studies* 12:365-86.
Knutsen, Oddbjorn. 1986. "Political Cleavages and Political Realignment in Norway: The New Politics Thesis Reexamined." *Scandinavian Political Studies* 9:235-63.
Koch, Koen. 1980. "The New Marxist Theory of the State or the Rediscovery of the Limitations of a Structure-Functionalist Paradigm." *Netherlands Journal of Sociology* 16:1- 19.
Kohl, Jurgen. 1981. "Trends and Problems in Postwar Public Expenditure Development in Western Europe and North America." In Peter Flora and Arnold J. Heidenheimer, eds., *The Development of Welfare States in Europe and America*, pp. 307-44. New Brunswick & London: Transaction Books.
Kohl, Jurgen. 1983. "The Functional Structure of Public Expenditures: Long-Term Changes." In Charles Lewis Taylor, ed. *Why Government Grow*, pp. 201-16. Beverly Hills: Sage.
Krasner, Stephen D., ed. 1983. *International Regimes*. Ithaca: Cornell University Press.
Ku, Sing-fai. 1987. *Ku Sing-fai's Discussion on Hong Kong*. Hong Kong: Mirror. (in Chinese)
Kuan, Hsin-chi. 1979. "Political Stability and Change in Hong Kong." In Lin Tzong-biau, Rance P.L. Lee and Udo-Ernst Simonis, eds. *Hong Kong: Economic, Social and Political Studies in Development*, pp. 145-66. New York & Kent: M. E. Sharpe & Dawson.
Kuan, Hsin-chi. 1991. "Power Dependence and Democratic Transition: The Case of Hong Kong." *China Quarterly* 128:774-93.

Kuan, Hsin-chi and Lau Siu-kai. 1987. "Hong Kong's Search for a Consensus: Barriers and Prospects." In Hungdah Chiu, Y.C. Jao, and Yuan-li Wu, eds. *The Future of Hong Kong: Toward 1997 and Beyond*, pp. 95-114. New York: Quorum.

Kuan, Hsin-chi, Lau Siu-kai, Louie Kin-sheun and Timothy K.Y. Wong, eds. 1996. *The 1995 Legislative Council Elections in Hong Kong*. Hong Kong: Hong Kong Institute of Asia-Pacific Studies, The Chinese University of Hong Kong.

Kurke, Lance B. 1992. "Repression and Restitution: Hong Kong and the PRC." *Journal of Contemporary Asia* 22:234-48.

Kwan, Siu-wah. 1988. "Hong Kong Walks Quietly into the Era of Party Politics." *Ming Pao Monthly* March:6-7. (in Chinese)

Kwok, Rowena Y.F., Joan Y.H. Leung and Ian Scott, eds. 1992. *Votes Without Power: The Hong Kong Legislative Council Elections 1991*. Hong Kong: Hong Kong University Press.

Lam, Jermain T.M. and Jane C.Y. Lee. 1992a. *The Political Culture of the Voters in Hong Kong: A Study of the Geographical Constituencies of the Legislative Council in Hong Kong*. Hong Kong: City Polytechnic of Hong Kong.

Lam, Jermain T.M. and Jane C.Y. Lee. 1992b. "Allegiance, Apathy, or Alienation? The Political Culture of Professional Constituency Voters in Hong Kong." *Issues & Studies* 28,7:76-109.

Lane, Jan-Erik, David McKay and Kenneth Newton. 1991. *Political Data Handbook: OECD Countries*. Oxford: Oxford University Press.

Lane, Kevin P. 1990. *Sovereignty and the Status Quo: The Historical Roots of China's Hong Kong Policy*. Boulder, Colorado: Westview.

LaPalombara, Joseph and Myron Weiner, eds. 1966. *Political Parties and Political Development*. Princeton, N.J.: Princeton University Press.

Larkey, Patrick D.; Chandler Stolp; and Mark Winer. 1981. "Theorizing About the Growth of Government: A Research Assessment." *Journal of Public Policy* 1:157-220.

Lau, Emily. 1988. "The Early History of the Drafting Process." In Peter Wesley-Smith and Albert H.Y. Chen, eds. *The Basic Law and Hong Kong's Future*, pp. 90-104. Hong Kong: Butterworths.

Lau, Siu-kai. 1981. "The Government, Intermediate Organizations, and Grass-Roots Politics in Hong Kong." *Asian Survey* 21:865-84.

Lau, Siu-kai. 1982. *Society and Politics in Hong Kong*. Hong Kong: Chinese University Press.

Lau, Siu-kai. 1983. "Social Change, Bureaucratic Rule, and Emergent Political Issues in Hong Kong." *World Politics* 35:544-62.

Lau, Siu-kai. 1987. *Decolonization without Independence: The Unfinished Political Reforms of the Hong Kong Government.* Hong Kong: Institute of Social Studies, Chinese University of Hong Kong.
Lau, Siu-kai. 1988a. *Basic Law and the New Political Order of Hong Kong.* Hong Kong: Institute of Social Studies, Chinese University of Hong Kong.
Lau, Siu-kai. 1988b. *Hong Kong's Political Structure Reform and Political Development.* Hong Kong: Wide Angle. (in Chinese)
Lau, Siu-kai. 1990. "Institutions Without Leaders: The Hong Kong Chinese View of Political Leadership." *Pacific Affairs* 63:191-209.
Lau, Siu-kai. 1992. *Political Attitude toward Political Parties in Hong Kong.* Hong Kong: Hong Kong Institute of Asia-Pacific Studies, Chinese University of Hong Kong.
Lau, Siu-kai and Kuan Hsin-chi. 1983. *District Board Elections in Hong Kong.* Hong Kong: Institute of Social Studies, Chinese University of Hong Kong.
Lau, Siu-kai and Kuan Hsin-chi. 1985. *The 1985 District Board Election in Hong Kong: The Limits of Political Mobilization in a Dependent Polity.* Hong Kong: Institute of Social Studies, Chinese University of Hong Kong.
Lau, Siu-kai and Kuan Hsin-chi. 1986. "Hong Kong After the Sino-British Agreement: The Limits to Change." *Pacific Affairs* 59:214-36.
Lau, Siu-kai and Kuan Hsin-chi. 1988. *The Ethos of the Hong Kong Chinese.* Hong Kong: Chinese University Press.
Lau, Siu-kai and Louie Kin-sheun, eds. 1993. *Hong Kong Tried Democracy: The 1991 Elections in Hong Kong.* Hong Kong: Hong Kong Institute of Asia-Pacific Studies, the Chinese University of Hong Kong.
Laver, Michael and W. Ben Hunt. 1992. *Policy and Party Competition.* New York: Routledge.
Lawson, Stephanie. 1993. "Conceptual Issues in the Comparative Study of Regime Change and Democratization." *Comparative Politics* 25:183-205.
Lee, J.M. 1967. *Colonial Development and Good Government.* Oxford: Clarendon.
Lee, Jane C.Y. and Anthony B.L. Cheung, eds. 1995. *Public Sector Reform in Hong Kong: Key Concepts, Progress-to-Date and Future Directions.* Hong Kong: The Chinese University Press.

Lee, Jane C.Y., Anthony B.L. Cheung, W.N. Ho, and Jermain T.M. Lam, eds. 1992. *A Report of the Conference Proceedings on Politics and 1991 Elections in Hong Kong*. Hong Kong: City Polytechnic of Hong Kong, Department of Public & Social Administration.

Lee, Martin C.M. 1988. "How Much Autonomy?" In William McGurn, ed. *Basic Law, Basic Questions: The Debate Continues*, pp. 37-52. Hong Kong: Review Publishing Co. Ltd.

Lee, M.K. 1982. "Emerging Patterns of Social Conflict in Hong Kong Society." In Joseph Y.S. Cheng, ed. *Hong Kong in the 1980s*, pp. 23-31. Hong Kong: Summerson.

Lee, M.K. 1993. "Issue-Position in the 1991 Legislative Council Election." In Lau Siu-kai and Louie Kin-sheun, eds. *Hong Kong Tried Democracy: The 1991 Elections in Hong Kong*, pp. 237-48. Hong Kong: Hong Kong Institute of Asia-Pacific Studies, the Chinese University of Hong Kong.

Lee, Su-Hoon. 1988. *State-Building in the Contemporary Third World*. Boulder: Westview.

Lehner, Franz and Ulrich Widmaier. 1983. "Market Failure and Growth of Government: A Sociological Explanation." In Charles Lewis Taylor, ed. *Why Government Grow*, pp. 240-60. Beverly Hills: Sage.

Lethbridge, H.J. 1978. *Hong Kong: Stability and Change*. Hong Kong: Oxford University Press.

Lethbridge, H.J. 1985. *Hard Graft in Hong Kong: Scandal, Corruption and the ICAC*. Hong Kong: Oxford University Press.

Leung, Benjamin and Stephen Chiu. 1991. *A Social History of Industrial Strikes and the Labour Movement in Hong Kong, 1946-1989*. Hong Kong: Social Sciences Research Centre, University of Hong Kong.

Leung, C.B. 1982. "Community Participation: From Kai Fong Association, Mutual Aid Committee to District Board." In Joseph Y.S. Cheng, ed. *Hong Kong in the 1980s*, pp. 152-70. Hong Kong: Summerson.

Leung, Chun-man. 1985. "The Criteria of Appointing District Boards Members and the Training of Leaders Capable for Governing Hong Kong: An Interview with Mr Albert C.C. Lam." *Hong Kong Economic Journal Monthly* 97:4-6. (in Chinese)

Leung, Joe. 1986. "Community Development in Hong Kong: Contributions Toward Democratization." *Community Development Journal* 21:3-10.

Leung Sai-wing, 1993. "The 'China Factor' in the 1991 Legislative Council Election: The June 4th Incident and Anti-Communist China Syndrome." In Lau Siu-kai and Louie Kin-sheun, eds., *Hong Kong Tried Democracy: The 1991 Elections in Hong Kong*, pp. 187-235. Hong Kong: Hong Kong Institute of Asia-Pacific Studies, Chinese University of Hong Kong.

Leung Sai-wing. 1996. "The 'China Factor' and Voters' Choice in the 1995 Legislative Council Election." In Kuan Hsin-chi, Lau Siu-kai, Louie Kin-sheun and Timothy K.Y. Wong, eds. *The 1995 Legislative Council Elections in Hong Kong*, pp. 201-44. Hong Kong: Hong Kong Institute of Asia-Pacific Studies, The Chinese University of Hong Kong.

Lewis, D.K. 1982. *The Prospects for Hong Kong*. London: Institute for the Study of Conflict.

Li, Pang-kwong. 1993. "An Exploratory Study of the Rural-Urban Cleavage in the 1991 Elections." In Lau Siu-kai and Louie Kin-sheun, eds. *Hong Kong Tried Democracy: The 1991 Elections in Hong Kong*, pp. 317-29. Hong Kong: Hong Kong Institute of Asia-Pacific Studies, The Chinese University of Hong Kong.

Li, Pang-kwong. 1995a. *Elections and Political Mobilisation: The Hong Kong 1991 Direct Elections*. Unpublished PhD thesis, The University of London, The London School of Economics and Political Science.

Li, Pang-kwong. 1995b. "Elections, Politicians, and Electoral Politics." In *The Other Hong Kong Report 1995*, pp. 51-66. Edited by S.Y.L. Cheung and S.M.H. Sze. Hong Kong: The Chinese University Press.

Li, Pang-kwong. 1996. "1995 Legislative Council Direct Election: A Political Cleavage Approach." In Kuan Hsin-chi, Lau Siu-kai, Louie Kin-sheun and Wong Ka-ying, eds., *The 1995 Legislative Council Elections in Hong Kong*, pp. 245-73. Hong Kong: The Hong Kong Institute of Asia-Pacific Studies, The Chinese University of Hong Kong.

Li, Pang-kwong, ed. 1997a. *Political Order and Power Transition in Hong Kong*. Hong Kong: The Chinese University Press.

Li, Pang-kwong. 1997b. "Executive and Legislature: Institutional Design, Electoral Dynamics and the Management of Conflicts in the Hong Kong Transition." In Li Pang-kwong, ed. *Political Order and Power Transition in Hong Kong*, pp. 53-78. Hong Kong: The Chinese University Press.

Li, Pang-kwong. 1998. "Electoral Cleavages and the Post-1997 Hong Kong's Political Dynamics." *Journal of Electoral Studies* 5 (1):161-80. (in Chinese)

Li, Pang-kwong and David Newman. 1997. "Give and Take: Electoral Politics in Transitional Hong Kong." *Asian Perspective* 21, 1:213-32.

Li, Si-ming and Yu Fu-lai. 1990. "The Redistributive Effects of Hong Kong's Public Housing Programme, 1976-86." *Urban Studies* 27:105-18.

Liang, Yu-ying. 1990. "Peking's Hong Kong Policy After Tienanmen." *Issues & Studies* 26(12):71-84.

Lijphart, Arend. 1981. "Political Parties: Ideologies and Programs." In David Butler, Howard R. Penniman, and Austin Ranney, eds. *Democracy at the Polls: A Comparative Study of Competitive National Elections*, pp. 26-51. Washington: American Enterprise Institute.

Lijphart, Arend. 1990. "The Cleavage Model and Electoral Geography: A Review." In R.J. Johnston, F.M. Shelley, and P.J. Taylor, eds. *Developments in Electoral Geography*, pp. 143-50. London: Routledge.

Lijphart, Arend and Bernard Grofman, eds. 1984. *Choosing An Electoral System: Issues and Alternatives*. New York: Praeger.

Lijphart, Arend; Ronald Rogowski and R. Kent Weaver. 1993. "Separation of Powers and Cleavage Management." In *Do Institutions Matter? Government Capabilities in the United States and Abroad*, pp. 302-44. Edited by R. Kent Weaver and Bert A. Rockman. Washington, D.C.: Brookings Institution.

Linz, J. Juan. 1973. "Opposition to and under an Authoritarian Regime: The Case of Spain." In Robert A. Dahl, ed. *Regimes and Oppositions*, pp. 171-259. New Haven & London: Yale University Press.

Lipset, Seymour M. 1960. *Political Man*. New York: Doubleday.

Lipset, Seymour M. and Stein Rokkan. 1967. "Cleavage Structures, Party Systems and Voter Alignment: An Introduction." In Seymour Lipset and Stein Rokkan, eds. *Party System and Voter Alignments*, pp. 1-64. New York: Free Press.

Liu, Yiu Chu. 1988. "Interpretation and Review of the Basic Law of the Hong Kong Special Administrative Region." *Journal of Chinese Law* 2:49-63.

Lo, Shiu-hing. 1988. "Decolonization and Political Development in Hong Kong: Citizen Participation." *Asian Survey* 28:613-29.

Lo, Shiu-hing. 1989. "Colonial Policy-Makers, Capitalist Class and China: Determinants of Electoral Reform in Hong Kong's and Macau's Legislatures." *Pacific Affairs* 62:204-18.

Lo, Shiu-hing. 1990. "Democratization in Hong Kong: Reasons, Phases, and Limits." *Issues and Studies* 26 (May 1990):100-17.
Lo, Shiu-hing. 1997. *The Politics of Democratisation in Hong Kong.* Hampshire: Macmillan.
Lo, Shiu-hing and Yu Wing-yat. 1996. "The Electoral System of Hong Kong's Legislative Council: Results under Different Proportional Representation Formulae." In Kuan Hsin-chi, Lau Siu-kai, Louie Kin-sheun and Timothy K.Y. Wong, eds. *The 1995 Legislative Council Elections in Hong Kong*, pp. 97-134. Hong Kong: Hong Kong Institute of Asia-Pacific Studies, The Chinese University of Hong Kong.
Lo, Wai. 1990. "Mr Fung Kin-kee Forms another Democratic Group." *Contemporary* 21 April:38-9. (in Chinese)
Louie, Kin-sheun and Wan Po-san. 1992. *Voting Behaviour of the Hong Kong Electorate: A Review of the Past Studies.* Paper submitted to Steering Group on Study of Voting Behaviour, Committee on the Promotion of Civic Education, Hong Kong, March 1992.
Louie, Kin-sheun et al. 1993. "Who Voted in the 1991 Elections? A Socio-Demographic Profile of the Hong Kong Electorate." In Lau Siu-kai and Louie Kin-sheun, eds. *Hong Kong Tried Democracy: The 1991 Elections in Hong Kong*, pp. 1-39. Hong Kong: Chinese University of Hong Kong, Hong Kong Institute of Asia-Pacific Studies, 1993.
Lui, T.L. and K.S. Kung. 1985. *Urban Movements and Politics in Hong Kong.* Hong Kong: Wide Angle. (in Chinese)
MacDonald, Stuart Elaine; Ola Listhaug; and George Rabinowitz. 1991. "Issues and Party Support in Multiparty Systems." *American Political Science Review* 85:1107- 1131.
Mainwaring, Scott. 1993. "Presidentialism, Multipartism, and Democracy. The Difficult Combination." *Comparative Political Studies* 26 (2):198-228.
Mainwaring, Scott and Timothy R. Scully, eds. 1995. *Building Democratic Institutions: Party Systems in Latin America.* Stanford, California: Stanford University Press.
Mann, Michael. 1984. "The Autonomous Power of the State: its Origins, Mechanisms and Result." *Archives Europeennes de Sociologie* 25:185-213.
Mann, Michael. 1986. *The Sources of Social Power.* Cambridge: Cambridge University Press.
Marx, Karl and Friedrich Engels. 1967. *The Communist Manifesto.* Middlesex: Penguin.

Mavrogordatos, George Th. 1987. "Downs Revisited: Spatial Models of Party Competition and Left-Right Measurements." *International Political Science Review* 8:333-42.

McGurn, William, ed. 1988. *Basic Law, Basic Questions: The Debate Continues.* Hong Kong: Review Publishing Co. Ltd.

McGurn, William. 1992. *Perfidious Albion: The Abandonment of Hong Kong 1997.* Washington, D.C.: Ethics and Public Policy Centre.

Migdal, Joel S. 1988. *Strong Societies and Weak State: State-Society Relations and State Capabilities in the Third World.* New Jersey: Princeton University Press.

Miners, Norman J. 1975. "Hong Kong: A Case Study in Political Stability" *Journal of Commonwealth and Comparative Politics* 13:26-39.

Miners, Norman J. 1988. "The Normal Pattern of Decolonisation of British Dependent Territories." In Peter Wesley-Smith & Albert H.Y. Chen, eds., *The Basic Law and Hong Kong's Future*, pp. 44-54. Hong Kong: Butterworths.

Miners, Norman J. 1989. "Constitutional Reform in Hong Kong, 1945-1952 and 1984-1989." *Asian Journal of Public Administration* 11:92-103.

Miners, Norman J. 1991. *The Government and Politics of Hong Kong.* 5th ed. Hong Kong: Oxford University Press.

Mitra, Subrata Kumar, ed. 1990. *The Post-Colonial State in Asia: Dialectics of Politics and Culture.* New York: Harvester Wheatsheaf.

Mok, Bong-ho. 1988. "Influence Through Political Power: The Emergence of Social Workers as Politicians in the Recent Political Reform in Hong Kong." *International Social Work* 31:249-62.

Morris, J.C. 1978. "Administration and Finance of Public Housing." In Luke S.K. Wong, ed. *Housing in Hong Kong*, pp. 55-71. Hong Kong: Heinemann.

Mushkat, Miron. 1990. "The Political Economy of Constitutional Change in Hong Kong." *Asian Economies* 75:33-53.

Nettl, J.P. 1967. *Political Mobilization: A Sociological Analysis of Methods and Concepts.* London: Faber and Faber.

Nettl, J.P. 1968. "The State as a Conceptual Variable." *World Politics* 20:559-92.

New Hong Kong Society. 1983. *New Hong Kong Society: 1st Anniversary Souvenir Publication.* Hong Kong: New Hong Kong Society. (in Chinese)

Ng, Yin. 1985. "The Outlook of the Hong Kong Multi-parties Politics." *Cheng Ming Monthly* June 1985:46-8. (in Chinese)

Nordlinger, Eric A. 1981. *On the Autonomy of the Democratic State.* Mass.: Harvard University Press.
Nossiter, T.J. 1982. *Communism in Kerala: A Study in Political Adaptation.* London: C. Hurst & Co.
Nthenda, Louis. 1979. "Recent Trends in Government and Industry Relationships in Hong Kong." In Tzong-biau Lin, Rance P.L. Lee, and Udo-Ernst Simonis, eds. *Hong Kong: Economic, Social and Political Studies in Development,* pp. 167-81. New York & Kent: M.E. Sharpe & Dawson.
O'Connor, James. 1973. *The Fiscal Crisis of the State.* New York: St. Martin's Press.
O'Donnell, Guillermo and Philippe C. Schmitter. 1986. *Transitions from Authoritarian Rule: Tentative Conclusions about Uncertain Democracies.* Baltimore & London: Johns Hopkins University Press.
Paddock, Joel. 1990. "Beyond the New Deal: Ideological Differences between Eleven State Democratic Parties, 1956-1980." *Western Political Quarterly* 43:181-90.
Patten, Chris. 1998. *East and West: The Last Governor of Hong Kong on Power, Freedom and the Future.* London and Basingstoke: Macmillan.
Peter, B. Guy and Martin O. Heisler. 1983. "Thinking About Public Sector Growth: Conceptual, Operational, Theoretical, and Policy Considerations." In Charles Lewis Taylor, ed., *Why Government Grow,* pp. 177-97. Beverly Hills: Sage.
Podmore, David. 1971. "Localisation in the Hong Kong Government Service 1948-1968." *Journal of Commonwealth Political Studies* 9:36-51.
Powell, G. Bingham, Jr. 1982. *Contemporary Democracies: Participation, Stability, and Violence.* Mass. and London: Harvard University Press.
Powell, G. Bingham, Jr.. 1989. "Constitutional Design and Citizen Electoral Control" *Journal of Theoretical Politics* 1:107-30.
Przeworski, Adam. 1975. "Institutionalization of Voting Patterns, or is Mobilization the Source of Decay?" *American Political Science Review* 69:49-67.
Przeworski, Adam and John Sprague. 1986. *Paper Stones: A History of Electoral Socialism.* Chicago: University of Chicago Press.
Rabushka, Alvin. 1973. *The Changing Face of Hong Kong: New Departures in Public Policy.* Washington, D.C.: American Enterprise Institute, and Stanford: Hoover Institution.
Rabushka, Alvin. 1976. *Value for Money: The Hong Kong Budgetary Process.* Stanford: Stanford University, Hoover Institution Press.

Rabushka, Alvin. 1979. *Hong Kong: A Study in Economic Freedom.* Chicago: University of Chicago.
Rae, Douglas W. and Michael Taylor. 1970. *The Analysis of Political Cleavages.* New Haven: Yale University Press.
Rear, John. 1971. "One Brand of Politics" In Keith Hopkins, ed., *Hong Kong: The industrial Colony,* pp. 55-139. Hong Kong: Oxford University Press.
Reeve, Andrew and Alan Ware. 1992. *Electoral Systems: A Comparative and Theoretical Introduction.* London and New York: Routledge.
Reform Club of Hong Kong. 1953. *Election Chronicle 1953.* Hong Kong: Reform Club of Hong Kong.
Reform Club of Hong Kong. 1959. *10th Anniversary, 1949-1959.* Hong Kong: Reform Club of Hong Kong.
Reform Club of Hong Kong. 1974. *Silver Jubilee Anniversary Souvenir Publication, 1949-1974.* Hong Kong: Reform Club of Hong Kong.
Remmer, Karen L. 1985. "Redemocratization and the Impact of Authoritarian Rule in Latin America." *Comparative Politics* 17:253-75.
Riggs, Fred W. 1988. "The Survival of Presidentialism in American: Para-constitutional Practices." *International Political Science Review* 9:247-78.
Riley, Mike. 1988. *Power, Politics and Voting Behaviour.* New York: Harvester Wheatsheaf.
Rokkan, Stein. 1970. *Citizens, Elections, Parties,* Oslo: Universitetsforlaget.
Rokkan, Stein. 1975. "Dimensions of State Formation and Nation-Building." In Charles Tilly, ed., *The Formation of National State in Western Europe,* pp. 562-600. New Jersey: Princeton University Press.
Rokkan, Stein and Derek W. Urwin, eds. 1982. *The Politics of Territorial Identity: Studies in European Regionalism.* London: Sage.
Rose, Richard, ed. 1980. *Electoral Participation: A Comparative Analysis.* Beverly Hills & London: Sage.
Rose, Richard. 1981. "What If Anything is Wrong with Big Government?" *Journal of Public Policy* 1:5-36.
Rose, Richard. 1983. "Disaggregating the Concept of Government." In Charles Lewis Taylor, ed., *Why Government Grow,* pp. 157-76. Beverly Hills: Sage.
Rose, Richard and Ian McAllister. 1990. *The Loyalties of Voters: A Lifetime Learning Model.* London: Sage.
Rose, Richard and Harve Mossawir. 1967. "Voting and Elections: A Functional Analysis." *Political Studies* 15:173-201.

Roy, Denny. 1991. "The Rabbit Awaits the Tiger: Hong Kong's View of the Peking Regime." *Issues & Studies* 27(7):61-78.

Rudolph, Susanne Hoeber. 1987. "State Formation in Asia--Prolegomenon to a Comparative Study." *Journal of Asian Studies* 46:731-46.

Rueschemeyer, Dietrich and Peter B. Evans. 1985. "The State and Economic Transformation: Toward an Analysis of the Conditions Underlying Effective Intervention." In Peter B. Evans, Dietrich Rueschemeyer, and Theda Skocpol, eds. *Bringing the State Back In*, pp. 44-77. Cambridge: Cambridge University Press.

Salisbury, Robert H. and Michael MacKuen. 1981. "On the Study of Party Realignment." *Journal of Politics* 43:523-30.

Sartori, Giovanni. 1976. *Parties and Party Systems: A Framework for Analysis*. Cambridge: Cambridge University Press.

Sartori, Giovanni. 1994. *Comparative Constitutional Engineering: An Inquiry into Structures, Incentives and Outcomes*. Hampshire: Macmillan.

Scarbrough, Elinor. 1991. "Micro and Macro Analysis of Elections." *European Journal of Political Research* 19:361-74.

Schiffer, Jonathan R. 1991. "State Policy and Economic Growth: A Note on the Hong Kong Model." *International Journal of Urban and Regional Research* 15:180-96.

Schmidt, Manfred G. 1983. "The Growth of the Tax State: The Industrial Democracies, 1950-1978." In Charles Lewis Taylor, ed. *Why Government Grow*, pp. 261-85. Beverly Hills: Sage.

Schneider, William. 1974. "Issues, Voting, and Cleavages: A Methodology and Some Tests." *American Behavioral Scientist* 18:111-46.

Schneider, William. 1980. "Styles of Electoral Competition." In Richard Rose, ed. *Electoral Participation: A Comparative Analysis*, pp. 75-100. Beverly Hills & London: Sage.

Scott, Ian. [1980]. *Administrative Adaptation and the New Towns Policy in Hong Kong*. mimeo. Hong Kong: Department of Political Science, University of Hong Kong.

Scott, Ian. 1986. "Sino-British Agreement and Political Power in Hong Kong." *Asian Pacific Community* 31:1-18.

Scott, Ian. 1989. *Political Change and the Crisis of Legitimacy in Hong Kong*. Honolulu: University of Hawaii Press.

Scott, Ian. 1992. "An Overview of the Hong Kong Legislative Council Elections of 1991." In Rowena Kwok, Loan Leung and Ian Scott, eds. *Votes Without Power: The Hong Kong Legislative Council Elections 1991*, pp. 1-28. Hong Kong: Hong Kong University Press.

Scott, Ian and John P. Burns, eds. 1988. *The Hong Kong Civil Service and Its Future.* Hong Kong: Oxford University Press.

Secretariat of the Consultative Committee for the Basic Law. 1988. *Drafting of the Basic Law and the "Mainstream Political Model".* Hong Kong: Consultative Committee for the Basic Law.

Secretariat of the Consultative Committee for the Basic Law. 1989a. *Reference Papers for the Basic Law of the Hong Kong Special Administrative Region of the People's Republic of China (Draft).* Hong Kong: Secretariat of the Consultative Committee for the Basic Law of the Hong Kong Special Administrative Region of the People's Republic of China.

Secretariat of the Consultative Committee for the Basic Law. 1989b. *The Basic Law of the Hong Kong Special Administrative Region of the People's Republic of China (Draft): Consultation report, Vol. 2.* Hong Kong: Secretariat of the Consultative Committee for the Basic Law of the Hong Kong Special Administrative Region of the People's Republic of China.

Shaffer, Bretigne. 1991. "Beijing, the West, and the Approaching Sack of Hong Kong." *Orbis* 35:327-45.

Shamir, Michal. 1984. "Are Western Party Systems 'Frozen'? A Comparative Dynamic Analysis." *Comparative Political Studies* 17:135-79.

Shawcross, William. 1989. *Kowtow!* London: Chatto & Windus.

Shively, W. Phillips. 1969. "'Ecological' Inference: The Use of Aggregate Data to Study Individuals." *American Political Science Review* 63:1183-96.

Shugart, Matthew Soberg and John M. Carey. 1992. *Presidents and Assemblies: Constitutional Design and Electoral Dynamics.* Cambridge: Cambridge University Press.

Silverman, Lawrence. 1991. "Beyond the Micro/Macro Distinction." *European Journal of Political Research* 19:375-97.

Skeldon, Ronald. 1990. "Emigration and the Future of Hong Kong." *Pacific Affairs* 63:500-23.

Skeldon, Ronald. 1991. "Emigration, Immigration and Fertility Decline: Demographic Integration or Disintegration?" In Sung Yun-wing and Lee Ming-kwan, eds., *The Other Hong Kong Report 1991*, pp. 233-58. Hong Kong: Chinese University Press.

Skocpol, Theda. 1985. "Bringing the State Back In: Strategies of Analysis in Current Research." In Peter B. Evans, Dietrich Rueschemeyer, and Theda Skocpol, eds., *Bringing the State Back In*, pp. 3-37. Cambridge: Cambridge University Press.

Slinn, Peter. 1987. "The Hong Kong Settlement: A Preliminary Assessment." *International Relations* 9:1-22.

Smith, Carl T. 1971. "The Emergence of a Chinese Elite in Hong Kong." *Journal of the Hong Kong Branch of the Royal Asiatic Society* 11:74-115.

So, Alvin Y. and Ludmilla Kwitko. 1990. "The New Middle Class and the Democratic Movement in Hong Kong." *Journal of Contemporary Asia* 20:384-98.

So, Alvin Y. and Ludmilla Kwitko. 1992. "The Transformation of Urban Movements in Hong Kong, 1970-90." *Bulletin of Concerned Asian Scholars* 24:32-43.

Skeldon, Ronald. 1992. "The Transformation of Urban Movements in Hong Kong, 1970-90." *Bulletin of Concerned Asian Scholars* 24:32-43.

Stepan, Alfred and Cindy Skach. 1993. "Constitutional Frameworks and Democratic Consolidation: Parliamentarianism versus Presidentialism." *World Politics* 46:1-22.

Strath, Bo and Rolf Torstendahl. 1992. "State Theory and State Development: State as Network Structure in Change in Modern European History." In Rolf Torstendahl, ed. *State Theory and State History*, pp. 12-37. London: Sage.

Sun Wai-see. 1987. *The Collection of Political Essays of Sun Wai-see.* Hong Kong: Ming Pao Publishing Co. (in Chinese)

Sun Wai-see. 1990. *The New Collection of Political Essays of Sun Wai-see.* Hong Kong: Ming Pao Publishing Co. (in Chinese)

Sundquist, James L. 1983. *Dynamics of the Party System: Alignment and Realignment of Political Parties in the United States.* rev. ed. Washington, D.C.: Brookings Institution.

Sung, Y.W. 1986. "Fiscal and Economic Policies in Hong Kong." In Joseph Y.S. Cheng, ed., *Hong Kong in Transition*, pp. 120-41. Hong Kong: Oxford university Press.

Szczepanik, Edward. 1958. *The Economic Growth of Hong Kong.* London: Oxford University Press.

Sze Ma, Yee. 1984. "The Negotiation of Hong Kong Future with All Glories Goes to Deng Xiaoping." *Hong Kong Economic Journal Monthly* 91:5-48. (in Chinese)

Tang, Shu-hung. 1991. "Fiscal Constitution, Income Distribution and the Basic law of Hong Kong." *Economy and Society* 20:281-305.

Tang, Shu-hung. 1992. *The Public Finance of Hong Kong in the Late-Transitional Period.* Hong Kong: Joint Publishing. (in Chinese)

Tang, Stephen Lung-wai. 1993. "Political Markets, Competition, and the Return to Monopoly: Evolution Amidst a Historical Tragedy." In Lau Siu-kai and Louie Kin-sheun, eds. *Hong Kong Tried Democracy: The 1991 Elections in Hong Kong*, pp. 249-96. Hong Kong: Hong Kong Institute of Asia-Pacific Studies, The Chinese University of Hong Kong.

Tarschys, Daniel. 1975. "The Growth of Public Expenditures: Nine Modes of Explanation." *Scandinavian Political Studies* 10:9-31.

Taylor, Charles Lewis, ed. 1983. *Why Governments Grow: Measuring Public Sector Size.* Beverly Hills: Sage.

Thatcher, Margaret. 1993. *The Downing Street Years.* London: Harper Collins.

Therborn, Goran. 1992. "The Right to Vote and the Four World Routes to/through Modernity." In Rolf Torstendahl, ed. *State Theory and State History*, pp. 62-92. London: Sage.

Thomas, George M., and John W. Meyer. 1984. "The Expansion of the State." *Annual Review of Sociology* 10:461-82.

Thomsen, Soren Risbjerg. 1987. *Danish Elections 1920-79: A Logit Approach to Ecological Analysis and Inference.* Aarhus: Politica.

Tilly, Charles, ed. 1975a. *The Formation of National State in Western Europe.* New Jersey: Princeton University Press.

Tilly, Charles. 1975b. "Reflections on the History of European State-Making." In Charles Tilly, ed. *The Formation of National State in Western Europe*, pp. 3-83. New Jersey: Princeton University Press.

Tilly, Charles. 1975c. "Western State-Making and Theories of Political Transformation." In Charles Tilly, ed., *The Formation of National State in Western Europe*, pp. 601-38. New Jersey: Princeton University Press.

Torstendahl, Rolf, ed. 1992. *State Theory and State History.* London: Sage.

Trench, David. 1971. *Hong Kong and Its Position in the Southeast Asia Region.* Hawaii: East-West Center, University of Hawaii.

Tsai, Jung-fang. 1993. *Hong Kong in Chinese History: Community and Social Unrest in the British Colony, 1842-1913.* New York: Columbia University Press.

Tsang, Steve Yui-sang. 1988. *Democracy Shelved: Great Britain, China, and Attempts at Constitutional Reform in Hong Kong, 1945-1952.* Hong Kong: Oxford University Press.

Tsang, Steve Yui-sang. 1989. "China and Political Reform in Hong Kong." *Pacific Review* 2:68-74.
Tsang Tak-shing. 1992. "On Chinese Official Attitudes towards Legislative Council Elections 1991." In Jane C.Y. Lee, W.N. Ho, and Jermain T.M. Lam, eds., *A Report of the Conference Proceedings on Politics and 1991 Elections in Hong Kong.* Hong Kong: City Polytechnic of Hong Kong, Department of Public & Social Administration.
Tsang, Wing-kwong. 1993. "Who Voted for the Democrats? An Analysis of the Electoral Choice of the 1991 Legislative Council Election." In Lau Siu-kai and Louie Kin-sheun, eds. *Hong Kong Tried Democracy: The 1991 Elections in Hong Kong,* pp. 115-55. Hong Kong: Chinese University of Hong Kong, Hong Kong Institute of Asia-Pacific Studies, 1993.
Tsim, T.L. 1984. "1997: Peking's Strategy for Hong Kong." *World Today* 40:37-45.
Tsim, T.L. 1984. 1991. "Beijing Hijacks Hong Kong Autonomy." *Asian Wall Street Journal* 29 January, p. 10.
Walden, John. 1983. *Excellency, Your Gap is Showing! Six Critiques on British Colonial Government in Hong Kong.* Hong Kong: Corporate Communication Ltd.
Walden, John. 1987. *Excellency, Your Gap is Growing! Six Talks on a Chinese Takeaway.* Hong Kong: All Noble Company Ltd.
Walden, John. 1988. "Accountability: Past, Present and Future." In William McGurn, ed. *Basic Law, Basic Questions: The Debate Continues,* pp. 53-68. Hong Kong: Review Publishing Co. Ltd.
Ware, Alan, ed. 1987. *Political Parties: Electoral Change and Structural Response.* Oxford: Basil Blackwell.
Weatherford, M. Stephen. 1987. "How Does Government Performance Influence Political Support?" *Political Behavior* 9:5-28.
Weaver, R. Kent. 1992. "Political Institutions and Canada's Constitutional Crisis." In R. Kent Weaver, ed. *The Collapse of Canada?,* pp. 7-75. Washington, D.C.: Brookings.
Weiner, Myron. 1987. "Empirical Democratic Theory." In Myron Weiner and Ergun Ozbudun, eds. *Competitive Elections in Developing Countries,* pp. 3-34. N.A.: Duke University Press, for American Enterprise Institute.
Weiner, Myron and Ergun Ozbudun, eds. 1987. *Competitive Elections in Developing Countries.* N.A.: Duke University Press, for American Enterprise Institute.

Weiss, Julian. 1988. "The Negotiation Style of The People's Republic of China: The Future of Hong Kong and Macao." *Journal of Social, Political and Economic Studies* 13:175-94.

Wellhofer, E. Spencer. 1991. "Confounding Sources of Variance in the Macro-Analysis of Electoral Data." *European Journal of Political Research* 19:425-39.

Welsh, Frank. 1993. *A History of Hong Kong*. London: Harper Collins.

Weng, Byron S.J. 1987-88. "The Hong Kong Model of 'One Country, Two Systems': Promises and Problems." *Asian Affairs* 14:193-209.

Wesley-Smith, Peter. 1980. *Unequal Treaty 1898-1997*. Hong Kong: Oxford University Press.

Wesley-Smith, Peter and Albert H.Y. Chen, eds. 1988. *The Basic Law and Hong Kong's Future*. Hong Kong: Butterworths.

Wight, Martin. 1946. *The Development of the Legislative Council 1606-1945*. London: Faber & Faber.

Wilkinson, Paul. 1983. "Hong Kong: a One-Way Ticket to an Unknown Destination." *Government and Opposition* 18:442-57.

Wong, Aline K. 1970-71. "Political Apathy and the Political System in Hong Kong." *United College Journal* 8:1-20.

Wong, Aline K. 1972a. *The Kaifong Associations and the Society of Hong Kong*. Taipei: Orient Cultural Service.

Wong, Aline K. 1972b. *The Study of Higher Non-Expatriate Civil Servants in Hong Kong*. Hong Kong: Social Research Centre, Chinese University of Hong Kong.

Wong, Aline K. 1972c. "Chinese Community Leadership in a Colonial Setting: The Hong Kong Neighbourhood Associations." *Asian Survey* 12:587-601.

Wong, C.K. 1990. "The Advocacy Role of Social Work in a Changing Political Environment: Its Dilemmas and Challenges in Hong Kong." *Community Development Journal* 25:399-404.

Wong, Chack-kie. 1993. *Social Work and Social Change: A Profile of the Activist Social Workers in Hong Kong*. Hong Kong: Hong Kong Institute of Asia-Pacific Studies, Chinese University of Hong Kong.

Wong, Fu-wing. 1990. "The Background and Problems of Forming Political Party among 'Democratic Groups'." *Contemporary* 10 February:23-4; 17 February:28-9; 24 February:28-9. (in Chinese)

Wong, Jeremiah K.H. 1982. "Separatism and Convergence: Pattern of Administrative Adaptation in the New Territories." In Joseph Y.S. Cheng, ed. *Hong Kong in the 1980s*, pp. 13-21. Hong Kong: Summerson.

Wong, Luke S. K., ed. 1978. *Housing in Hong Kong: A Multi-Disciplinary Study*. Hong Kong: Heinemann.

Wong, Man-fong. 1994. "My Forty-Two Years of Life and Works in the New China News Agency's Hong Kong Branch." *Eastweek* 90 (13 July 1994):160-4. (series and in Chinese)

Wong, Man-fong. 1997. *China's Resumption of Sovereignty over Hong Kong*. Hong Kong: The David C. Lam Institute for East-West Studies, Hong Kong Baptist University.

Wong, Richard Y.C. and Joseph Y.S. Cheng, eds. 1990. *The Other Hong Kong Report 1990*. Hong Kong: Chinese University Press.

Xiao, Weiyun. 1988. "A Study of the Political System of the Hong Kong Special Administrative Region Under the Basic Law." *Journal of Chinese Law* 2:95-113.

Xu, Jiatun. 1993. *Xu Jiatun's Hong Kong Memoirs*. 2 Vols. Hong Kong: Hong Kong United Daily News. (in Chinese)

Yahuda, Michael. 1993. "Hong Kong's Future: Sino-British Negotiations, Perceptions, Organization and Political Culture." *International Affairs* 69:245-66.

Yahuda, Michael. 1996. *Hong Kong: China's Challenge*. London and New York: Routledge.

Yee, Herbert S. and Wong Yiu-chung. 1987. "Hong Kong: The Politics of the Daya Bay Nuclear Plant Debate." *International Affairs* 63:617-30.

Yip, Tze-chin. 1984. "The Political Wake-up of Hong Kong's New Generation of Intelligentsia." *Hong Kong Economic Journal Monthly* 92:40-3. (in Chinese)

Yip, Chi-chao. 1991. "The Chinese Deployment Towards the 1991 Direct Elections." *Hong Kong Economic Times*, 12 September 1991. (in Chinese)

Yu, Fu-lai and Li Si-ming. 1985. "The Welfare Cost of Hong Kong's Public Housing Programme." *Urban Studies* 22:133-40.

Zhang, Youyu. 1988. "The Reasons for and Basic Principles in Formulating the Hong Kong Special Administrative Region Basic Law, And Its Essential Contents and Mode of Expression." *Journal of Chinese Law* 2:5-19.

Zuckerman, Alan S. 1982. "New Approaches to Political Cleavage: A Theoretical Introduction." *Comparative Political Studies* 15:131-44.

Index

1984 Green and White Papers, 58-9, 62, 66
1987-88 Green and White Papers, 65-9
1994-95 Elections: arrangement of, 194; seven diplomatic documents, 82

Akers-Jones, David, 63
anti-Communist China syndrome, 5
anti-nuclear movement (Daya Bay), 95
Assessment Office, 50, 242
Association of Democracy and Justice (ADJ), 155, 157

Basic Law: appointment of drafters, 72; informal British involvement, 72; discussions on post-1997 political model, 74-82; Selection Committee and Provisional LegCo, 100; elections and, 196; constitutional framework, 213-6
Basic Law Consultative Committee (BLCC): confidence towards, 73
Basic Law Drafting Committee BLDC): composition, 213
Big Three merger plan, 161
Bray, Denis, 156

centre-periphery cleavage, 37, 69-71, 82-4; definition, 220; transformation after 1997, 233
Cha Chi-min, 76
Cha, Louis, 76
Cha-Cha formula, 77
Chan Choi-hei, 204
Chan Kam-chuen: on popular elections, 60
Chan Pun, 156
Chan Yat-sun, 153
Chan Ying-lun, 158
Chan Yuen-han, 193

Chang, Alexander Yau-hung, 194
Chen, Edward, 156
Cheng Kai-nam, 193
Cheong, Stephen Kam-chuen, 158, 160, 165
Cheung Hon-chung, 194
Cheung Man-kwong, 160
Cheung Yan-lung, 156
Chief Executive (CE): Sino-British joint Declaration, 45; 1984 Green Paper, 58; proposals of returning, 74-82; appointment of ExCo members, 188; election of, 196, 214; popular election of, 206; relationship with LegCo, 215-6; Selection Committee, 217-8; conflict management and alternative arrangements, 225-8
China: 1967 riots, 27; policy towards Hong Kong, 30-1; views on party formation, 158-60; supports pro-Beijing candidates, 186-8
Chinese Communist Party (CCP): the leftists and, 19n; activities in Hong Kong, 137-8, 159; HKPTU and Szeto Wah, 145
Chow, Selina, 158
Chow Yick-hay, 201
Chung Sze-yuen: met with Deng Xiaoping, 47, 49; on representative government, 59-60; on political parties, 159
City District Officer Scheme, 92, 247
constitution-making: objective dimension, 210; subjective dimension, 209; access to, 218
consumption cleavage: Patrict Dunleavy, 11; state expansion and, 86; concept, 124; election dynamics, 220-2

Index

Cooperative Resources Centre (CRC), 166
Cradock, Percy: China policy, 41, 71; Hong Kong's involvement in Basic Law drafting process, 72; on Beijing policy towards Hong Kong after 1989, 78; on proportion of popularly-elected seats, 82

decolonization: in early 1980s, 31-5
Democratic Alliance for Betterment of Hong Kong (DAB): founding declaration, 167; role transformation, 168; in 1994 DBs' elections, 197-9; in 1995 Municipal Councils elections, 199-201; in 1995 LegCo elections, 201-3; in Provisional and 1998 LegCo elections, 203-6
Democratic Party (DP): formation, 164; 1994-95 elections, 197-203; 1998 LegCo elections, 204-6
democratization: elections and, 6-9; centre-periphery cleavage and, 37-8, 230-3; China's resistance to, 53-4; conflicting ideas of, 64-9; RCHK on,138; the Frontier and, 164-5; the conservatives and, 168-9; the democrats and, 169-70; the leftists, 170-1; electoral support and, 237-9
Deng, Xiaoping: reclaim Hong Kong's sovereignty, 39; on "three-legged stool", 47; on popular election, 65; on separation of power, 74
Ding Lik-kiu, 66, 157, 163
District Affairs Advisors, 176
District Boards (DBs): preparatory stage for decolonization, 31; number of seats and candidates, 33, 103, 176-7; in 1987 Green Paper, 65; electoral college, 69; composition, 105; 1985 DBs' elections, 152-4; 1994 DBs' elections, 196-9
double-rent policy, 133
Dunn, Lydia, 47, 49

electoral market: sure win thesis, 193; "Distorted", 235
electoral system: different kinds of, 205
electorate: relaxation of franchise restriction in 1965, 140-1; UrbCo, 142; and population, 176-7
encapsulated conflicts, 17
Executive Council (ExCo): composition, 101
executive-led government: appointment system and, 211; "opposition" legislature, 236-7

Fan, Rita, 158
Federation of Trade Unions (FTU): democracy, 66-7; in BLDC, 72; support "Bicameral Model", 79; 1985 DBs elections, 152; 1991 LegCo elections, 181, 184; Lu Ping, 187; LegCo election results, 190
Forsgate, Gerry, 156
Frontier, 164-5
Fung Ho-lap, 145
Fung, Kenneth, 156
Fung Kin-kee, 157
Fung, Victor, 156

Grantham, Alexander, 89
Group of 190: 190 Proposal, 75
Group of 89: 89 Proposal, 75; Assorted Model, 80; party-building, 160-1, 165

Hariela, Hari, 164
Hau Shui-pui, 193
Ho, Albert, 163
Hong Kong: financial autonomy, 20, 90, 93, 102; British Crown colony, 20; autonomy in the face of capitalists' challenge, 22; Chinese society under British rule, 24; socio-economic condition, 25; influx of refugees, 25-6, 87; colonialism without serious challenge, 28; local-born Hong Kong people, 28, 91; unusual decolonisation in early 1980s, 31; democratization of, 51; growth of expenditure and revenue, 109; high land price policy, 234
Hong Kong Affairs Society (HKAS): formation, 151-2; 1985 DBs elections, 153-4; 1988 DBs election, 157; merger plan, 160-3

Hong Kong Alliance in Support of the Patriotic Democratic Movement in China (HKASPDMC), 162-3
Hong Kong Association for Democracy and People's Livelihood (HKADPL): formation, 157; merger plan, 160, 163-4; 1991 LegCo elections, 180-1; membership, 183; LegCo election results, 189, 197-206; Patten's reform, 195
Hong Kong Christian Industrial Committee (HKCIC), 144, 161
Hong Kong Civic Association (HKCA), 138, 182
Hong Kong Democratic Foundation (HKDF), 164, 181, 189
Hong Kong General Chamber of Commerce: non-official LegCo member, 24; termination of informal practice, 92
Hong Kong Observers (HKO), 146, 153
Hong Kong people governing Hong Kong: Beijing's strategic move, 48, 53; stop using the phrase, 63; and democratic reforms, 70; origin, 84, n5; and the leftists, 152
Hong Kong People's Association, 151
Hong Kong Professional Teachers' Union (HKPTU), 144-5, 161
Hong Kong Progressive Alliance (HKPA), 166, 190, 199
Hong Kong Special Administrative Region (HKSAR): Preliminary Working Committee, 195-6; Preparatory Committee, 195, 203, 216-9; Selection Committee, 203-4, 214, 217-9; Provisional LegCo and 1998 LegCo elections, 203-6; political model of, 214-6; possible political developments, 239-41
Hong Kong state: development of, 86; functional expansion, 107; state development in pre-1945 period, 23; structural expansion, 99
Howe, Geoffrey, 44, 59
Hu Fa-kuang, 165

individual-collective consumption cleavage, 234 (see consumption cleavage)
institutional design and conflict management, 15, 208
Ip Kwok-chung, 198

Ji Pengfei, 49, 63
Joint Liaison Group (JLG), 45, 64, 66, 158
Justices of the Peace: as LegCo member, 24, 92

Kan Fook-yee, 156, 161
Ko, Vincent, 151
Kuomintang (KMT): activities in Hong Kong, 136-7; the rightists and, 173n
Kwok, Philip, 155, 161, 165

Lam, Albert C.C., 152
Lam Chak-piu, 156
Lam Kui-shing, 193
Lam Wai-keung, 200
land sales: repid decline in, 115; privatization, 131-2
Lau Chin-shek, 73, 157, 160-1, 191
Lau, Emily Wai-hing, 195
Lau Wong-fat, 153
Lee, Allen, 158, 160, 165-6, 169, 180, 206-7
Lee Fung-ying, 156
Lee, J.K., 156
Lee Kai-ming, 156
Lee, Martin, 69, 78, 85, 158, 160, 162-4, 187-8, 191
Lee Ming-kwan, 151
Lee Wah-ming, 200
Lee Wing-tat, 157
Legislative Council (LegCo): non-official majority, 93, 100; 1991 elections, 179; Election Committee, 199; 1995 elections, 201; 1998 elections, 204; political orientations of LegCo members, 223; Provisional LegCo, 100-1, 196, 203-4, 215, 217-9; right to initial bills, 214; separate vote count mechanism, 215, 227; segmented methods of returning members, 216, 223

Leong Che-hung, 164
Leung Chun-ying, 156
Leung, Ronald Ding-bong, 200
Li Chu-wen, 48
Li Hou, 66, 74, 159, 187
Liberal Democratic Federation (LDF): formation, 166; 1991 LegCo elections, 181; LegCo election results, 190-4, 197-200
Liberal Party (LP): formation, 166; LegCo election results, 190, 195, 197, 199-200, 202-6; "distorted" electoral market, 235
Liu Ching-leung, 201
Lo King-man, 151
Lo Lung-kwong, 157
Lo Tak-shing, 79, 160-1, 165, 174n
Lo, Vincent, 66, 85, 156, 165
Lobo motion, 49
local-born Hong Kong people, 28, 91
Lu Ping, 63, 74, 159, 187, 196
Luk Yan-lung, 151

MacLehose, Murray, 39, 93, 132
McGregor, Jimmy, 164
Meeting Point (MP): formation, 150-1; 1985 DBs elections 153; merger plan, 163-4; 1991 LegCo elections, 180-2, 184, 189, 191; 1994 DBs elections, 196-7
Municipal Council Ordinance 1949, 88

Neoh, Anthony, 151
New Hong Kong Alliance (NHKA): Bicameral Model, 79-81; fromation, 161; split of, 165; 1991 LegCo elections, 180-2; membership, 183
New Hong Kong Society (NHKS), 150, 153, 157, 232
New Territories Association of Societies (NTAS), 152, 187
Ngan Kam-chuen, 201

Oram, Matthew, 164

Pao Yue-kong, 73
party systems and voter alignments, 13
Pattern, Christopher: 150, 166; reform package, 194-5

political change of Hong Kong: uniqueness, 1
political cleavages: concept, 9
political reforms: different attitudes towards, 52; accountability of the executive to the legislature, 73; "190 Proposal", 75; "89 Proposal", 75; Mainstream Model, 76; OMELCO Consensus Model, 78-80; Bicameral Model, 79-81, 165; New Compromise Model (4-4-2 Model), 79-80, 165; Assorted Model, 80-1; New Mainstream Model, 81-2
pressure group politics, 143
privatization: logic, 131; and public housing, 133-4; and consumption cleavage, 234-5; electoral support, 237-9
Progressive Hong Kong Society (PHKS): formation, 155-6; close relationship with NHKA, 161; coalition-building, 165; membership, 182
public housing: government contribution to, 127-8, 130; and privatization, 132-4
Public Sector Reform, 131

Reform Club of Hong Kong (RCHK), 138-40, 181
refugees: political instability in China, 29-30; attitude towards China, 56; in late 1940s, 87-9
Regional Council (RegCo): number of seats and candidates, 33, 176-8; formation and composition, 102-4; 1995 RegCo elections, 199-201
rent policy 132-3
Renton, Timothy, 64
representation: threshold of, 74-5, 147, 194; institutional barriers of, 46

salaries tax, 119-23, 235
second "stove", 195
separate vote count mechanism, 215, 227
Sino-British Joint Declaration: non-official ExCo and LegCo members' position on, 49; land lease

arrangements, 115; constitutional parameters, 211-3; public access, 219
Sino-British Negotiation: setting, 40-2; institutional barriers of representation, 46-8; three-legged stool, 47, 49, 211
Sital, Kewlram, 164
Society for Community Organisation (SoCO), 144-6
Standing Committee on Pressure Groups (SCOPG), 143-6
Survey Office, 65, 67-9
synarchical rule, 30
Szeto Wah, 72, 78, 144, 162, 169, 187-8, 191

Tam, Maria, 79, 81, 106, 155, 160-1, 165-6, 174n, 180, 184, 194
Tam Yiu-chung, 72, 204
Thatcher, Margaret, 39, 42-5, 69
three-tier legislature, 33, 36n, 176
Tiananmen Incident: impact on Hong Kong, 78-9
Tiananmen Incident complex, 5
Tomlin, Ian, 164
Tong, Carl, 153
Tong Kam-biu, 156
Tsang Tak-shing, 184
Tsang Yok-sing, 66, 85, 204

United Ants (UA), 165, 189

United Democrats of Hong Kong (UDHK): formation, 163-4; 1991 LegCo elections, 180-2, 184, 188-9, 191-3; 1994 DBs elections, 197
Urban Council (UrbCo): 36n, reform proposal, 93-4; composition, 102, 104; electorate, 142; numbers of seats and candidates, 176-8; 1995 UrbCo elections, 199-201

Walden, John, 20
Wong, Johnny Chi-keung, 194
Wong Man-fong, 31, 36
Wong, Peter Hong-yuen, 161, 165
Wong Siu-lun, 151
Wong Wai-hung, 156
Wong Yuen-cheung, 153
Wu, Raymond, 156, 161, 165
Wu, Veronica, 156, 161, 165

Xu Jiatun, 62, 72, 80, 145, 158-60

Yeung Sum, 150-1, 169, 174n, 191
Youde, Edward, 47, 57, 84n, 158, 211
Young Plan, 88-90

Zhao Ziyang, 43
Zhou Nan, 187